L.M. Montgomery and the Matter of Nature(s)

L.M. Montgomery
and the Matter of Nature(s)

Edited by

Rita Bode and Jean Mitchell

McGill-Queen's University Press
Montreal & Kingston | London | Chicago

ISBN 978-0-7735-5274-6 (cloth)
ISBN 978-0-7735-5275-3 (paper)
ISBN 978-0-7735-5399-6 (ePDF)
ISBN 978-0-7735-5400-9 (ePUB)

Legal deposit second quarter 2018
Bibliothèque nationale du Québec

Printed in Canada on acid-free paper that is 100% ancient forest free (100% post-consumer recycled), processed chlorine free

This book has been published with the help of a grant from the Canadian Federation for the Humanities and Social Sciences, through the Awards to Scholarly Publications Program, using funds provided by the Social Sciences and Humanities Research Council of Canada.

Funded by the Government of Canada | Financé par le gouvernement du Canada | Canada | Canada Council for the Arts | Conseil des arts du Canada

We acknowledge the support of the Canada Council for the Arts, which last year invested $153 million to bring the arts to Canadians throughout the country. Nous remercions le Conseil des arts du Canada de son soutien. L'an dernier, le Conseil a investi 153 millions de dollars pour mettre de l'art dans la vie des Canadiennes et des Canadiens de tout le pays.

Library and Archives Canada Cataloguing in Publication

L.M. Montgomery and the matter of nature(s) / edited by Rita Bode and Jean Mitchell.

Includes bibliographical references and index.
Issued in print and electronic formats.
ISBN 978-0-7735-5274-6 (hardcover).
–ISBN 978-0-7735-5275-3 (softcover).
–ISBN 978-0-7735-5399-6 (ePDF).
–ISBN 978-0-7735-5400-9 (ePUB)

1. Montgomery, L.M. (Lucy Maud), 1874–1942 – Criticism and interpretation. 2. Nature in literature. 3. Human ecology in literature. I. Bode, Rita, 1950–, editor II. Mitchell, Jean, 1953–, editor

PS8526.O55Z756 2018 C813'.52 C2017-907580-2
C2017-907581-0

This book was designed and typeset by studio oneonone in Minion 11/14.

Contents

Illustrations

Acknowledgments

The idea for this book emerged from the L.M. Montgomery Institute's ninth biennial international conference on the theme of "L.M. Montgomery and the Matter of Nature." Our first thanks is to our contributors who, in addition to their own fine scholarly perspectives, thoughtfully engaged each other's work initiating conversations across disciplines about Montgomery and the matter of nature(s). We have very much appreciated the opportunity to work with them.

We extend a special thanks to Elizabeth Epperly, founder of the L.M. Montgomery Institute, for her scholarship, sustained support, and generous humanity. Montgomery scholarship owes a special thanks to Mary Rubio, Elizabeth Waterston, and Jen Rubio for their work on the Montgomery journals. We are also grateful to the Montgomery community of scholars and readers worldwide.

We thank Benjamin Lefebvre for his significant editorial work on an early version of this volume. His contribution is greatly appreciated by the editors and authors in this final collection. We are grateful to Lesley Clement and Wendy Shilton who provided valuable insights into an earlier version of the introduction and to the anonymous readers at McGill-Queen's University Press for their helpful and constructive feedback, which helped to sharpen the focus of the volume. We also thank Lesley for being a generous source of helpful information. We appreciate the help that the staff at the L.M. Montgomery Collection, Archival and Special Collections, University of Guelph, are always prompt to provide.

We owe great thanks to our editor at the press, Mark Abley, whose perceptive reading and thoughtful enthusiasm make working with him a true pleasure. We also appreciate the work of the various departments at the press that produce and market the publications.

We thank Kate MacDonald Butler, the heirs of L.M. Montgomery, and Sally Keefe-Cohen for their ongoing support of Montgomery scholarship.

At the University of Prince Edward Island, we appreciate the knowledge and support of Simon Lloyd, archivist and special collections librarian; Donald Moses, university librarian; Philip Smith, chair of the LMM Institute; and Mike Newland, university photographer.

We gratefully acknowledge that this book has been published with the assistance of a grant from the Federation for the Humanities and Social Sciences through the Awards to Scholarly Publications Program, using funds provided by the Social Sciences and Humanities Research Council of Canada.

Rita Bode would like to thank her colleagues at Trent University, both in the Department of English Literature and on the Durham campus, and other friends and family, with special thanks to Brian O'Byrne, Adam O'Byrne, and Julia O'Byrne.

Jean Mitchell thanks colleagues at the University of Prince Edward Island especially Doreley Coll, Udo Krautwurst, Sharon Myers, and Kate Tilleczek. She is also grateful to her friends, Lissant Bolton, Dolores Levangie, Emily Niras, and Usha Rangan. Special thanks are due to her family, Gerard, Mary J., Mary, Bill, Helen, Lonnie, Joseph, George, and Marian.

Permissions

Material written by L.M. Montgomery is excerpted with permission of the heirs of L.M. Montgomery Inc. *L.M. Montgomery*, *Emily of New Moon*, *The Story Girl, and Blue Castle* are trademarks of the heirs of L.M. Montgomery Inc., and are used with permission.

Anne of Green Gables, *Rainbow Valleys*, *Rilla of Ingleside*, and other indicia of "Anne" are trademarks and/or Canadian official marks of the Anne of Green Gables Licensing Authority Inc. and are used with permission.

Permission for use of the photograph of the "Natural Bridge," Virginia is granted courtesy of Matt Rutigliano, Natural Bridge Historic Hotel and Conference Center and the Caverns at Natural Bridge, Natural Bridge, VA.

Permission for use of the photographs entitled "The Wine Gate of the Alhambra, Granada, Spain" and "Sunnyside," home of Washington Irving, is granted by Jessica Brookes-Parkhill.

Permission for use of the L.M. Montgomery photograph entitled "Lover's Lane" is granted by the L.M. Montgomery Collection, Archival and Special Collections, University of Guelph Library.

Cover Photo: Permission for use of the photograph, "View of Cavendish shore with group of figures," is granted by the L.M. Montgomery Collection, Archival and Special Collections, University of Guelph Library.

L.M. Montgomery and the Matter of Nature(s)

INTRODUCTION

L.M. Montgomery and the Matter of Nature(s)

Rita Bode and Jean Mitchell

On 20 December 1908, L.M. Montgomery entered into her journal a personal and deeply felt comment on the subject of nature. "I am thankful above all else," she writes, "for my love of nature and my capacity for finding fullness of joy in her companionship. I would rather lose everything else I possess than that," she concludes.[1] Her reflection seems straightforward. Montgomery's writing, from early to late in her career, from life-writing to poetry and prose, is replete with depictions of an enchanting nature that conveys the entry's intense appreciation. Her relationship with nature aligns well with the critical view that places her in the literary tradition of the British Romantics. As Elizabeth Epperly affirms, "Montgomery's nature descriptions are strongly influenced by the Romantic poets and by late-Victorian Romanticism";[2] but like much else about Montgomery's life and work, which are a continuing and rich source for critical reappraisal, the subject of her journal entry may be more nuanced than at first appears, for the nature that Montgomery explores is both subtle and fluid. *L.M. Montgomery and the Matter of Nature(s)* brings a new understanding to Montgomery and the subject of nature through a multidisciplinary approach and a critical environmental awareness that embraces the concept of nature as expansive, inclusive, and varied.

The subject of Montgomery and the "matter of nature(s)" presents a particularly meaningful area for exploration at a time when anxieties about environmental crises are intensifying, ecocritical perspectives burgeoning, and new approaches to understanding human and nonhuman relationships continually emerging. Political ecologist Jane Bennett, for example, in speaking of "vital materiality" and "material vitality," advocates a sharpened focus on the materiality of humans and the vitality of nature.[3] By reframing both matter and agency, she challenges the boundaries between culture and nature and engages the many ways in which, in Serenella Iovino and Serpil Oppermann's words, "material realities are enmeshed with meaning and narratives."[4] Critical reassessments of Romanticism, the aesthetic tradition closely involved with nature, also offer new insights into the past representations of human and nonhuman relationships. Such developments introduce a range of opportunities for enriched readings of Montgomery who, as her journal entry suggests, clearly privileged her own relationship to nature. In this collection, two key aspects of environmental perspectives inform the volume's various strands: interrelatedness and materiality. The chapters seek to locate, rather than dislocate, the human presence in the natural world; that is, they all examine the relationship of the human with the nonhuman or, in the words of philosopher and environmentalist David Abram, "more-than-human world" that includes the life beside, around, and beyond the human presence.[5] Out of this interrelatedness emerges the volume's second aspect: the materiality of this close involvement between human and nonhuman life. In this introduction, we locate Montgomery's approach to nature within British and American Romanticism and the Canadian literary context, and at the same time, we draw attention to theoretical innovations about nature and, specifically, literature and the environment that suggest new ways of approaching Montgomery's work.

Montgomery's approach to nature, both human and nonhuman, was by no means time-bound or static. Jennifer Litster, in this volume, notes that Montgomery began writing in Prince Edward Island as an "imaginative young woman who experienced the natural world in a different way to those around her" and ended her writing career as an "aging exile" in Toronto. During her lifetime of writing, she experienced profound changes wrought by modernity and the horrors of two world wars. A prolific writer in several genres, Montgomery was an astute observer of humans and their environments.[6] She tracked her observations of everyday life and environs in her journals allowing us to understand the intensity that she brought to experiencing and imagining nature in both her life-writing and fiction. Her writing contributed to the development of a consciousness about nature in her readers. Margaret Atwood suggests that Montgomery's influence is "subcutaneous,"[7] exerting material and embodied effects on generations of readers that critical enquiry continues to discover.

Approaching Nature and Literature

"Nature," as Raymond Williams famously states "is perhaps the most complex word in the [English] language."[8] Timothy Clark elaborates on nature's often incompatible meanings: at its narrowest usage, nature qualifies something definitively, as in "the nature of 'nature'," while at "its broadest *nature* is the sum total of structures, substances and causal powers that are the universe." Clark reminds us that nature is framed in opposition to culture and subsequently positioned "as an object of human contemplation, exploitation, wonder or terror."[9] Embedded in this human-centric approach to nature are the problematic tensions between nature–culture, mind–matter, self–other, and subject–object relations which many environmental theorists, across multiple disciplines, challenge. Anthropologist Donna Haraway, for example, insists that "natureculture" be simultaneously articulated underlining how the material and discursive processes are intertwined and how dualistic formulations have informed our thinking about nature.[10] Abram's designation of a more-than-human environment makes a similar point privileging contiguity rather than separation of human and nonhuman nature.

In the discourse of the late twentieth and early twenty-first centuries, the critical understanding of nature and its representations comes from a range of standpoints, most notably ecocriticism. Lawrence Buell, the literary critic at the forefront in the development of environmental criticism, opens his 2011 article on emerging trends in ecocriticism with the question, "What *is* ecocriticism?"[11] Fifteen years earlier in the introduction to the highly influential *Ecocriticism Reader*, Cheryll Glotfelty asked and answered this same question: "Simply put," Glotfelty states, "ecocriticism is the study of the relationship between literature and the physical environment."[12] As evidenced by Buell's return to the question, and his description of the expansion of ecocriticism, Glotfelty's answer leaves the issue wide open and has proven not so simple. More recently, in *Greening the Maple: Canadian Ecocriticism in Context*, Ella Soper and Nicholas Bradley contend that "ecocriticism can be described in very general terms as the investigation of the many ways in which culture and the environment – the realm that both includes and exceeds the human – are interrelated and conceptualized."[13] In "Ecocriticism, What Is It Good For?," first published in 2000, Robert Kern offers as one of ecocriticism's objectives "reading against the grain" to expose "a whole range of anthropocentric attitudes and assumptions whose authority and even hegemony in reading and criticism are often still taken for granted."[14] These critical insights provide possibilities for rereading, and for reconsidering genres and traditions such as Romanticism, that have been foundational to articulating human relationships to nature. Buell's ongoing revision of the critical discourse on Romantic nature, for instance, allows for a shift from the study of Romantic aesthetic alone to a recognition of the Romantic ecology that may be part of it, and opens up new avenues for reappraisals of writers like Montgomery.

Romanticism(s)

The Romantic designation of Montgomery not only links her to a British tradition but also aligns her with her Canadian contemporaries, specifically the group of poets whom Malcolm Ross would later come to designate the Confederation poets. They, too, valued nature and aimed to recreate in their poetry the kind of "spontaneous overflow of powerful feelings" that Wordsworth articulates for Romantic poetry.[15] In invoking nature, Montgomery's diction reflects their language. Like Montgomery, they speak about their "companionship" with nature. The poem that Carl Y. Connor, in his 1929 assessment of Archibald Lampman, deemed the best reflection of the poet's "attitude to Nature" is entitled, "On the Companionship with Nature."[16] Bliss Carman was the Canadian poet to whom Montgomery was most closely drawn, as reflected in her many allusions to his work, especially in the semiautobiographical *Emily* series. Not surprisingly, Carman's 1903 collection of essays on nature is titled "The Kinship of Nature."[17] The writings of the Confederation poets, like Montgomery's, appealed to the reading public but as the twentieth century wore on, neither benefitted critically from their powerful, romantic renderings of nature.[18] The aesthetic shift toward modernism in the first decades of the twentieth-century intensified after the First World War. The move toward a more Darwinian view of nature was already amply present in Tennyson and his late Romantic contemporaries, and reinforced the disruptive urgings of the new century to break with past literary traditions. Modernism's demands for starker realities and more abstract forms of expression detracted from the critical appeal of the Confederation poets and Montgomery's work alike and made them seem traditional, sometimes mistakenly, in a time that was privileging the new and experimental in both content and form. The Confederation poets, nonetheless, were allotted a place in the formation of a Canadian literary history. Their work appeared in the first anthology of Canadian literature to include both prose and verse, *Our Canadian Literature: Representative Prose and Verse* edited by Albert Durrant Watson and Lorne Pierce (1922), and in the canon-forming anthologies of Canadian literature that emerged in the mid and latter half of the twentieth century.[19] In contrast, Montgomery's writing, with its intensely appreciative renderings of the natural world that made her work synonymous with Canadian literature worldwide, finds no place in these early anthologies of Canadian literature. Her deep involvement with nature, her environmental explorations, and her relation to a Canadian literary tradition or traditions are missing.

The Romanticism of Montgomery and the Confederation poets along with their placement in literary traditions, either established or emerging, is further complicated by its North American context since their Romanticism did not follow a straight line from the British influence. The Confederation poets looked to Wordsworth and his contemporaries, and their Victorian practitioners, but they also read widely among their American predecessors and counterparts who themselves were influenced by a European and British Romanticism, adapting it to the outlook of a new nation. D.M.R. Bentley suggests that "in turning towards the natural environment for materials that were recognizably original because local or indigenous and, therefore, outside the existing repertoire of English Romantic and Victorian Poetry, the Confederation poets were largely guided by American nature writers."[20] Like the Confederation poets, Montgomery, too, was drawn to influential figures in American Romanticism. Her characters speak about and quote Keats, and Tennyson alongside Emerson. She, too, read the American naturalist, John Burroughs, a favourite of the Confederation poets, and possibly based her own naturalist writer, John Foster, on him.[21] American influences on and modifications of the British Romantic outlook became a part of Canadian writers' Romanticism; in its new world setting, Romanticism confronts the wild without necessarily turning from the cultivated or the bucolic. It is drawn to view the natural world not only as a retreat and source of healing but also as an object of exploration. The Romanticism of Montgomery and other North American writers generally privilege immediacy and observation over Wordsworthian recollection; Montgomery's work puts poetic subjectivity into creative tension with nature's autonomy. Like Victorian critic, John Ruskin, who through his critical principles and especially his term, pathetic fallacy,[22] warned against making excessive emotional response the basis of art, Montgomery resists the disappearance of the nonhuman organic world into the human consciousness observing and describing it; she rejects an art that depicts nature as only a mirror for human emotions and sensations. In its nuanced resistance to the "assimilat[ion]" of nature into the representation of "the thoughts, reflections and memories of the individual mind," as Aidan Day describes British Romanticism,[23] the increased emphasis on interaction in Montgomery and others reveals their broad conceptualizations of nature which facilitates new lines of critical enquiry. A focus on Montgomery's representations of the relationship between the human and nonhuman, which this variation invites, seems timely and warranted as evidenced by this volume's studies.

Modernism and Its Legacies

While Mary Rubio and others rightly identify the shift toward modernism and the divide between canonical and popular literature as significant in the resistance to Montgomery, other factors involving perspectives on nature have also affected Montgomery's critical position for most of the twentieth century.[24] The influential formulations of a distinct Canadian literature in the 1960s and 1970s interpreted Canadian writing as a response to the presence of a hostile, alien natural environment. Montgomery's "Haunted Wood," however thrilling and chilling for her fictional Anne, does not fit Northrop Frye's well-known designation of the Canadian imagination as a "garrison mentality" emerging from the country's "huge, unthinking, menacing, and formidable physical setting," or Margaret Atwood's premise that physical and mental survival in the face of "nature the monster" is the dominant theme of Canadian literature.[25] Soper and Bradley identify the relationship between nature and nation as central to the development of a distinct Canadian literature, but they also confirm that multiple expanding directions in environmental criticism are effectively moving the markers for a "national literature" beyond the "overarching and distinguishing motifs and concerns" initially defining it. Such reappraisals do not diminish "nature's importance to Canadian culture" but rather highlight its diversity and simultaneity. For Soper and Bradley, the subject of nature is contentious, but they offer the theoretical perspective of a "comparatist paradigm" that is open to a range of variants.[26] Their perspective allows for the challenging of environments, as well as for appreciative visions.

Montgomery seems closer to some of the viable, alternative views of nature in Canadian literature that have emerged in more recent decades especially in studies on women's writing. Diana Relke's *Greenwor(l)ds* argues that Frye's notions of "deep terror" as a distinguishing feature of Canadian poetry excludes the nation's female poets whose approaches to the physical environment are not necessarily premised on confrontation and subjugation. More recently, Shelley Boyd privileges the garden over the wilderness in her reading of five Canadian women writers from the nineteenth through to the twenty-first century.[27] Suggestive for Montgomery studies, too, are readings of individual authors in which the human presence sees its interactions with its surroundings as actively and mutually relational. Helen M. Buss, for instance, finds in the life writings of nineteenth-century Ontario settlers such as Elizabeth Simcoe and Mary O'Brien the development of a "unique relation to the land" that is optimistic and ultimately liberating "from the strictures the old life put on women."[28] Extending Michael Peterman and Carl Ballstadt's view of

Catharine Parr Traill's "ecological conservatism," Margaret Steffler and Neill Steffler discuss the way in which Traill's botanical eye balances her "perceptive observations and analysis of the position of Canadian plants and flowers within their ecosystems" with "assessments of her own position and circumstances in the 'new world.'"[29] The approaches in these studies offer possible further directions in exploring Montgomery's relationship to and representations of nature – how, for instance, do her depictions of landscapes interact with her inclusions of gardens and gardeners? – and also confirm the viability of the multiple critical perspectives in this volume's chapters and in the handful of studies on which they build.

In her study of Montgomery in the "extraordinary Canadians" series, Jane Urquhart observes that "given to writing about landscape and how it shapes character, [Montgomery] was accused of writing purple prose."[30] In associating her approach to nature with denigrations of Romantic writing, Urquhart accurately pinpoints Montgomery's vulnerability to critical dismissal. As this collection shows, Montgomery's work defies ready classification and the many designations that include not only "purple prose" but "nostalgic," "sentimental," "regional idyllic," "romantic," "pastoral," "local colour," and others. These categories, which often marginalize women writers, are the subject of reappraisals by feminist scholars such as Judith Fetterley, Marjorie Pryse, and more recently, Karen L. Kilcup. In *Fallen Forests: Emotion, Embodiment, and Ethics in American Women's Environmental Writing*, Kilcup attends to "the literary, historical, and theoretical contexts for some of our most pressing environmental debates," arguing that women writers "have engendered awareness of environmental concerns" through strategies that include "logic, ethics, and, particularly, emotion."[31]

Urquhart's association of landscape and characters is astute and in the second decade of the twenty-first century reveals the present irony in earlier critical dismissals of Montgomery. Abram's "more-than-human" formulation is significant not for premising a qualitative inclusion (or exclusion) but for its quantitative recognition of the vast sentient life of which the human is one significant part of that larger whole. This is a premise with which Montgomery's writings are fully engaged and which offers possibilities for rereading her work. Iovino and Oppermann, for example, note that landscapes, so often seen as passive objects of the human gaze, display a vibrant agency affecting human and nonhuman life. Landscapes may possess "a strong character" that interacts with and shapes human figures.[32] This presents a familiar idea to Montgomery readers who have recognized the "character" of Avonlea/Cavendish. Readings of lively landscapes and their many animated elements also serve to counter the well-versed limitations of anthropomorphism. Bennett's reevaluation of the practice of anthropomorphism suggests that it works against the dominant human-centric approaches to nature by striking "a chord ... between person and thing," and thus, she observes, "I am no longer above or outside a nonhuman 'environment.'"[33] The nature–culture and the mind–matter dualisms are predicated on the idea that the matter of nature is stable and passive, but as physicist Karen Barad succinctly states in her ground breaking book, *Meeting the Universe Halfway*, "matter is produced and productive, generated and generative. Matter is agentive, not a fixed essence or property of things."[34] This view opens the way for alternative understandings of the matter of nature and points toward nature(s)' plurality. Iovino and Oppermann contend that reframing matter and extending agency beyond the domain of the human recognizes the "kinship between out-side and in-side, the mind and the world, embracing life, language, mind and sensorial perception in a non-dualistic perspective."[35] While Montgomery's vivid appreciations of the natural world reflect at times a Romantic sensibility that embraces the picturesque and deploys personification, she nonetheless continually reverts to an acknowledgement of nature's and her own autonomy. Her writings represent the human and nonhuman as equal participants in the act of living, engaged in the necessity and challenge of a beneficial coexistence. The chapters in this collection involve Montgomery studies in the kinds of explorations that these ways of thinking suggest.

The volume's intent is not strictly environmentalist in a conventional sense; the volume aims, rather, to open up a broad conversation about the matter of nature(s) in Montgomery's work. This strategy is evident in the collection's title, which pluralizes nature – "L.M. Montgomery and the Matter of Nature(s)" – underlining the multiplicities embedded in the notion of nature. Our inclusion of chapters on kinship (Paul Keen; Laura Robinson), natural law (Kate Sutherland) and illness (Jean Mitchell), subjects that may initially seem beyond the topic of nature, are integral to studying Montgomery's "nature(s)" since these chapters suggest how nature is constituted in diverse and frequently "un-natural" ways in Montgomery's work. The emphasis on materiality and interrelatedness extends the understanding of "the matter of nature(s)" to encompass the human (including the nature in human nature) and the more-than-human world. The collection, committed to a multi- and interdisciplinary approach that is broadly in accord with the inherent interdisciplinarity of ecocriticism, includes literary, anthropological, gender, ecological, legal, queer, and postcolonial perspectives which provoke new critical entries into Montgomery's work in the context of the matter of nature.

Critical Assessments of Montgomery

Critical studies of Montgomery underline the range and strength of her literary and cultural achievements and challenge the narrow positioning of her as a popular writer or a children's writer. Critical and biographical work by Mary Rubio and Elizabeth Waterston, including their editing of Montgomery's journals (1985–2012), have established Montgomery as a strong subject of scholarly pursuit. Several collections of essays have illuminated Montgomery and her work through specific contexts, such as Montgomery and Canadian culture, Montgomery and popular culture, and Montgomery's darker side.[36] Multiple studies of *Anne of Green Gables* emerged out of its centennial year of 2008.[37] Benjamin Lefebvre's three-volume edition, *The L.M. Montgomery Reader*, consisting of hitherto unpublished journal and magazine articles, by and about Montgomery (2013), a selection of scholarly articles (2014), and "her legacy in review" (2015), continue to make accessible valuable primary materials and secondary sources. Two recent collections of essays, *L.M. Montgomery's Rainbow Valleys: the Ontario Years, 1911–1942* (2015) coedited by Rita Bode and Lesley D. Clement, and *L.M. Montgomery and War* (2017), coedited by Andrea McKenzie and Jane Ledwell, extend the investigations of Montgomery's work in these new geographical and historical directions. Elizabeth Epperly's influential study, *The Fragrance of Sweet-Grass: L.M. Montgomery's Heroines and the Pursuit of Romance* (1992; reissued, 2014), with its particular focus on the Romantic tradition, threads the place of nature into Montgomery's exploration of her young female protagonists' development throughout the work.

Drawing on Epperly's lead, other studies focus closely on Montgomery's representations and conceptions of landscapes. Janice Fiamengo's discussion in the *Making Avonlea* collection about the "popular landscape in *Anne of Green Gables*" suggests that part of Montgomery's enduring popularity lies in her ability to transform "physical space into an imaginative geography" through language and emotion creating "portable landscapes" that have universal appeal. Fiamengo goes on to acknowledge the problematic dismissal of colonial dispossession but also sees in Anne's need to belong to a place an alternative to the drive for domination over nature and the living beings inhabiting it.[38] A special issue of CREArTA, edited by Rosemary Ross Johnston, considers what the volume's title suggests, the close connections between "L.M. Montgomery's Interior and Exterior Landscapes" (2006). The articles in this issue interpret Montgomery's landscapes as central to the subjectivity of both her writerly self and her protagonists' identity; they see landscape as consistently entwined with an inner space that is closely linked to concepts of home and a sense of spirituality. Invoking Margaret Doody's observation in her Introduction to *The Annotated Anne of Green Gables*, that Montgomery "will be freshly discovered as a 'Green writer,'" Nancy Holmes, in her contribution to the *Storm and Dissonance* volume, shifts the discussion more directly into current environmental approaches by invoking ecofeminist theory to explore Montgomery's attempts "to envision solutions to the conflicts that environmentalists come up against all the time: how to reconcile perceptions of nature as sacred ground and as our home yet also as something subject to our desires to ravish and profit from, as well as to use for our genuine, legitimate, needs."[39] Several articles by Irene Gammel draw on different disciplines for their analyses of Montgomery's landscapes: her ethnographic approach in *Making Avonlea* finds in Montgomery's landscapes "the *erotic* and the *sensual* qualities that solicit desire" and argues that Montgomery presents "her girl readers with a rich arena of erotic alternatives" by encouraging her girl heroines "to take control of their pleasure and [by] put[ting] them in touch with their bodies and their surroundings."[40] Gammel's later article in *The Lion and the Unicorn* opens up the visual appreciation of Montgomery's landscapes, which is always a starting point for her appeal, to somatic theories that privilege a multisensory "embodied ... aesthetics." Located "at the intersection of ecology, aesthetics, body theory, and gender," Gammel calls "for future research to look beyond the ... visual conventions" in Montgomery's work, and "to recognize the painterly appreciation of nature inscribed in the text[s] as a screen for covering more radical and covert subtexts that effectively break the Cartesian body/mind split."[41] Two essays in Terri Doughty and Dawn Thompson's collection *Knowing Their Place?* (2011) examine issues of "identity and space" in Montgomery's representations of nature. Rather than critiquing the tendency of Montgomery's heroines to personify and bestow names on nature as a form of imposition, Catherine Posey argues that the "personification of elements in nature ... are ... strategies Montgomery uses in [*Anne of Green Gables*] to show that a connectedness between the individual and the natural world is positive, as Anne continually helps to widen the vision of those around her."[42] Focusing on *Jane of Lantern Hill*, Jane Grafton interprets Jane's transformations in terms of an "ecocritical ... experience," that distinguishes "between being in nature, and being active in a natural environment."[43] Christiana Salah, in turn, pursues the interest in Montgomery's darker side in interpreting Montgomery's landscape depictions in her short stories. In her article in *Tulsa Studies in Women's Literature*, she argues that Montgomery's natural setting at times transforms into a "prehensile place" with threatening gothic associations for her girl protagonists.[44]

The Chapters

The chapters in this collection build on previous Montgomery scholarship, extending it in ways that reflect the far reaches of environmental studies. Their focus remains on Montgomery's prose fiction and life writing, but their ideas and approaches suggest possibilities for further critical inquiries, most notably, perhaps, into Montgomery's verse, which often looks to nature and environmental themes for its subject.[45] The volume's diverse approaches recognize the urgency of the issues at stake in the framing of the matter of nature at this time. The studies on kinship, law, and illness support the volume's aim to trouble the boundary between nature and culture, and mind and body by suggesting how specific deployments of nature may disrupt and/or affirm assumptions about nature. As already suggested, environmental perspectives foregrounding the materiality of humans and the vitality of nature create challenges but also offer productive openings for rereading Montgomery. We have structured the chapters around three main themes: nature's places, nature's embodiments, and nature's otherness. Each of these themes emphasizes the linked issues of the interrelatedness and materiality of nature in Montgomery's work.

Part One: Nature's Places

The chapters in this section acknowledge the ways in which compelling descriptions of place connect language and landscape, and the human and nonhuman in Montgomery's work. The authors reconceptualize Montgomery's ideas and practices of place by extending them from the singular to the multiple. Anthropologist Margaret Rodman, argues that "places like voices are local and multiple."[46] Place is a conduit for understanding the complex relational dimensions of nature and human nature. While "the local" remains important, this section's critical discussions also challenge the idea that the specificity of place is sufficient to anchor a productive environmental or ecological vision. Ursula Heise, who suggests that an emphasis on place too often privileges humans and culture, cautions against the uncritical reliance on ideas of place, rootedness, and the local. Nature, argues Heise, "in its local manifestation does not appear as a stable ground in which identities can be firmly rooted but as a dynamic force of constant transformations."[47]

In "Queer Ecology Visits Silver Bush: Fire, Fantasy, and Futurity," Catriona Sandilands challenges conventional interpretations of Pat's attachment to Silver Bush as pathological by reframing the *Pat* novels around "Montgomery's opposition between love of place and heterosexual futurity." Pat's aversion to change and her deep attachment to her place, eventually destroyed by fire, is read as resistance to heterosexual and patrilocal conventions that dictate the need for women to sever ties to their places upon marriage. Sandilands's chapter probes these normalizing conventions and denaturalizes place while underlining the "inevitability of both social transformation and ecological succession," specifically through island settings and occurrences of fire. By bringing Montgomery's novels into conversation with Jane Rule's contemporary novel, *After the Fire,* Sandilands suggests the regenerative capacities and possibilities of social–ecological transformations.

In "The Scotsman, the Scribe, and the Spyglass: Going Back with L.M. Montgomery to Prince Edward Island," Jennifer Litster explores how Montgomery remembered and fictionalized the natural world of her childhood when in 1924 she transcribed Cavendish farmer Charles Macneill's fragmentary diary that documented farming and social life in their community between 1892 and 1896. This exercise, according to Litster, allowed Montgomery to reflect on her childhood in Cavendish transporting her to an earlier happier time and place before modern changes such as mechanization transformed the landscape. The novel *Jane of Lantern Hill,* written in 1936, argues Litster, was shaped by Montgomery's immersion in the diary with its quotidian details of rural life providing a sharp contrast to the urban and class-based snobbery depicted in the novel. Jane, who revels in the domestic and agricultural tasks of everyday rural life, unlike Montgomery's other heroines, "reads the world through a farmer's eyes." By returning to Cavendish via Macneill's diary, suggests Litster, Montgomery was able to acquire a different perspective on nature and nature's work recreating Prince Edward Island landscapes anew.

As already noted, Sandilands, in this section's first chapter, places Montgomery's writing into a late twentieth-century Canadian literary context; Nancy Holmes effectively draws Montgomery into a North American frame of reference by comparing Montgomery and American writer, Gene Stratton-Porter. In "Romantic Novelist as Naturalist: John Foster and the Bird Woman," Holmes locates the authors as contemporaries who loved their places, an island and swamp lands, places that are often essentialized and marginalized. Place, in Montgomery's work, writes Nancy Holmes, "is charged with narrative vitality through an engagement with and love of nature." Holmes explores the profound relationship between places and persons arguing that both authors "not merely enhance nature appreciation" in their respective descriptions of beloved places but "radicalize narrative in fascinating ways" that render them precursors of "ecofiction." The authors, argues Holmes, were innovative in their attempts to find narrative strategies that privilege place rather than plot, in the same way nature writing does.

In the section's final chapter, Rita Bode suggests that indoors and outdoors, the rural and the urban alike, made strong claims on Montgomery. "L.M. Montgomery's 'Indoors and Out': Imagining an Organic Architecture" affirms the extent to which Montgomery's views on nature eschewed divisive binaries in favour of a "partnership ethic" beneficial to human and nonhuman nature. The chapter traces Montgomery's enduring engagement with built environments and the ways in which her fictional houses, the creations of culture, reconcile with rather than oppose nature's presence. The chapter demonstrates how Montgomery's fiction "articulates a dynamic architecture ... in which the constructed is not only a shelter for its human inhabitants but is itself contained in harmony with and by the land on which it is situated." Bode's analysis finds in Montgomery's built environments models of modern architectural principles, such as the "organic architecture" espoused by Montgomery's contemporary, the architect, Frank Lloyd Wright.

Part Two: Embodied Nature

The contributors in this section look to new or different ways of understanding how nature is imagined, observed, and embodied in Montgomery's work by exploring practices that connect the material and social in human experience. They examine both limitations and strengths in Montgomery's engagements with nature, exploring questions about the extent to which her work undermines dualities and forges an ethos of sustainability for life on the planet. The chapters attempt to further the understanding of the role that nonhuman nature plays in the formation of human knowledge and values. Several chapters draw on the intersection of science and the humanities, illuminating how ideas of nature are mobilized in law, medicine, and education as well as materialized in bodies and metaphors. As Kilcup points out, tracking "metaphor's role in shaping attitudes toward nature … and effecting agency" is a vital thread in contemporary ecocriticism.[48]

With her enduring interest in Montgomery's figurative language and evocative depictions of nature, Elizabeth Epperly in "Natural Bridge: L.M. Montgomery and the Architecture of Imaginative Landscapes," argues that the effectiveness of Montgomery's metaphors is tied to the ways in which they engage nature. Focusing on "bridges and bridging," Epperly draws on American transcendentalism, iconic places, and current theories in neuroscience to trace the connections among mind, metaphor, and nature. Her chapter seeks to explain the deeply engaging effects of Montgomery's imaginative landscapes on her readers. Epperly suggests that Montgomery's metaphors render her writing "accessible" and "transformative." She argues that Emerson's notion of "Nature" provided Montgomery with "a convincing description for the kind of power she experienced in and through her reading and her environment. She gives this experience of power to all of the heroines of her novels; it is the grounding for her metaphors as well as for theirs."

In "L.M. Montgomery's Neurasthenia: Embodied Nature and the Matter of Nerves," Jean Mitchell contextualizes the emergence of neurasthenia and explores Montgomery's observations of her own experience with the nervous disorder. Prevalent in the late Victorian and early Edwardian eras, neurasthenia provided a language linking nature, culture and society. Montgomery's identification with the nervous disorder, a common condition among writers and intellectuals, validated both her creativity and anxiety. The gender-specific causes and treatments of the nervous disorder are discussed in the context of Montgomery's life and times. The body most often depicted as simply "natural" is shown in this chapter to be riveted by social, cultural, and political processes. While the body is privileged as the site of exhausted nerves under duress from modernity, the treatment of neurasthenia often entailed a simultaneous move away from locating bodies within social and ecological contexts and an increasing reliance on medicalization. Neurasthenia, suggests Mitchell, was innovative in underlining the adverse effects of modernizing society on humans but subscribed to a limited view of nature as a source of human revitalization while underplaying the devastation that modernity's expanding capitalism also imposed on nature. In contrast, Montgomery's view of nature, while restorative, was far more complex and expansive.

Kate Sutherland's "The Education of Emily: Tempering a Force of Nature through Lessons in Law" examines the use of "natural law" in children's literature and the cultivation of a critical understanding of morals and law. The essay draws on the distinction between natural law based on moral truths derived from human nature in contrast to positive law that emerged in the nineteenth century and effectively separated law and morality. In this chapter Sutherland examines Montgomery's journals, which outline her own legal battles, and the novel *Emily of New Moon*, written during the 1920s while Montgomery was preoccupied with lawsuits. According to Sutherland, Montgomery displays scepticism toward positive law and a commitment to natural law. Novels, as Sutherland shows, can embrace a form of natural law and provide a basis to critically assess positive law on moral grounds. The novel extends and complicates ideas of law as well as assumptions about nature and morality. Sutherland demonstrates how natural law derived from truths about human nature opens up an inquiry about both the conjunctions and contradictions of nature, law, and morality

In the final chapter of this section, "The Spirit of Inquiry: Nature Study and the Sense of Wonder in L.M. Montgomery's Anne Books," Tara K. Parmiter traces the nature study movement in these novels. The movement emphasized the direct observation of the natural world to teach science and to generate a love of nature among children. The chapter charts the ways in which this movement informed teaching and writing about nature at the turn of the century. Parmiter locates Montgomery within this movement arguing that for her "the natural world is not only a site of wonder but of learning, where the matter of nature is also a matter of education." Nature study, according to Parmiter, addressed the contradictory goals of preparing school children for scientific study in a modern society and renewing the link between humans and the nonhuman in North America which is increasingly urbanized and removed from "wild" nature. Nature study, argues Parmiter, privileged the imagination as well as observation both of which were essential to Montgomery's approach to nature.

Part Three: Nature's Otherness

In the volume's final section, the chapters emphasize the dynamic and ambivalent interplay between and among nature and nurture, the human and animal, organic and constructed nature in Montgomery's work. They address the ways in which her writing explores difference within an interconnected world where nature, as Kate Soper suggests, "is the concept through which humanity thinks its difference and specificity."[49] The chapters in this section call attention to how received ideas about nature and human nature are deployed to bolster or dispute claims pertaining to gender, sexuality, animality, biology, and race. The chapters involving kinship show how biology and society are never truly separate despite human efforts to create boundaries between them. The authors strive to show how the nonhuman material realm informs the narratives and meanings attached to the everyday lives of humans. Kinship, for example, is often determined by blood and construed as "natural" while orphans, bereft of kin, are rendered "unnatural."

Paul Keen in " No London street Arabs for me': The Unnatural Orphan in *Anne of Green Gables*," posits that nature implies "a range of meanings, many of them in contradiction with one another." He uses the figure of the orphan to challenge the binary limitations of the nature-versus-nurture debate, arguing that it is better read as nature-and-nurture. His chapter explores how *Anne of Green Gables* questions the influence of biology and environment on human character to disrupt "a domestic ideology grounded in narrowly conceived definitions of the happy home and the happy child." According to Keen, it is Anne's lack of difference and her inability to reinforce the self–other distinction that prove to be most threatening to the always tenuous collective identity. Keen alerts us to the slippages in the various categories of race, class, and foreigner that are used to index morality and "otherness " in the novel.

In the next chapter, "Kindred Spirits: Kinship and the Nature of Nature in *Anne's House of Dreams* and *The Blue Castle*," Laura Robinson uses an anthropological lens to examine the role of biology and nature in kinship relationships in two of Montgomery's novels. Robinson argues that the author disrupts kinship relations by demonstrating how the operations of the traditional biological family work to reinforce gender roles while questioning what constitutes "natural" and kinship. The "natural" is represented by the biological family and heterosexual marriage, but, as Robinson argues, the novels show that the "natural" is often most unnatural. Montgomery casts doubt on the belief that "the family must be a specifically biologically-determined entity." In a nuanced analysis, Robinson shows how Montgomery troubles the opposition between nature and nurture by privileging affiliation over filiation. Montgomery, argues Robinson, is ambivalent about the "naturalness" invested in kinship even as she appears to validate it.

Lesley D. Clement's chapter, "The Poetic Sensibility: Empathy and Discerning Nature's Secrets," examines the self–other dichotomy in a discussion of the human apprehension of nature through human empathy and creativity. Drawing on the work of primatologist and ethnologist, Frans de Waal, Clement distinguishes between two relationships to nature: one based on intimacy and accessibility and another, prevalent among artists, that privileges a more complex empathetic approach to nature encompassing not only its beauty but its "otherness." The author contrasts Montgomery's protagonists, Anne and Emily, to demonstrate the two very different approaches to nature and to creativity. Anne's personification of nature, argues Clement, epitomizes her search for intimacy with nature, which is depicted as beautiful, familiar and accessible. In contrast, Emily cultivates an empathetic approach to nature that informs her poetic capacity and encompasses "the menacing face of nature."

Idette Noomé brings the volume to a close with "The Nature of the Beast: Pets and People in L.M. Montgomery's Fiction," in which she draws on the expanding field of animal studies to consider Montgomery's approach to domestic animals in her life-writing and novels. Noomé argues that Montgomery's depictions of people's relationships with pets inform us about the "moral worth and potential for empathy" of humans. The chapter also tracks the "changing discourse about human-animal relations and the place of animals in the world" during Montgomery's time. While Montgomery does not anthropomorphize animals, according to Noomé, there are examples of the capacity of animals such as Jem's dog, Monday, in *Rilla of Ingleside*, to comprehend complex scenarios. It is striking, as Noomé points out, that farm animals, so ubiquitous in rural life, are not given attention in Montgomery's fiction. This omission supports

Litster's contention in this volume that "the hard graft of the farm rarely impinges on her child characters." However, violence against animals, as Noomé suggests, escalates in Montgomery's later fiction and serves as a barometer for her own concerns about the world and her family.

Conclusion

The various perspectives in this volume acknowledge coexistence, but they also suggest that the human and more-than-human are coextensive and even codeterminant, occupying but also subject to the same space and time and to each other within these parameters. They recognize that material embodiment, like social factors, is an active, multidirectional environmental force. In their diverse approaches, the chapters look to the kind of embodied materialism that Stacy Alaimo articulates in her theory of porous bodies. In Alaimo's words, "imagining human corporeality as trans-corporeality, in which the human is always enmeshed with the more-than-human world, underlines the extent to which the substance of the human is always ultimately inseparable from 'the environment' … [which] is not located somewhere out there, but is always the very substance of ourselves."[50] Alaimo's contemporary thoughts align with ideas found in the literary traditions of previous centuries and, applied to Montgomery, suggest that her nineteenth-century literary roots not only honed her nature descriptions but also developed her awareness of an expansive nature that is both material and interrelated.

Singing of himself, Walt Whitman, more than a century and a half ago, recounts a child asking him: "*What is the grass*?" The chapters in this collection suggest that in the early decades of the twentieth century, Montgomery was exploring a similar question, but from a twenty-first-century perspective, the question sounds perhaps a bit different; what we hear her asking is, "what is nature"? Whitman's initial response acknowledges the complexity of the child's question: "How could I answer the child? I do not know what it is any more than he," but as he probes for an explanation, he finds multiple answers that are both inclusive and expansive. From thinking first that the grass is "the flag of my disposition, out of hopeful green stuff woven," to finding, more than four hundred lines later, that it is "no less than the journey-work of the stars," Whitman finally bequeaths himself at the poem's end "to the dirt to grow from the grass I love, / If you want me again look for me under your boot-soles," he declares.[51] The effect of Whitman's direction is a startling defamiliarization of the human presence that places the poet, and us, his readers, in kinship with the dirt and the life it bears, the grass. The concept is both Biblical and modern. The chapters in this volume make similar claims for the "matter of nature(s)"; they reveal startling connections and uncover a multiplicity of approaches to the complex questions that Montgomery's work poses. As environmental awareness continues to permeate our social and cultural thinking and enters into a wide range of disciplinary research and methodologies, these chapters expand critical directions in Montgomery studies bringing new insights into her life and work and into the broader field of Canadian literary and cultural studies.

PART ONE

Nature's Places

CHAPTER ONE

Fire, Fantasy, and Futurity: Queer Ecology Visits Silver Bush[1]

Catriona Sandilands

L.M. Montgomery's *Mistress Pat* (1935), the sequel to *Pat of Silver Bush* (1933), ends with a fire. Specifically, it ends with a blaze that not only sees Silver Bush, "a home that had been a home for generations[,] wiped out," but also marks the final destruction of the lifelong anchor of Patricia Gardiner's self-concept: "She felt horribly old. Her love for Silver Bush had kept her young … and now it was gone. Nothing was left … there was only a dreadful, unbearable emptiness."[2] Pat has loved Silver Bush all her life, loved its fields and buildings as people; every change that she has experienced, from the birth of her sister Rachel in the early chapters of *Pat of Silver Bush* to the death of beloved servant Judy Plum a year before the fire, has been accompanied by an intensified identification with the place itself. As Montgomery tells us clearly and repeatedly, in Pat's world, the place of Silver Bush stands as a refuge against change, a rich island of presence and stability in the midst of the inevitable – for Pat, generally unwelcome – transformations of family and community that are a routine part of everyday life: "The house remembered her whole life. *It* has always been the same … *it* had never changed … not really. Only little surface changes. How she loved it! She loved it in morning rose and sunset amber, and best of all in the darkness of night, when it loomed palely through the gloom and was all her own. This beauty was hers … all hers. Life could never be empty at Silver Bush."[3]

One particularly revealing aspect of Pat's intense and detailed attachment to place – and, as Jean Mitchell points out in her introduction to *Storm and Dissonance: L.M. Montgomery and Conflict*, of Pat's concomitant pleasure and skill in "the incessant work of place-making"[4] – is that

Montgomery opposes Pat's love of place to most possibilities for her full participation in the usual social rituals of patrilocal heterosexuality:[5] despite abundant pressure to the contrary, Pat cannot marry because marrying would mean leaving home. Indeed, with one possible exception, childhood friend Hilary (Jingle) Gordon, Pat simply cannot love any man as well as she loves Silver Bush; she rejects one suitor because he demands that she think about him rather than the weather, another because he dares to demean the place, and most of the rest because she realizes that place is more central to her emotional universe than any person (notably, Montgomery's descriptions of Silver Bush are more vivid than those of any of the various suitors). In the middle of a serious marriage proposal from one such suitor, for instance, "Pat turned a little away from his flushed, eager face. Through a gap in the trees she saw the dark purple of the woods on Robinson's hill … the blue sheen of the gulf … the green of the clover aftermath in the Field of the Pool … the misty opal sky … and Silver Bush." In the midst of such detailed and sensual emplacement, the reader knows that this suitor is doomed long before he does. Although Pat has intended to accept his proposal, what comes out of her mouth is yet another refusal: "I can't marry you. I thought I could but I can't."[6]

And so, it is only when Silver Bush burns down that patrilocal heterosexuality is able to find a lasting purchase in Pat's life. Two weeks after the fire, Pat makes her first grieving visit to the remains of her home. She finds not only a house reduced to ashes but the eponymous birch grove more than half burned and Judy Plum's lovingly tended flower beds completely obliterated; with these three elements damaged beyond repair, there is no question that Silver Bush is dead.[7] Just as Pat is mournfully contemplating her new, miserable placelessness, she hears Hilary's voice behind her: having heard of the fire (and thus knowing his main rival is out of the picture), he has come home with the intent of claiming Pat and taking her to the new house that he has built her in Vancouver after a lifetime's ambition: "I've made you mine forever with that kiss … You can never belong to anyone else. And I've waited long enough for it." Pat at last realizes that her true happiness has always been with Hilary: "that old, old, unacknowledged ache of *loneliness she had tried to stifle with Silver Bush* vanished forever. His lips were on hers … it was like a tide turning home."[8]

I find this "happy" ending remarkably sad, not least because it feels like a last-minute attempt to reassert the supremacy of heterosexual romance over all other kinds of love: Pat's deep affection for Silver Bush is revealed to have been a pathological fantasy all along, her marriage refusals all about a repressed desire for Hilary and nothing to do with a potentially rather laudable commitment to the stewardship of a farm and family in resistance to the imperatives of heteronormativity. Other critics are more sympathetic to this ending, however: Margaret Doody argues that Pat's attachment to Silver Bush is obsessive and incestuous (she does not want her older brother Sid to marry because that would mean someone other than herself as mistress of Silver Bush, "mistress" of Sid); the Silver Bush fire shatters the mirror of her "passionately unreasonable" narcissism.[9] Heidi MacDonald adds that after the fire Pat "finally enters adulthood by agreeing to marry Jingle,"[10] as if Pat's commitment to Silver Bush has been nothing but a fantastic extension of childhood "playing house." Although there is clearly a fantasy element in Pat's desire to keep Silver Bush as unchanged as possible – in the face of the inevitability of both social transformation and ecological succession – I would like to argue in this chapter that Montgomery's choice to emphasize the incommensurability of Pat's love of place with participation in heterosexual convention is also amenable to a rather more queer ecological interpretation: Silver Bush dries up and burns not because of Pat's insularity but because of the conditions in which Pat's painstaking attention to the intricacies of place are rendered irrelevant under the social rituals of patrilocal (and patriarchal) residence and inheritance that, ultimately, determine Silver Bush's fate. Further, I would like to suggest that a queer ecological reading of the Pat books asks readers to challenge not only the heteronormative conventions undergirding the destruction of place in the novel but also some of the popular understandings of nature, including islands, fires, and the nature of ecological change, on which Montgomery's opposition between love of place and heterosexual futurity rests.

Queer Ecologies: Islands, Fires, and *After the Fire*

In his book on the "island motif" in Canadian women's fiction, Theodore Sheckels argues that Silver Bush is an "island on an island."[11] Islands, according to Sheckels, tend to be implicated in fantasies of insularity and stasis: they suggest places out of time, and in Canadian women's fiction they become sites of fictional escape, retreat, isolation, and idyll. In this view, islands are both problems and escapes from problems, partly incestuous traps, partly paradisial flirtations with *jouissance*, but certainly other-worldly. More ecologically, however, as Greg Garrard documents, islands have also been understood as natural laboratories in which environmental and evolutionary changes are seen in especially concentrated form. Drawing from the work of Charles Darwin, Garrard argues that islands foster unique forms of speciation in which isolated populations adapt to their particular isolated biogeographies, over time becoming quite distinct from their mainland cousins. As he expands, "Islands [also] tend to have a far higher proportion of endemic species than mainlands (i.e., ones found nowhere else), and their species tend to be exceptionally vulnerable to extinction."[12] And for environmental historian Alfred Crosby, both of these factors suggest the particular vulnerability of islands to imperialism of both the biological and the social variety: epidemic diseases eradicate species and peoples with no built-up resistances, whereas introduced species (including colonizing settler humans) easily decimate, for example, flightless birds that have no experience of being prey.[13] Thus, as Garrard emphasizes, relying on the work of ecologist Daniel Botkin, islands may be insular but they are most certainly *not* static; islands are not so much other-worldly as they are places where the world unfolds in particularly concentrated ways. According to Botkin, they are sites in which the ecological fact of constant transformation is most especially apparent: there is no ideal "steady-state" for nature, and it has turned out to be fairly disastrous to imagine that there is an optimum balance in which a given island ecosystem exists and to which it should return if disturbed.[14] Islands may be peculiar and fragile but on any given island on any given day, something is changing.

Although in *Mistress Pat* fire is represented primarily as the obliteration of Pat's "ecosystem," fire is part of the concentrated movement of islands, no matter how much a given human community might wish to avoid it (not all human communities do and broadcast burning was and is culturally important to many Indigenous and other peoples). Botkin offers us further insight. Many species, like the Kirtland's Warbler that only nests in the dead branches of "jack-pine woodlands that are between 6 and 21 years old,"[15] *require* fire: the jack-pines on which the warblers are entirely dependent germinate only in the heat of a fire and grow only when their leaves can reach into full sunlight, as in a fire-produced clearing. In a view of islands as idyllic "places out of time," fires are pure, lapsarian destruction; in a more ecological view, they are part of an ongoing transformative process in which new species and relationships are enabled by the physical, chemical, and biotic changes wrought by combustion.[16]

In Jane Rule's novel *After the Fire* (1989), set on Galiano Island in British Columbia, we can see this more ecological view take literary shape. In contrast to *Mistress Pat*, in which the fire ends an era, in *After the Fire* all of the seeding and nesting and growing and changing in the novel occurs, as the title indicates, in the *wake* of a fire that "bloomed into the winter night before the fire truck could get there."[17] This novel clearly considers fire not as an ending but as part of a concentrated process of transformation. Specifically, the fire acts as both a literal and a metaphoric space-clearing: both obviously and subtly, the five women through whom the story moves find their lives transformed by the fire and also by the chains of events that the fire lets loose: just as Kirtland's Warblers find a generative space in the low branches of new growth, in *After the Fire* each woman finds a new trajectory of becoming in the midst of the events that the fire directly and indirectly causes to occur.

By way of a specifically queer ecological reading, the generative capacity set in motion in Rule's novel is clearly set *against* heteronormative convention. The most obvious example concerns Red, who we discover later is pregnant with the child of the man, Dickie John (yes, really), whose house is destroyed and whose charred body is found in the ashes. Red is not in love with Dickie, who has a swaggering reputation for sleeping around, and she does not respond publicly to his death; she had a relationship with him to conceive a child and notes wryly that she "just got pregnant before he got bored."[18] Although it is doubtful that Dickie would have defended his paternal rights in any case, the fire quite literally clears the island of any of the heteronormative requirements that might have arisen around the baby's birth. With Dickie's death, Red is free to form the family of her choosing on the island that is also of her choosing: Red, her dog Blackie, and her baby daughter Blue. Even their names defy convention: the cross-species trio is constellated by Red as a set of bruise-like colours, and not according to any patronymy.

Even beyond Red's post-infernal "rebirth," Rule is quite clear in her opinion of islands, fires, and new possibilities. Each of the four other main characters – young Karen Tasuki, middle-aged Milly Forbes, older Henrietta Hawkins, and elderly Miss James – finds her relationship to the Galiano community profoundly changed over the course of the novel, changes all set narratively in motion by the fire. Henrietta Hawkins has been in a holding pattern for years, visiting her nonresponsive husband in a nursing home in Vancouver twice weekly; his eventual death releases a torrent of grief and guilt that threatens to destroy her, but Red and Karen take care of her and help her to return to her community. Racist and class-obsessed Milly Forbes, deposited on Galiano by her ex-husband to keep her out of the way of his new marriage, festers with bigotry and resentment until she has a hysterectomy (with serious complications) and is forced to rely on the other women around her. Ancient Miss James has never married and had retired to the island after years of globally itinerant teaching; after preparing herself for death, she dies and leaves her tiny, perfect house to Red, clearing the space of her elderly self so that a new life can move in. And Karen Tasuki, who retreated to the island in the aftermath of a lesbian relationship that seemed predicated on her loss of an independent identity, finds on Galiano both a strong community of women among whom to live and the need, like Miss James before her, to go elsewhere to find out where she "belongs": she plans to go to Japan to explore the part of her identity that her father demanded she forget, a choice to explore herself anew in the wake of old intimate relationships and demands.

For all of these characters, the fire and the changes that echo it throughout the novel are a form of creative destruction. On this island, in this fire, a whole array of calcified, heteronormative patterns of relationship, identity, and belief is set alight, and in the smoking aftermath the seeds of the jack-pines open. Specifically, a new kind of community emerges. Rule's Galiano is not an escape, not a fantasy, not an idyll, not a haven: in short, it is not a place out of time. Despite our desires to the contrary, fires happen, and in this case, the burning of a dense thicket of over-determined heterosexual conventions allows five island women, after the fire, to rethink how they wish to grow.

After the Fire, as well as the ecological relations of islands and fires that generated my reading of it, thus highlights a number of important questions with which to return to the Pat novels. First, rather than consider Silver Bush as an idyllic "island on an island" in which no change occurs – Pat's apparent desires notwithstanding – we can examine the relations of the novel in terms of their ongoing and concentrated transformation, including the fire as part of that change rather than as a fall from some fantastical version of grace or innocence. Second, we can pay particular attention to the ways in which Montgomery depicts the *nature* of the change that Pat so dreads and that threatens her ecological niche at Silver Bush; perhaps it is not *all* change that is at issue, but rather change that reasserts an especially heteronormative framework of ownership and occupancy (reproductive futurity) on a landscape that has, for Pat at least – crucially, including Judy Plum – resisted this framework fairly well for the majority of her life. Finally, we can consider the larger question: what does it mean to read the Pat novels through a different (in this case, queerer) set of nature metaphors? Certainly, a queer ecological reading disrupts the pathologization of Pat's detailed "sense of place" as inherently narcissistic and childish; I would like to argue that it also draws attention more broadly to the ways in which certain kinds of sex and gender relations are naturalized in the novels, creating a situation in which it is not so much Pat's fantasy that is tinder-dry and unsustainable but rather the social relations in the midst of which her dream of a life is *rendered* the stuff of fantasy.

"Niver the Same Again": A Queer Ecology of Silver Bush

For Jane Rule, writing in the late 1980s while living on the island, Galiano is a unique and dynamic biotic and social community in which fire has the potential to release possibility, rather than simply destroy it: fire and death can clear the way for alternative forms of life (not that everyone on

Galiano, Rule included, does not go out of their way to prevent it[19]). For Montgomery, writing unhappily in the early 1930s in Norval, Ontario and reflecting nostalgically on the place and time of her childhood by rereading her journals,[20] Prince Edward Island comes to resemble much more an impossible pastoral idyll than a site of ecological succession and social possibility: the island (the house and lands of Silver Bush in particular) offers a fantastic landscape of enormous Romantic proportions, full of golden-pink skies, velvety green hills, birch trees sparkling in the winter sun, and warm conversations in the family kitchen that Montgomery describes in intimate detail, especially in *Pat of Silver Bush*: "Every field she looked on was a friend. The asters along the path were letters of the poem in her heart."[21] With this kind of perfect ecological and familial loveliness at stake, any change can appear as a destruction rather than an opening; the Golden Age of Silver Bush (and of Pat's self, given the twinning of the two) is indeed a state of childhood. In this reading, it is not at all surprising that Silver Bush burns down; the litany of losses that the place undergoes, especially in the latter half of *Mistress Pat*, leaves it dried out and lifeless, given that no new beings or relationships (except May Binnie) come to make it into a new home.

With this idyllic view in mind, Sheckels offers an account of the Pat books that focuses on Pat's increasing "entrapment" in the ultimately tinder-dry fantasy of her childhood. For him as for Doody and MacDonald, Pat's resistance to change is pathological and contrasts with the normal, healthy, transformative unfolding of births, marriages, and deaths at Silver Bush. As Sheckels states, "the change [Montgomery] depicts is positive. However, she also makes it clear that the effect of these positive changes to others' lives is negative on Pat."[22] As a result, Pat's obsessive devotion to Silver Bush makes her more and more isolated as she grows older; her love of place is ultimately tragic because the place she loves leaves her behind. Moreover, as Doody writes even more emphatically, in the conflict between change and stasis Pat "is an absurd and tragic figure. Other objectives may be met, partially or wholly .... But an unchanging world is not to be had. Nobody can give it. Change is the law of life."[23]

I would like to argue that this sharp opposition between change/nature/normalcy and Pat/stasis/pathology misses two crucial points that are revealed in a queer ecological reading of the novels. First, as Montgomery underscores (both narratively and structurally), Silver Bush *is* constantly changing, and despite Pat's general reluctance and occasionally vocal opposition, she actually adapts quite readily, often remarkably quickly, to most of the changes depicted in the novels. For example, when Rachel is born, Pat accepts her presence as entirely "natural" in their very first encounter: "Only a few minutes ago she had been thinking of the baby as an interloper, only to be tolerated for mother's sake. But now it was one of the family and it seemed as if it had always been at Silver Bush."[24] Similarly, when Joe leaves, she (like everyone else in her family) is initially distraught but comes to recognize, almost guiltily, that life at Silver Bush continues vigorously in his absence: "The life of Silver Bush closed over his going with hardly a ripple."[25] When Winnie marries and leaves, Pat comes to love their changed relationship (including her new niece, Little Mary, who is very much like Pat). Tillytuck arrives and enhances the life of the kitchen. Suzanne and David Kirk ease the pain of Bets's absence from the Long House and enrich Pat's life thoroughly, despite the fact that she does not love David as more than a friend. In short, although Montgomery tells us repeatedly that Pat hates any and all change, what Pat actually *does* belies her adaptability: she accepts transformation both effectively and reflectively, pausing to think far more than any of her siblings or friends about the nature of change itself, such as the differences between cyclical changes (including the movement of the seasons, which Pat loves: "I'll have nothing to do with anything to-day but spring") and linear ones (departures, deaths, marriages).[26]

It seems that Pat is able to adapt to changes, and even to *enjoy* them, because she is part of a vibrant web of ecological and interpersonal relations that temper and moderate the effects of any single transformative event and that also work away at Pat to nurture her adaptive capacities. At one level, of course, Pat is sustained by Silver Bush – *not* just by a fantasy of Silver Bush – and by the regularity of its cycles and the familiarity of its daily and annual rituals. Her "sense of place," here, is a source of tremendous strength; her friends include the trees, flowers, fields, and built structures, and this ecological network is her lifeworld. At another level, I would argue that certain of Pat's human companions are especially important:

her network of sisters and female friends is rich with intimacy and, so long as the spectre of patriarchy does not loom, so are her relations with Sid, Hilary, and David.

It is, however, Judy Plum who is really Pat's most important companion and, especially in *Pat of Silver Bush*, Montgomery offers readers as much of Judy's view of the world as she does of Pat's; as a result, much of our ability to appreciate and sympathize with Pat's arguably obsessive tendencies is shaped by the fact that Judy both loves and understands her.[27] Judy is Pat's symbiote, without whom she would not be able to respond to changing conditions at Silver Bush; Judy helps Pat digest changing relations and adapt to transformative events, so that she even learns to enjoy them. Judy shapes Pat by telling her stories to soften the edges of her reality (such as the one about finding babies in the parsley bed); Judy also shapes the often highly repressive forces that act on Pat from a position of heightened tolerance and sympathy (lambasting the Gardiners for their harshly punitive response to Pat's naked moonbathing, for instance). Even more, Judy fills Silver Bush with stories that exceed the present and beckon to a time when Silver Bush was not what it is now; her stories locate Pat's present in a historical past, and she remarks, over and over, that people and places are "niver the same again" in response to events. Things are always changing, and Judy coaxes Pat into an understanding of herself, however fragile, as part of the *constantly shifting* landscape of Silver Bush. When Judy dies, her symbiotic presence and interpretive embeddedness dies with her; when the fire destroys Silver Bush, Pat has to face life after the fire *without* the crucial interlocutor who has always allowed her to be comfortable in the changing landscape. Thus, I would argue that it is not really that a fantasy of stasis has rendered Pat's life at Silver Bush unsustainable; it is that the interdependent relations that sustained her existence died away, leaving a withered community ripe for burning.

Second, it also seems that there are certain *kinds* of change that Pat cannot tolerate and that, as it turns out, also contribute to the combustibility of Silver Bush. Specifically, the things Pat hates the most are marriages, not because she dislikes men but because the institution of marriage is so thoroughly steeped in compulsory heterosexuality and patrilocal institutions that insist that men stay "in their place" and women move to meet them. Marriage, for Pat, can only *ever* mean that she will leave Silver Bush and that some other woman will arrive, which she does, in the form of hated May Binnie (which, MacDonald argues, is "the most painful change that Pat has to endure in her first thirty-one years"[28]). In *Pat of Silver Bush*, seven-year-old Pat clearly recognizes heteronormative patrilocality and says "no" to it quite earnestly: "I'm never going to marry either, Judy," she says, "[b]ecause if I got married I'd have to go away from Silver Bush, and I couldn't bear that. We're going to stay here always ... Sid and me."[29] As opposed to Doody's invocations of incest, Sheckels locates Pat's unwavering attachment to Silver Bush rather more positively in what he calls Montgomery's "proto-feminism," in which many of her female characters visibly butt up against heteropatriarchal conventions in their desires to live lives of their own choosing and are often prevented from doing so because, as Montgomery likely understood of her own situation, "a woman's choices in life are limited [and] marriage can be a trap."[30] Silver Bush can thus be seen as protecting Pat, however temporarily and partially, from the storms of *male*-defined change and relocation. When Pat's family is threatened by a westward move that none of the Gardiner women wants, Judy tells it like it is: "Oh, oh, it's a man's world, so it is, and we women must just be putting up wid it."[31] And so, it is not surprising that Pat's consistent refusal of all of her various suitors is accompanied by an equally consistent recapitulation of her intense love for Silver Bush: as she contemplates a marriage proposal while lying among the trees in the Secret Field, for example, the place itself "cleared the matter up for her. No, liking wasn't enough ... There must be something more before she could dream of leaving Silver Bush."[32] At the end of the novel, however, patrilocality wins: it is May Binnie who torches Silver Bush, in which process she finally establishes the heteronormative right to be mistress of Silver Bush by destroying the last remnants of Pat's social and ecological network in order to establish a better habitat for her own placemaking desires.[33]

I would go so far as to argue that Silver Bush itself participates in resisting heteronormative overdetermination to the very end. Although Montgomery's tendency to personify nature through "virginal girl figures" declines in her later novels, as Nancy Holmes has pointed out in her ecofeminist reading of *Anne of Green Gables*,[34] there is in the two Pat books a repeated feminization of nature: Silver Bush is a sister to Pat, and she "a sister to all the loveliness of the world." Her identification with the landscape as sister is not exactly erotic (although it is in the bathing in moonlight episode) but it is definitely the case that Pat prefers the company of the grove of very *feminine*, slender "white-skinned trees and ferny hollows" that named Silver Bush to any of the many male options otherwise offered to her.[35] The space of Silver Bush is domestic and feminine despite the fact that it is ultimately organized and owned by men. This reading does not make Montgomery a closet lesbian separatist – her biography suggests very strongly otherwise[36] – but it *does* suggest that Montgomery railed against the limited options available for women who might choose not to marry or who might choose vocation or, in this case, *location*, over heterosexual coupling. Pat's love of the place is only pathological, on this reading, if one considers heteronormativity a "natural" organization of space and life and opposite-sex romance the only love that really matters.

There is, then, an overdetermined relationship between change and heteronormativity at Silver Bush, in which Pat's desire to live with Silver Bush comes to appear as static and immature (I have argued that it is neither) in relation to a patrilocal and patriarchal understanding of futurity and in which the "natural" course of a woman's life (and her life space) comes to be rendered as always and only heterosexual. Throughout the novels, this tension is traced most fully in the relation between Pat's love for her home and her affection for Hilary. Shortly after we are introduced to Hilary, we learn that he is "always building houses" and that he fully intends to build one eventually for Pat.[37] Much as he shares Pat's aesthetic, fantastic, architectural, and social appreciation of Silver Bush, he also has aspirations that will clearly take him away from Prince Edward Island – as they do, in *Mistress Pat*, to architectural school and eventually to the west coast – but that clearly still include Pat as a wife and partner. Pat makes a clear choice for the vast majority of both novels: she loves Hilary but not in the same passionate way that she loves Silver Bush. Once Silver Bush has burned down, however, the space is cleared for Hilary to enter at the very end of the novel: "I know," he says, "what this tragedy of Silver Bush must have meant to you … but I've a home for you by another sea, Pat. And in it we'll build up a new life and the old will become just a treasury of dear and sacred memories … of things time cannot destroy."[38] Pat, it seems, is revealed as a Kirtland's Warbler: she can now nest in the low branches of a young, fire-opened jack pine, where previously she was caught in an over-mature, overgrown forest that held no possibilities but an increasingly uncomfortable spinsterhood, mistress of Silver Bush or no.

Perhaps to please her readers or perhaps to take a step back from the "proto-feminist" tension between Pat's abundant desires for life at Silver Bush and the constrained heteronormative opportunities open to her, Montgomery thus slips in a romantic "happy ending" in which Pat realizes that her refusal of marriage was not about her home and place but about Hilary all along: "I thought I couldn't marry them because I couldn't leave Silver Bush … but I know now it was because they weren't *you*."[39] But Pat has had plenty of opportunity to reflect on the possibility of a life with Hilary in the face of the many changes to Silver Bush; it seems to me, rather, that Pat could not leave Silver Bush so long as it held together as an ecosystem and that her choice to leave and form a new life with Hilary is not, as her post-facto exclamation suggests, a discovery of some inner and ongoing aim but rather a final acceptance of the constrained choices available to her. Perhaps Silver Bush *had* to burn; perhaps the changes that are documented throughout the two Pat books are really a long prelude *to* the fire; perhaps the island fantasy to which Pat was so attached is really, for Montgomery, an anachronistic refuge of female desire in the face of overwhelming, immolating heteronormative convention. Nonetheless, the seed of Hilary's love did *not* germinate in Pat's heart until the fire cleared the space and allowed, or forced, the seed to open.

Conclusion

What, then, does this queer ecological reading matter for the Pat books or for studies of Montgomery more generally? What does it matter for us that islands are, ecologically speaking, not really the stuff of their frequent metaphoric production as atemporal refuges or incestuous traps? What does it matter that Rule's island fire enables new forms of female becoming, where Montgomery's seems to close it down as part of the progression of a rigidly heteronormative future? What does it matter, following Holmes, to read Montgomery more or less ecologically, rather than as simply "green" because of her pastoral invocations of Prince Edward Island?

I think there are many possibilities, but by way of a conclusion I would like to suggest two. First, the two Pat books outline precisely the ecological and social unsustainability (and metaphoric inadequacy) of a view in which islands are "places out of time." Especially with the interpretive presence of Judy Plum, it is clear from the outset that Silver Bush is not immune to change; we might sympathize with Pat's desire to hold on to the forms of life and sociality that are unique and essential to her place at any given moment, but it is apparent throughout that Pat can either adapt or die, such is the inevitability of movement. Pat turns out to be the unlikely embodiment of Botkin's ecological understanding. However much we would like things to stay the same and however exceptionally interesting an "island" ecosystem might be, there is no optimal, harmonious, and eternal balance: it will all change, whether due to fire or invasion, predator abundance or species extinction, and it will "niver be the same again." Here, an ecological reading demands an understanding of islands as dynamic and vulnerable, as unique subjects of ecological and social processes that are not in themselves unique. Metaphorically, then, even if Silver Bush did not burn, it would have been taken over anyway, eventually, with new life forms. Pat may have adapted (she did and would have continued to do so without the death-dealing blows wrought by heteropatriarchy), but Silver Bush was always already a ripe field of possibility and not only an archaic remnant of past desires.

Second, I think Silver Bush makes clear that the "natural" progress of change should not be understood as the same thing as the unfolding of reproductive futurity. Pat tries to choose a life that defies patrilocal convention, and succeeds for quite a long time, surrounded by a web of sustaining ecological and social relations; although some critics read this defiance as unnatural, I think it is more important to highlight the fact that Pat's intensive and caring sense of place – which is, one could argue, quite sustainable insofar as it is embedded in a symbiotic web of social and ecological relationships – is ultimately incommensurable with the requirements of heteropatriarchy, in which men and not women are tied to the land and in which marriage and not lifelong attentiveness is the relation that ultimately counts in terms of belonging. In this reading, Pat's resistance to patrilocal heterosexuality ultimately fails but *not* because it was pathologically insistent on stasis. Rather, Pat recognizes – as I think Montgomery recognized – that the organization of change according to constraining heteronormative assumptions about the "natural" progression of futurity is not especially good for women (and, perhaps, not especially good for environmental sustainability, either[40]).

After all: why could not Hilary just have built a house at Silver Bush?

CHAPTER TWO

The Scotsman, the Scribe, and the Spyglass: Going Back with L.M. Montgomery to Prince Edward Island

Jennifer H. Litster

> Timothy Salt lets me look through his spy-glass. It's such fun looking at things through the wrong end. They seem so small and far away as if you were in another world.
> – *Jane of Lantern Hill*[1]

In an article on Japanese tourists and "Anne" tourism, American journalist Calvin Trillin observes that the Anne books "are so imbued with the look and feel of Prince Edward Island that the province itself practically qualifies as one of the characters."[2] Reviews of her first published novel, *Anne of Green Gables*, made Montgomery aware that some measure of its success was due to the resonance of the Prince Edward Island setting with readers. For example, a review in *The Spectator* (London) gushed that "no better advertisement of the charm of [PEI's] landscape could be devised than the admirable descriptions of its sylvan glories which lend decorative relief to the narrative. Miss Montgomery … makes us fall in love with [the] surroundings, and long to visit the Lake of Shining Waters, the White Way of Delight, Idlewild, and other favourite resorts of 'the Anne-girl.'"[3] Avonlea – a fictionalized version of the rural community of Cavendish where Maud Montgomery was raised – joined the ranks of "local color" idylls (Drumtochty, Thrums, Glengarry, Glenoro, Dunnet Landing) that were in vogue in Britain, the United States, and Canada around the turn of the twentieth century.

For her part, Montgomery expressed surprise that a story "written in and of a simple PEI farming settlement" was such a hit with the "busy world."[4] As Janice Fiamengo explains, however, Montgomery's skill as an author lies partly in her ability to find, in the landscape of her particular childhood, a "comforting myth of belonging" that is universally and enduringly popular. Although based on a real location in a real past, Avonlea according to this reading is "subject to the ambiguities of memory" and the scene is "always deliberately crafted and creatively transformed."[5] Fiamengo argues that Montgomery "not only borrowed landscapes at will but also created them anew to suit her purposes"; in the act of so doing, "Avonlea, unlike Cavendish, became a portable landscape" situated in a "portable past time" that tapped into individual readers' nostalgia and became, in time, "a metaphor for pre-war innocence."[6]

To trace the complex process whereby the real world of rural Prince Edward Island is transformed into fiction, critics can turn to the ten volumes of L.M. Montgomery's handwritten journals; for example, in 1911 she laid out the explicit connections between the real Cavendish and the imaginary Avonlea.[7] This chapter, in looking at how Montgomery lived, reminisced about, and fictionalized the *natural* world of her childhood and youth, makes use of another and as yet unexplored source. In the sixth volume of her handwritten journal, Montgomery broke from writing about her own life to transcribe into her ledger the diary of a Cavendish farmer, Charles Macneill (1832–1908). A close neighbour of Maud Montgomery's, Macneill was also the father of Pensie Macneill (1872–1898), one of her closest childhood friends, and of Alec Macneill (1870–1951), who with his wife May (1876–1947) played host to Maud Montgomery in her later years at Gartmore Farm, the old Macneill homestead.[8]

Charles Macneill was the son of one Alexander Macneill (no blood relation to Montgomery's Macneill ancestors) who migrated to Prince Edward Island from Perthshire, Scotland, in 1804. As L.M. Montgomery later reflected, Charles Macneill was by way of a "local joke."[9] From Gartmore Farm's vantage point on the road that led east from central Cavendish, a thoroughfare popular for "after-meeting drives," he was well placed to monitor comings and goings. He also kept "a spy-glass in the house and it was invariably trained on everybody who walked or drove down the road," hence the local joke (and also, perhaps, Mrs

Rachel Lynde's "all-seeing eye"): Montgomery remarked that she "never went down that road in daytime without feeling that spy glass focussed on the small of my back."[10] It is the Cavendish world Macneill saw through his spyglass that lends his diary an interest to scholars of Montgomery's work.

In drawing attention to the diary and Montgomery's reactions to it, this chapter has three aims. First, it introduces to a wider readership a lengthy portion of Montgomery's handwritten journal that is almost entirely unknown. (Macneill's diary was edited out of the published *Selected Journals*, as was the commentary by Montgomery that follows it.) Second, it looks at the natural world portrayed in Macneill's diary and considers the ways in which Montgomery interacted with this environment and the creative process she engaged in when translating and editing the landscapes of her childhood into fiction. Lastly, this chapter ends by speculating on a more direct impact Macneill's diary may have had on her 1937 novel *Jane of Lantern Hill*. By borrowing from and finding inspiration in its commonplace and at times classless agricultural world, Montgomery sourced a slice of the natural world that was a fitting backdrop for one of the novel's main themes – the conflict between Jane Stuart's egalitarianism and Grandmother Kennedy's snobbery.

"[T]edious to read and unthinkably tedious to copy"

Montgomery borrowed Macneill's diary from Alec and May Macneill in July 1924 and, knowing that she would have to return it when she next visited the Island, she copied the three surviving portions – dated from 7 August 1892 to 15 March 1893, 14 January to 7 June 1896, and 6 February 1897 to 4 November 1898 – into a journal entry dated 1 March 1925. Macneill's diary alone occupies some eighty-five pages of the sixth handwritten volume and is followed by more than thirty handwritten pages of Montgomery's reminiscences. She wrote that to transcribe the diary faithfully took her "several Sunday afternoons,"[11] during which time her own diary was kept in a separate notebook, to be copied into the journal proper at a later date.

Her decision to turn over a fifth of this volume to someone else's diary is a bold and a curious one. One explanation may be that her journal offered a secure home for a diary she believed would have "a certain value in the future."[12] This would certainly be in keeping with the message Montgomery gave in her public addresses of the 1920s and 1930s, where she urged audiences to preserve similar family and community histories before they were lost, not least because tales of ordinary Canadian life represented potential material for stories and contained "a tremendous amount of literary material" for Canadian writers.[13] By this stage of her literary career, Montgomery recognised that the written record of her life would be a legacy for her sons and read by others after her death.

Transcribing Macneill's diary served a more immediate purpose: it kept Montgomery occupied and distracted her from "a world of intolerable realities."[14] Immediately prior to this she had alleviated the multiple stresses of ill health, Church Union, legal battles, and domestic staff by revising the manuscript of her romantic fantasy, *The Blue Castle*. Although it is surprising that a mundane farming diary could provide similar escapism, Mary Henley Rubio speculates that Montgomery, who was "in an abnormal state" – depressed, shaky, and flu-ridden and "on the brink of a nervous collapse" – probably found that the old, dull diary "took her mind off herself."[15]

Lastly, however, in much the same way as when she preserved the comic diary kept with her friend Nora Lefurgey in an edited typescript of the journal compiled in the 1930s,[16] Montgomery was writing another "self" in absorbing Macneill's diary into her daily life-writing. Removing herself from her present day woes, Montgomery was transported back to carefree girlhood or, more accurately, to being the girl, at thirty years' remove, she nostalgically remembered she had been:

> I was back again in a world where happiness reigned and problems were non-existent – for me at least. I was so much at [Charles Macneill's] home when a child and young girl that every word he wrote brought back vividly some sweet memory of those past days and childish frolics and delights. The most commonplace statement seemed like a finger touching the keys of an organ and evoking

> melodies of haunting sweetness – sights, sounds, of that old north shore farm that came back like the faint appealing voices of ghosts heard long ago many shadowy years agone. Pensie was alive to run with me under the moon and together we slipped back into that garden where the sword is set and mortals may not pass – the Eden of childhood.[17]

Although it invoked happy memories, Montgomery's verdict that for anyone else Macneill's diary would be "tedious to read and unthinkably tedious to copy"[18] is, in most respects, a fair one (thus its excision by Rubio and Waterston from their third volume of her *Selected Journals*). In fairness to Charles Macneill, however, his diary was not intended to be read by anyone but himself, let alone the subject of academic scrutiny. Its content suggests that its primary function was as a logbook and accounting system; in documenting the annual round of farming life, such as which crops were planted where and when and how they fared, monies paid and monies owed, the barter of goods and the visits of local sows to his boar, Charles Macneill created an agricultural record that could be consulted year on year to improve his husbandry or track changes in prices or yields. Presumably the surviving notebooks were just some of many written over the years at Gartmore Farm.

The first daily entries are invariably brief – four or five staccato sentences at most, especially in the portion that covers the first five months of 1896 – and almost always begin with a weather summary, before Macneill delivers a cursory statement of that day's activities on his own and neighbouring farms and an update on his health woes. (Montgomery, from whom one might have expected a sympathetic ear given the space her own diary devotes to health problems, is rather dismissive of Macneill's "pathetic" entries about his failing eyesight.[19]) "Very cold windy day. Boys went to plough on the road farm. I was cutting wood and boiling for the pigs. Fixed the back fence. My eye very sore." "Colder. 2 butchers here from town after fat cattle. J. Clark hauling house. Went through the ice. Went down to Rustico with flour to Doucette and Gallant. Got shoe on mare. Cost 20 ¢. Bought a bag of salt, 75 ¢, 20 lbs of sugar 90 ¢. 2 lbs of tea 50 ¢, Broom 25 ¢ in all $2.40." "Fine day. Fencing on Mackenzie farm all day. Turned very cold."[20]

Entries from the winter of 1897 until the summer of 1898 are somewhat longer, although still no more than ten to fifteen short sentences. Some of the additional content comes in the form of sarcastic jibes by Macneill at his family and neighbours, their faith, good works, parsimony, and frivolousness.

> A fine day. Very bright. Preaching in Cavendish. Mr Robertson and Mr Jackson had service together. They are going to hold their meetings together this week of prayer. There was a good many people in church to-day but they seem very much inclined for horse racing on their way home. It is a poor sign. It shows that they don't mind what they hear.

> Soft snowy day. Boys hauling manure. Russell went to Eddy Toombs' boy's funeral. After that to Lorenzo Toombs with the children. They were up getting dresses made. Lelia was up to Alberts' all day. Went up to Murray Robertson's with Ma and Lelia. After that with Letty up to James Robert Stewart's. On the go all the time. She has gone for a time. I hope for a long time so we can have some quiet times without so much rush.

> Showery morning. Moved the sheep from Montana to the shore field. Hope they will do better now. Cleared up fine. Russell scuffling the potatoes. Alexander not doing much. I am hoeing turnips. After that turning hay. It is very wet. Will try and rake it up this evening. Had 198 coils of hay. Very faire [*sic*] if saved well. Races up at J.T. Cosgrove's to-day. Bad time there I hear. Too much beer and too little sense showed by people that ought to know better.[21]

Workaday and commonplace Charles Macneill's diary undoubtedly is, and yet there is perhaps more to interest the casual reader than Montgomery allowed. To the historian it sheds light on the hard graft of farming life and the intricacies of the rural economy, especially at a time when financially motivated out-migration from Prince Edward Island was in full swing. Its pages are rich with references to travelling pedlars (of the type that leads Anne Shirley to grief), horses and sleigh driving, dressmaking and socializing, births, illnesses, funerals, and – in the case of Montgomery's Grandfather Macneill – wills. (Charles Macneill's account of Alexander Marquis Macneill's funeral includes the comment "He left the farm to John Franklin [his son] and his money in the bank and stock to his wife. So John Franklin and Campbell says.")[22] The snide asides from the misanthropic diarist lend it a certain comic charm to anyone familiar with the stereotype of the repressed and gruff Scot. His use of language is, at times, appealingly colourful, and Montgomery was not above borrowing his turns of phrase: Mr Carpenter utters Macneill's "she-weasels" on his deathbed in *Emily's Quest*, and Judy Plum uses his "too many bushels for a small canoe"; Tillytuck's dig at Matilda Binnie, who has "a new set of teeth and a new fur coat[, but] if she could get a new set of brains she might do very well for a while," was aimed by Charles Macneill at Montgomery's aunt, Ann Maria Macneill.[23]

Although the diary gives the impression that Macneill strongly disapproved of his gallivanting children,[24] he was in fact a sociable man: as Montgomery recalled, "No one liked better than he to see folks drop in … He loved to talk to everyone, getting all the local news. You always heard all the current gossip at 'Charles's.' They were not malicious. But they never read books or papers and their only amusement was their interest in the doings of their small world."[25] In fact, it is this interest in the small world around him that makes Macneill's logbook worth reading and worth preserving, not least because it is the same interest that fuels Montgomery's life writing and story writing. Like Macneill, Montgomery took an active interest in her neighbours, "even if" she, like him, "might write a sarcastic sentence about them in [her] diary that evening" or sarcastic words in her fiction.[26]

The Narrow Groove

Looking more closely at the parts of this farming diary that were particularly evocative to Montgomery expands our understanding of the connections between Cavendish and Avonlea in two ways. In the first instance, Montgomery's reminiscences come from earlier childhood, *before* she began keeping her own journal at the age of fourteen. Although her journal is rich with *memories* of these years, the agricultural focus of Macneill's diary exposes memories that show an unfamiliar side of young Maud Montgomery and her connection to the natural world around her. Second, her reminiscences provide insights on the process she engaged in when recreating a "simple PEI farming settlement" as a romantic idyll. In both these matters, it is the very dullness of Macneill's diary that is of interest. It is an unedited world, where the wintery weather is recorded with grim repetitiveness and no extraordinary dramas happen. As Montgomery recalled, "His life was a very narrow one but in its groove, it was as happy, peaceful and prosperous a one as I ever knew."[27]

Montgomery's reminiscences are inspired by four types of diary entries: those about the weather, those about farm work, about Cavendish as a place, and about Cavendish people. (In another tranche of recollections Montgomery either provides the backstory to one of Charles Macneill's sarcastic comments or supplies information on "what happened next.") Two of these groups – the weather and farm work – most clearly illustrate the matter of nature.

Macneill's diary entries may succumb to a Scottish tendency to err on the bleak side where weather is concerned, but reflective of Cavendish's "sylvan glories" they are not. For eight months of the year, weeks of "cold" are broken only by rain, snow, and blustery winds. Farm work involved guarding crops and livestock from the elements – on 5 September 1892 Macneill rose at two in the morning to take in his wheat as it threatened to rain. The Island weather in all but the summer months frequently led to the roads, just red earth and apt to turn sludgy, becoming "heavy" or blocked. Macneill's diary contains several references to travel "abroad" being curtailed or to gangs of local men gathering to dig the community out. The privation and isolation brought by the weather is captured in tales of the minister's weekly struggle to preach in the rural churches and the inability of his flock to attend: "Stormy day. Nobody went to church to-day. Snowing very thick. Roads very heavy."[28]

For Montgomery, Macneill's terse weather reports are a short cut back to the Island. News of heavy rain and thunder takes her back to the doorstep of Gartmore Farm, "and I see the huge black clouds riding up over the tiny house and the giant willows behind it and Pensie and I run from the door and crouch in the parlor that has grown almost dark, and out to sea a shaft of lightning pierces the sky and the woods have grown dim in their skirts of shadow." When Charles Macneill jots down that it is "blowing hard," Montgomery follows the west wind as it "thrashes the tops of the trees and howls in the dog-woods" and then the wind from the south, "a lonesome thing, purring softly down over the slopes behind the house and laughing in the garden and blowing leaves crazily across the yard." Though the ground is solid with ice and the roads are very rough, Montgomery flies over the frosty terrain in bright snapshots of Cavendish's natural beauty: "No mud now. Household lights gleaming warmly out along the road. Melody of storm in the wind that is swooping down over the sleeping fields; a big round silvery moon floating up over a frosty hill; the gnomish beauty of dark lombardies against the moonrise; bars of moonlight and shadow on the road under the trees and Pensie laughing beside me – always laughing."[29]

Montgomery's word-pictures do more than prettify the Scotsman's barren outlook. His brief descriptions are a springboard for Montgomery to rise from the prosaic (a "foggy day") to the panoramic ("An evening fog filled me with a strange deep joy – that mournful ghostly thing hanging low over the fields and drifting in phantom-like waves through the spruces"). Macneill's everyday language appears to trigger such a reaction in Montgomery for the same reason that his diary was not tedious for her to transcribe. It might be commonplace, but it is Cavendish – it is not a foggy day anywhere but a foggy day on her beloved north shore. The natural world of her childhood acquires both the soft focus of nostalgic recollection and a high-definition resolution. In this process, the relentlessness of rural life, the sheer drudgery of working the soil in miserable weather, is almost completely overlooked. In her recollections, memories inspired by "fine bright" days – "Vast sky gardens where white cloud flowers bloomed. Great golden fields with the magic of dark spruce woods behind them. Musky, spicy garden flowers. Triangles of sea shimmering into violet" – do not differ in essence from memories of cold and squally ones. Every day in childhood is a fair weather day even when the actual weather is foul.[30]

The fact that Montgomery can rewrite Charles Macneill's world into a world where "happiness reigned and problems were non-existent" comes as no surprise if we stop to think about weather in her fiction. Clearly, a novel in which the protagonists spend six months of the year huddled around the fire would have limited appeal, and Montgomery was bound to concentrate the action of her stories in times and climes when her characters can be either sociable or outdoors. (*The Story Girl* is a good example of this; with its plot set entirely within the months of May to November, it is self-consciously the story of a golden summer.) Nonetheless, *Anne of Green Gables*, where the action takes place over a period of almost five years, contains only two rainy days (the Saturday before the Sunday School picnic and a Sunday, when "the rain poured down in torrents from dawn till dusk"); other promised rainy days fail to materialize. When the "wind" blows it is as a gentle breeze that stirs the flowers ("a little gypsy wind came down [the lane] to meet them, laden with the spicy perfume of young dew-wet ferns.")[31] The winter of Miss Stacy's Christmas concert is "unusually mild" and January weather does not prevent Marilla and the Lyndes from travelling to Charlottetown to hear John A. Macdonald nor Anne from crossing the snow-crusted fields to Orchard Slope.[32] Winter in Avonlea means fur-robes and sleigh rides in a world where "the plowed fields were stretches of snowy dimples; and there was a crisp tang in the air that was glorious."[33] *Anne of Avonlea* does introduce atrocious weather – the thunderstorm on the Tory Road and Uncle Abe's storm where "the hail swooped down and blotted the landscape out in one white fury"[34] – but purely as a dramatic device.

L.M. Montgomery's memories of weather are surprising given that her Cavendish journal frequently chronicles the impact of bad weather on her social life and mental health. Of course, Montgomery's recollections are self-consciously a stylistic exercise, artistic fodder she could poach at a later date. But here she also supplies a window on how, in Fiamengo's perspective, memories of landscapes of the real past, in the form of Charles Macneill's diary, are transformed for her fiction. The "real" Cavendish was edited by the imaginative young woman who experienced the natural world in a different way to those around her and later revised by the aging exile who uses her own nostalgia to create the landscape anew. Montgomery went through a similar process with different aspects of her past; she tapped into the slights and miseries of her childhood when dreaming up her orphaned and abandoned heroines even though, on the whole, her childhood was not "actually unhappy [but] it was never as happy as childhood should be."[35]

Charles Macneill starts each diary entry with the weather because of its substantial impact on the life and work of the farmstead. And where his Scottish heritage is hinted at in his weather reports, his work ethic is solidly Presbyterian. Each entry catalogues tasks done, whether sowing hay seed, stumping trees, ploughing fields, or feeding livestock. Other days he would share threshing machinery, barter wood for apples, buy mackerel or codfish, sell pork or cow hides. If the Macneill men needed boots or suits, mending or buying, they went to Stanley Bridge; Macneill journeyed to Summerside or Charlottetown to lay in supplies of tea, sugar, beans, and rice. Animals were taken to market in the larger towns with links off-Island, although butchers visited rural districts, like Mr Shearer who buys Anne's rampant Jersey cow in *Anne of Avonlea*. For seasonal farm labour, Charles Macneill depended on local Acadians, and his diary is "scattered all through," as Montgomery noted, with the French names that "were so well known to my childhood."[36] This is a world where the agricultural landscape is kept in motion by different communities pulling together.

Montgomery's recollections of this world of work provide a hitherto unseen glimpse of her childhood. She recalls how "every summer there came an afternoon when rain threatened and men were scarce and 'we youngsters' were pressed into emergency service" to build loads of grain. Montgomery also notes that she had "'stoked' grain in my time, too" – building wheat into "stooks" (a Scottish term for what Ontarians called "shocks") and that the children in the community were always excited by "threshing days" when they were allowed to stay home from school to "tramp straw" in the lofts and sheds: "It was gorgeous fun. I loved it all – the whir and roar and dust – and the clouds of grain pouring out of the drum, while the straw was coughed furiously out beyond to the waiting man with the fork who tossed it to us."[37] Although Montgomery is clear that such days were infrequent, driven by the necessity of securing a quick and successful harvest, her recollections situate her firmly within the democratized agricultural world. Montgomery's connection to her environment was anchored in the ways that nature was managed and controlled, harnessed and tamed by her community.

Although *Anne of Green Gables* nails its agricultural colours to the mast in chapter 1 – "Thomas Lynde … was sowing his late turnip seed on the hill field beyond the barn; and Matthew Cuthbert ought to have been sowing his on the red brook field"[38] – the daily tasks of farming life are but a murmur in the background of Montgomery's fiction. She faithfully attends to matters of seasons and farming lore when writing her novels, but the hard graft of the farm rarely impinges on her child characters.[39] Little girls undertake certain farm chores: Anne and Emily take charge of the cows, the children in the two "Story Girl" books earn "egg money" from the hens, and Emily plants potatoes. However, Anne and her friends are never excused from school for an afternoon's haying. (When prim Diana cuts potato sets she does her "hands up in lemon juice and kid gloves every night."[40]) In the First World War, it is Mary Vance and Susan Baker who help stack grain in lieu of the absent menfolk, but genteel Rilla elects to work in the store, believing she would not "be much use in a harvest field … though lots of girls are."[41] Jane Stuart alone, as we shall see, engages in a variety of farm labours.

Generally farm work in Montgomery's novels is gentler stuff – characters plough the fields and scatter – not the back-breaking labour Macneill describes where dulse is hauled from the seashore and longers made into fence poles and fields cleared of tree stumps nor is it the dirt and grease of annual sheep shearing and wool washing, women's work in Cavendish. (There are no sheep near Avonlea, apart from the one that Mrs Lynde says Mrs Isaac Wright's grandfather stole.[42]) When Montgomery recalls how the local farmers chased and captured seals that had been driven onto the shoreline with incoming ice, it seems outlandish and a world away from her fictional landscapes: "enormous quantities of oil could be obtained from the carcass and a farmer was lucky if he captured a seal or two. I recall a particularly huge one grandfather caught. Its white and gray hide was nailed to the side of the barn to dry."[43] For all that Avonlea is associated with "local color" schools, it appears that anything in Cavendish that was too regional – or maybe too Canadian, like the unfortunate seals – was tamed by Montgomery when creating a pastoral agrarian world that could appeal to readers off-Island.

Charles Macneill's diary may be dull but it is an intriguing companion piece to Montgomery's journals of Cavendish life, especially as for much of the period it covers (1892–98) Montgomery lived elsewhere.[44] This last reason may account for the fact her reminiscences of these times are those of a schoolgirl, not of the schoolma'am that she was in these years. In effect, Montgomery reimagines the Cavendish of Macneill's diary as a "portable past time," a time before change and a time before machines transformed the landscape, how it was worked, and who worked it.

Perhaps what is most interesting about Montgomery's recollections is how she uses her spyglass on the past to transport this world before change to the modern day where readers experience the intricacies of Macneill's world in a way that is miniature and immediate – the "black-eyed French girls" chattering in the fields as they bind the grain; the three Jack girls carrying their bundles of sheep shearing clothes; the codfish eaten "with only an hour between sea and pot" – only then to reverse the glass to make it become "small and far away as if you were in another world." The past she remembers is almost tangible but ultimately a will-o'-the-wisp. Her reminiscences end when she summons the ghost of Pensie Macneill, to mourn the loss of this friend and the world she inhabited: "She is gone – and Mr and Mrs Charles have gone – and the old Cavendish has gone … and there are times when I envy Pensie, asleep in her unmarked grave on the New Glasgow hillside."[45]

"The very essence of PE Islandism"

The influence of Mr Charles's words on Montgomery's writing is not confined to her life-writing. However, it is not in *Anne of Green Gables* (set around the 1880s) that readers will find late-nineteenth-century Prince Edward Island as presented in Charles Macneill's diary but, I would argue, in *Jane of Lantern Hill* (1937), one of Montgomery's final novels and one of the few books she wrote where the action happens in a similar period to its composition (the others being *Rilla of Ingleside*, *A Tangled Web*, and the last sections of *The Blythes Are Quoted*). Shortly before beginning work on *Jane* in the summer of 1936, Montgomery drew heavily on Macneill's diary when she was commissioned to write about Prince Edward Island for the *Maritime Advocate and Busy East*, one of several magazine articles she wrote in this period as a means of generating income.[46] As the original diary was back with the Macneills, Montgomery used her journal transcription and commentary as a source for "Come Back with Me to Prince Edward Island," which was published in a special edition on the province in spring 1936. Commenting on a few short paragraphs of publicity material that accompanied the article, Montgomery wrote that, "in one happy moment of inspiration I captured the very essence of PE Islandism."[47]

The article is a shortened, edited (Macneill is not named and in all cases the real Prince Edward Island names are substituted) version of the commentary she had written ten years previously but more explicitly takes the changing world as a central theme. Montgomery tells readers about a farmer's diary from her childhood (although it was not) that "fell" into her hands and which "made me realize as I had never realized before how many changes have come to Abegweit [PEI] since my youth." In this piece, Macneill's diary serves as the baseline against which change is measured, as readers are transported from a simple past to a complicated present.[48] Although Montgomery ends the article by stating that these changes have not altered nature in her home province – "it still rains and shines and blows and 'fogs' and blossoms on the farm he tilled and still in breeze and flower and meadow the old charm lingers yet. For our Island is still '*the* Island' and what other is there?"[49] – the tone of the article is overwhelmingly elegiac.

That this recent article was fresh in Montgomery's mind when writing *Jane of Lantern Hill* seems apparent firstly in the descriptions of the natural world Jane Stuart encounters when she arrives on the Island to meet the father who has been long lost to her. As Elizabeth Waterston comments, "Jane's first impressions of the Island scenes are like a set of postcards for us to take home":[50] "The road was full of lovely surprises … a glimpse of far-off hills that seemed made of opal dust … a whiff of wind that had been blowing over a clover field … brooks that appeared from nowhere and ran off into green shadowy woods where long branches of spicy fir hung over the laced water … great white cloud mountains towering up in the blue sky … a hollow of tipsy buttercups … a tidal river unbelievably blue."[51] This snapshot style – and what Waterston calls the "kinetic force" of Montgomery's prose which goes beyond "mere prettiness"[52] – evokes the soaring passages in her journal that were prompted by Macneill's diary. The picture in the journal of a rainy day and "the long red road growing darker and redder and richer under the wet" becomes in *Jane of Lantern Hill* a country road "almost blood-red in its glistening wetness."[53]

In *Jane*, as in Macneill's diary but not as in *Anne*, weather can be boring – "The sun rose without any unusual fuss" – and can be fierce as a matter of course: "The storm broke presently and lasted for two days. The wind that night didn't sound like wind at all … it sounded like the roar of a wild beast. For two days you could see nothing but a swirl of grey rain over a greyer sea … hear nothing but the tremendous music of huge breakers booming against the stubborn rocks of lower Queen's Shore." On Jane's return to the Island late in the book, when she fears her father is about to remarry, the weather contains a greyness that has taken months to build: "The train whirled over the sodden land. Her Island was not beautiful now. It was just like every other place in the ugliness of very early spring."[54]

It is unsurprising that a piece of writing that contained "the very essence" of the Island should be in Montgomery's mind when she was writing *Jane*. The fact that Jane Stuart was born on the Island although raised in Toronto is critical to the plot; Prince Edward Island – and the water that surrounds it ("You are the sea's child and you have come home") – is in Jane's blood. In *Jane of Lantern Hill*, however, Montgomery goes beyond her familiar strategy of employing Prince Edward Island as a land where dreams come true. As Waterston observes, in *Jane of Lantern Hill* readers find "a new, dramatically energetic version of the dream world."[55] The heart of Jane's connection to her Island home is that she learns to read the world around her through a farmer's eyes: "She learned that a mackerel sky was a sign of fine weather and mare's tails meant wind. She learned that red sky at morning foretokened rain, as did the dark firs on Little Donald's hill when they looked so near and clear." More than any of Montgomery's heroines, Jane Stuart is at one with the land and those who live simply off it – she is a child of the soil as well as the sea. She hauls "well-rotted cow manure," shingles barn roofs, drives in the hay, and bugs potatoes. Her friends are the local farmers, and each one owes something to Charles Macneill: Timothy Salt with his spyglass who teaches Jane to swim, saw, hammer, and fish; Step-a-yard the hired man who gossips about his neighbours' morals and discusses with Jane "green feed and the price of pork and what made cows chew wood."[56]

Jane of Lantern Hill is a novel of dualities and contradictions: city and countryside, east and west, reality and fantasy, incarceration and freedom, Kennedys and Stuarts, mother and father, the old and the new. At the core of this novel's dramatic tension is the conflict between Jane's "low tastes" and her Grandmother Kennedy's place in Toronto's high society. Jane's pursuit of domestic and, importantly, agricultural accomplishments, sets her on a collision course with her grandmother. To Grandmother Kennedy, embracing Prince Edward Island ways is akin to going backwards (or "savage"); for Jane, her relationship with the soil and the people who till it is forward-looking – it is a move toward a modernity that sees her cast off the shackles of outmoded snobbery and embrace egalitarianism. While the influence of Charles Macneill's diary as literary material on this novel should not be exaggerated, it does seem that in returning to it at this time, L.M. Montgomery was able to take from its perspectives on looking at nature (the weather) and controlling nature (farming) a way in which she might create Prince Edward Island anew while retaining the essence of simplicity, tradition, and changelessness. Girlhood memories of helping the harvest home might belong to another, faraway world, but they could be invoked fifty years later to symbolize something new, modern, and true.

CHAPTER THREE

Romantic Novelist as Naturalist: John Foster and the Bird Woman

Nancy Holmes

DR BLYTHE: "Don't you really think, Anne-girl, that you love places too much?"
ANNE, *sighing*: "I'm afraid I do …"
– *The Blythes Are Quoted*[1]

Is it possible to "love places too much," as Gilbert Blythe asks of Anne in the late L.M. Montgomery book, *The Blythes Are Quoted*? Are we unable to imagine an emotionally profound relationship between a person and a place or is it too hurtful to love places since they will likely be changed beyond recognition by development or by our own rejection? These questions are raised in Montgomery's novels in a variety of ways. For many readers, Montgomery and her work are associated with a love of places, in the form of both homes and natural landscapes. An American novelist of the same era, Gene Stratton-Porter (1863–1924), is as strongly connected to the landscape of the mid-western US, specifically Indiana, as Montgomery is with Prince Edward Island. National historic sites are dedicated to each writer in these regions, although in true North American fashion each writer eventually went to live elsewhere (Montgomery to Southern Ontario and Stratton-Porter to California). In the novels of these two authors, particularly Stratton-Porter's *Freckles* (1904) and *A Girl of the Limberlost* (1909) and Montgomery's *The Blue Castle* (1926), place is charged with narrative vitality through an engagement with and a love of nature. As two women and two North Americans who loved "place," Montgomery and Stratton-Porter struggled in these novels to find narrative strategies that foreground place rather than plot, in the same way that nature writing does. Although all three novels ultimately fail to deliver a narrative that fully adapts itself to place, Montgomery and Stratton-Porter were at the forefront of an experiment that is only now being appreciated and recalibrated: the attempt to write ecopastoral text or econarrative.

For each author, part of this experiment includes creating a character who is a naturalist, that is, a person who studies natural history, especially plants and animals in their natural surroundings. In *The Blue Castle*, John Foster is a popular nature writer and eventually is revealed to be the pseudonym of the hero, Barney Snaith, alias Bernard Redfern. Appearing in both *Freckles* and *A Girl of the Limberlost*, the Bird Woman is a photographer and naturalist. These two characters are emblematic of the rise of the literary or journalistic naturalist, a cultural phenomenon that began in the latter half of the nineteenth century with writers like John Muir (1838–1914) and Henry David Thoreau (1817–1862) and continued through to the 1940s, if we consider the naturalist and writer Aldo Leopold (1887–1948) as the transitional figure of nature writer to ecocritic. While Leopold took a great leap forward in beginning to describe a reciprocal ethical relation between humans and nature, naturalist writers and photographers prior to 1940 set the groundwork for the ecological thought of the latter half of the twentieth century by contributing a new perception of nature in North America, urging a modification to the worst excesses of resource exploitation. Although there is no direct evidence that Montgomery and Stratton-Porter knew or read each other's work, they were both bestselling authors in the period between the first decade of the twentieth century and the 1920s. Though both authors wrote for a particular demographic – the middle-class female reader – it is Stratton-Porter who is most often credited with bringing "generations of readers into this kind of intimate relationship with nature … [and having] immeasurable influence on the developing attitudes toward conservation of land and animals in the 20th century."[2] These perceptions of Stratton-Porter's central role in enhancing popular appreciation of nature needs to be modified by the awareness that Montgomery was engaged in a very similar kind of project; through their work, both Montgomery and Stratton-Porter contributed to this perceptual shift by leading countless readers, especially women, to an appreciation of the world outdoors, sometimes in overtly deliberate ways, as in the nature study lessons in the Anne books discussed by Tara K. Parmiter in her chapter in this volume.

Montgomery's effusive descriptions of natural beauty are part of the texture of her stories, and readers around the world associate her characters with love of nature – Jennifer H. Litster in her chapter in this volume reminds us of Calvin Trillin's statement that Prince Edward Island nature qualifies as a character in Montgomery's fiction. Indeed, the attachment to nature is arguably the only attachment in Montgomery's novels that is regularly elevated to a spiritual condition. While her characters are often dutiful towards family and their healthiest romances are often merely friendly, the love of the natural world is imbued unequivocally with spiritual power and value. In her short article "Spring in the Woods," the first of four nature essays published in *The Canadian Magazine* in 1911, the words "worshipper," "soul," "spiritual," and "immortal" appear several times along with similar otherworldly terms such as "haunt," "heaven," and "reincarnate." In Stratton-Porter's work, nature is likewise spiritually affecting: as the narrator notes in *Freckles*, "Nature can be trusted to work her own miracle in the heart of any man whose daily task keeps him alone among her sights, sounds, and silences," and indeed, Freckles calls his particular grove in the Limberlost "the cathedral."[3] As Paul Brooks remarks in *Speaking for Nature* (1980), Stratton-Porter's fiction and nonfiction works alike "transmute the veneration of nature into something close to a religion." The character of Freckles, he adds, "won the hearts of millions of readers who were convinced by his creator's comfortable philosophy that wildness, far from being evil as the Church had once assumed, was one with God."[4] Brooks includes Stratton-Porter among the influential writers of the early twentieth century who radically transformed the general public's ideas about nature, and as I show in this chapter, this claim can be extended to L.M. Montgomery, her Canadian near contemporary. However, what is most radical about these two women, and what can be learned through a comparative analysis of their work, is that they do not merely enhance nature appreciation, but they also radicalize narrative in fascinating ways, both becoming precursors to what we might now call "ecofiction."

From the late-nineteenth century to the mid-twentieth, when Montgomery and Stratton-Porter both were writing, people began to realize the horror of the mass extinctions and slaughter of North American flora and fauna and the destruction of places of great natural beauty. Stratton-Porter's first published article, "A New Experience in Millinery," in 1900, was part of a protest against the use of birds' feathers for hat decoration.[5] Because of campaigns to preserve wilderness areas in nearly every region of the continent, many treasured national parks were established in the late nineteenth century, including Yellowstone National Park in 1872, Banff in 1885, and Yosemite in 1890. In fact, as Alan MacEachern notes, the prevailing attitude in the Canadian federal parks branch was that, due to such a long and prolonged campaign of preservation, "the [national park] system was … complete" after 1930.[6] Although this was a premature statement (Cape Breton Highlands, Fundy, and Prince Edward Island were all established in the 1930s and 40s), 1930 is a convenient date to identify as the culmination of decades of conservation lobbying and history as this was the year the National Parks Act was established by the Canadian government.[7] The years when Stratton-Porter and Montgomery wrote their first novels were particularly important in the development of nature consciousness. Historian George Altmeyer notes that the years 1893 to 1914 were characterized by a significant "back to nature" movement in both Canada and the United States.[8] The "new" attitudes that Altmeyer outlines – nature as benevolent, for example – are evident in the work of both Montgomery and Stratton-Porter. The dual belief that the natural world is healthy and invigorating and that urban or indoor life is enervating and unhealthy is clearly referred to in *The Blue Castle* when Olive implicitly compares her city-boy fiancé to outdoorsman Barney: "I really think, Cecil, you should exercise more. It doesn't do to get too fleshy." Similarly, in *A Girl of the Limberlost*, Phillip Ammon, Elnora's love interest, "had a fever and he has to stay outdoors until he grows strong again," much like schoolteacher Walter Blythe in *Rilla of Ingleside*, who needs an "idle summer in the open air and sunshine" as part of his recovery from typhoid.[9] Hearty outdoor exercise is the recipe for manly health and vigour; as Altmeyer notes, quoting a 1904 editorial in *Rod & Gun*, it was considered important that "every Canadian male [should] get into the woods and lakes at least once a year in order to prevent them from becoming 'helplessly soft and luxurious.'"[10] Back-to-nature movements, country health resorts, summer camps for children, and the rise of cottage country are all characteristics of this era in both Canada and the United States. Both Stratton-Porter's novels have a scene in Mackinaw, a summer resort; many of Montgomery's stories refer to the "summer" people who visit Prince Edward Island as tourists, and *The Blue Castle* is set in Muskoka country, where rich men have summer palaces and where Montgomery and her family spent their summer vacation in 1922.[11] Thus, throughout their writing careers from the early 1900s to the 1920s and 30s, Montgomery and Stratton-Porter were influenced by and contributed to this era's changing attitudes in North America about natural places, particularly the perception of human relations to the natural world from one of religiously sanctioned domination and capitalist utilitarian views towards preservation and appreciation, similar to the shift in the treatment of animals, discussed in Idette Noomé's chapter in this volume, albeit with the accompanying commercialization of the tourist industry.

Clearly, the "nature focus" of the books by Montgomery and Stratton-Porter is not anomalous and can be seen as representative of new attitudes to nature that were prevalent in the first decades of the twentieth century. They wrote just after the rise of popularizers of the "nature essay" like John Burroughs (1837–1921) and John Muir. However, the nature writing that is often now considered the mainstream of the ecocritical tradition is usually nonfiction and, with a few exceptions such as Mary Austin (1868–1934) and Rachel Carson (1907–1964), written by men. John Burroughs, for instance, wrote nonfiction nature essays that were extremely popular. As Brooks notes, he produced "innumerable magazine pieces, twenty-seven volumes [that] would reach a vast audience and make their author one of the best loved of all American writers."[12] Burroughs had an aphoristic, American vernacular style with a poetic slant and also an anthropomorphizing tendency; as Mary Rubio notes, he seems to be the closest model for Montgomery's John Foster.[13] Fiction writers like Charles G.D. Roberts (1860–1943) and Ernest Thompson Seton (1860–1946) wrote animal stories, a genre Stratton-Porter herself attempted in her first book, *The Song of the Cardinal* (1903), which she wrote to instil appreciation for the indigenous songbirds and forest birds of eastern North America – a *Black Beauty* for birds of the forest, as one reviewer noted.[14] Stratton-Porter was distressed by the small audience of the book, noting in a 1916 article published in the *Ladies Home Journal* that it "started so slowly that soon I came to the realization that, if I could not reach people faster, so far as my work was concerned, the cardinals might all go as had the [passenger] pigeons."[15] After the tepid response to *The Song of the Cardinal*, she turned to writing romance novels with a strong nature bent.

The naturalist characters in the three novels under consideration here are indications of a latent nonfictional discourse that underpins the romantic plot of the novels, reflected in the fact, not made explicit in the texts, that the naturalist characters are also the novelists themselves. Stratton-Porter claimed that fiction was not her primary interest: she "never considered herself a novelist," according to biographer Bertrand F. Richards, who claims that "[s]he maintained that her books were all nature studies 'sugar-coated with fiction.'"[16] Stratton-Porter was known as the Bird Woman of Geneva, Indiana, a successful nature journalist and photographer of birds and moths. By 1901, two years before the publication of *The Song of the Cardinal*, she had made a reputation as a professional writer, photographer, and illustrator. In her memoir, Stratton-Porter's daughter recalls a visit that her mother paid to her sister in Michigan that year: "when it was known that the 'Bird Woman' was in the city, she was besieged with invitations to address one of the meetings."[17] Not only does Stratton-Porter use her experiences in the field as situations in her novels, such as the key scene in *Freckles* in which the Bird Woman photographs a black vulture,[18] but the Bird Woman character – who has no other name in the book and who does little in the narrative in terms of plot – is the author "intruding in her own text," according to Elizabeth Ford, "a projection that would help explain the Bird Woman's absence from the list of characters" at the front of the book.[19]

In Montgomery's *The Blue Castle*, a string of aliases disguises the nature writer John Foster, but the aliases ultimately disguise the fact that the Foster texts in the novel are the nature writing of Montgomery herself.[20] The first paragraph of Montgomery's "Spring in the Woods," published in *The Canadian Magazine* in May 1911, is nearly identical to the first passage by John Foster that appears in *The Blue Castle*. The only difference in the passages is that in the *Blue Castle* version, the last Foster sentence is extracted from a later section in the "Woods" article and has a very slight variation, which appears here between square brackets: "Then the immortal heart of the woods will beat against ours and its subtle life will steal into our veins and make us its own forever, so that no matter where we go or how widely we wander [*in the noisy ways of cities or over lone paths of sea*,] we shall yet be drawn back to the forest to find our most enduring kinship."[21] Valancy (called "Doss" by the members of her family) is reading this passage when she is interrupted by her dreadful mother shouting at her, attempting to thwart her "wandering" out of the home to go the library. As Laura M. Robinson notes later in this volume in her discussion of kinship ties in this novel and in *Anne's House of Dreams*, ambivalence about the sickness, dysfunction, and misery of home prompts the desire to escape, not for noisy cities or paths of sea but eventually to a marriage and a new home in the woods. Until that ultimate escape happens, Valancy gets her "escape" from reading John Foster (and, more implicitly, L.M. Montgomery).

Like the Bird Woman, John Foster also has a shadowy half-life in the novel. Barney dons the mask of John Foster when he goes into a small lean-to to write, a place forbidden to Valancy. Both naturalists are nearly transparent characters, ghostly versions of the flesh-and-blood authors Stratton-Porter and Montgomery. They are as if Wayne Booth's implied author half-manifests materially in the narrative. In his famous critical work *The Rhetoric of Fiction* (1961), Booth distinguishes between the actual author (the human being outside the book who wrote the fiction), the narrator (the teller of the story within the fiction) and the implied author, the author's "second self," that impression of personality created by the author (through style, technique, exposition, tone, moral compass, and choice of scene or illumination) about the kind of person he or she is.[22] In both Montgomery's and Stratton-Porter's narrations, this implied author materializes as an oddly shadowy character in the novel. The naturalists are not the works' narrators nor explicit commentators; they are characters but they are simultaneously projections of the authors scribing in the barely acknowledged recesses of the novel, imprinting the texts with assumptions about the readers and their relation to the natural world, in a way that is very similar to the work of literary naturalists. The impression of authorial personality that Booth identifies as a feature of the "implied author" is located in the attitudes each author conveys about how the presumed audience thinks about the natural world. The Bird Woman is an impersonal wise woman figure; she provides a stable, disinterested ground for the various melodramatic stories and love affairs that are going on in the Limberlost. The tone she provides underscores Stratton-Porter's sense that the romance is the sugar coating for the important work of nature conservation awareness. The Bird Woman's cool, impersonal presence provides a subterranean resistance to the intense emotion of the books; as a young girl when I read the books, I felt the Bird Woman to be almost inexplicable: her purpose and who she was were mysterious to me, as if there were something going on in this world that I didn't understand or as if there existed another book, a prequel, about the Bird Woman's story that I had never read. (There is no such book.) The implied author lurking in the background functions in some ways like the setting itself, as a palpable but nearly invisible wisdom, like the enveloping natural world. Stratton-Porter seems to suggest that, for her readers, the natural world is incomprehensible and unseen, so using the entertainment value of the roller coaster of the melodramatic plots of *Freckles* and *Girl of the Limberlost*, readers can be guided towards more nature awareness. The implied author accepts the ignorance of the reader while projecting a barely perceptible scorn on the reader who seems to prefer romance to birding. In contrast, the impression of authorial personality in *The Blue Castle*, centred around Barney/John Foster, is less mysterious and distant; the tone he gives to the fiction is of a friendly, witty chum who has a great deal of nature-knowledge. Mary Rubio suggests that Barney/John Foster is "slightly embarrassed by his books";[23] this embarrassment or self-deprecation can be seen as an element of Montgomery's own perception that expressing a love of nature in the "purple prose" of John Foster is increasingly held up for ridicule in her era. However, the hidden, shadowy author lurking in his lean-to is also a trope for secret knowledge. Foster's knowledge is shared but only to a select few readers and, of course, Valancy. Montgomery presents Barney/herself as a "best friend" or "kindred spirit," an intimate balm for the deeply lonely Valancy as well as the reader, the solitary reader of romances, who is gently directed not only to conventional expectations about finding happiness in heterosexual romance but also to the message that people really should be "finding fullness of joy in [nature's] companionship" (as Rita Bode and Jean Mitchell state in their introduction). This latter route to happiness is, in fact, surer and deeper. The effect of Montgomery's implied personality is that it sets up an "in-group," a sense that by entering the woods and nature books of John Foster, the reader is among the "race of

Joseph" who are witty and generous and fun, but also who are the select: true lovers of the natural world.

With these author/naturalist characters rooted so firmly in both the fictional (as characters) and the "real" world (the naturalist work done outside the fictional texts as well as the authors' personalities infusing the texts), the conventionally narrated world and the nonfictional "actual" world seem to meet in an odd liminal zone between the fiction and the nonfiction "nature writing" texts. This instability tends to give the fictional world a friable or fragile surface, where the "real" can erupt at any moment into the fiction, often signalling an earthy, solid presence beneath the fabric of the story, in much the way geocritic Sten Moslund describes setting or place as capable of "presencing" in literary works.[24] Moslund notes that "presencing" is "a mode of reading that moves away from the *representation* of place in literature to a direct presencing of place or sensation of place."[25] Moslund quotes philosopher Maurice Merleau-Ponty as noting that some art "thrusts us once again into the presence of the world of lived experience."[26] Merleau-Ponty's phenomenological thought is central to much current ecocritical discourse, a validation of embodied and sense-based experience in writing that can provide "a genuine cognitive insight into the natural world";[27] Stratton-Porter and Montgomery are early, fervent, and skilled protopractitioners of these perceptual and ecoliterary tools. While the naturalist characters and their shadowy connections to the authors' perceptions "presence" in the text, in a more conventional ecofictional way, so too does place unsettle the fiction.

In the novels, some interesting gender-blurring tendencies lead to a surprising awareness of how place affects the identities of the characters and the course of the fiction. Again, the figures of the naturalists in the novels reveal this slippage or slipperiness of identity. The Bird Woman lacks any patriarchal trappings such as a surname, and John Foster/Barney Snaith has also shed his surname, trading his father's (Redfern) in favour of his late mother's (Snaith). These unstably named naturalists gesture towards androgyny, a quality that subtly intrudes into the other characters in the novels. This is where the plot thickens or rather begins to disappear, not hybridly into nonfictional discourse but instead into a role subordinate to setting. Valancy/Doss is doubly named, as is Freckles/Terence O'More, and each name-pair is associated with place: "Doss" in town, "Valancy" in the natural world; "Freckles" in the woods, "Terence" in town. Many of the heroes and heroines, as well as the naturalists, have nature-determined identities. What seems to be at first the slipperiness of only the naturalists, in fact, is the first step to realizing that all central identities are changed in these books by emplacement. In this system of place-based name shifting, the naturalists as experts of place are the catalysts to the romantic plot. In *The Blue Castle*, John Foster/L.M. Montgomery encourages Valancy to get out of her oppressive life in town to the woods where she will find love and freedom, and in *Freckles* the Bird Woman/Gene Stratton-Porter brings the Angel into the Limberlost woods so Freckles, the abandoned orphan, can find true love and social status. The main characters shift selves and roles through the catalyzing force of the naturalists' presence as well as the characters' physical locations.

A Girl of the Limberlost is complex in its place-shifting identity instability. Elnora and Philip as a couple are strongly associated with Freckles and the Angel who are the couple from *Freckles* and who appear briefly in *Girl*. (*The Girl of the Limberlost* is a semisequel to *Freckles*). However, the four characters map ambiguously onto each other. Elnora is like Freckles (red-haired, a nature lover of the Limberlost, musical) but also like the Angel, an angelic woman and lover; Philip Ammon is like the Angel (who is from the town and who has a father who looks out for him) but also the wealthy male lover who gets ill and must be made healthy (similar to how Freckles becomes an invalid and must be made healthy by the Angel.) Elnora is like the female Angel in town and like the male Freckles when she is in the woods; Philip is most like the male Terence O'More/Freckles in town and most like the Angel in the Limberlost woods. In this novel, the characters shift roles according to place and acquire strange gender-blending associations especially when the novels are compared.

What is key, though, is that in all three novels, the shifting identities revolve – literally – around specific places: the island in the Muskoka back country (*Blue Castle*) and the Limberlost (*Freckles* and *Girl of the Limberlost*). Barney and Valancy prowl about the countryside and always come back to their island in the middle of a lake. Freckles literally patrols the Limberlost in a circuit each day as he guards the valuable timber within it, and in *A Girl of the Limberlost* the Comstock farm is an island of pristine, untouched trees and swamp in the middle of developing agricultural and oil production, a place where time has stopped.

Once the main characters are situated in the primary landscape, beginnings and endings disintegrate and cyclical rhythms dominate – *The Blue Castle* is a seasonal chain, spring to spring, and *Freckles* also cycles through a seasonal year. *A Girl of the Limberlost* is again more complex but it too has a plot problem, similar to the one in *Anne of Green Gables*, where significant "change" in a character occurs to a subordinate character, where the "story" is not, in fact, about the heroine. In *Green Gables*, Marilla undergoes her transformation over several years, in a slow and believable development of character; in *Girl*, Mrs Comstock ceases to pathologically grieve for her husband after discovering that he was an unfaithful philanderer. She then undergoes a sudden and profound change of heart and realizes she had neglected her extraordinary daughter, Elnora. One week when Elnora is away, Mrs Comstock undergoes a "road to Damascus" conversion when she peels off her brown skin in a painful "facial," essentially coming out of a chrysalis. A similar metamorphosis occurs to Edith, Elnora's rival, whose initial revulsion for insects and whose superficial, cold character transforms through an experience of wonderment when she carries on her finger a moth just moments out of its cocoon. The wonder triggers a new empathy and compassion as she carries the valuable creature to the unchanged and unchanging Elnora. These two women have the real "stories" in *A Girl of the Limberlost*, but in *The Blue Castle* and *Freckles* the "stories" are pure, unbelievable melodrama. Valancy escapes her awful home and finds a new one, but she never essentially changes; she stays what she always is. Like a fairy-tale heroine, she is a jewel hidden in an ash pit; in the novel, her concealed inner self is revealed so that worthwhile people begin to value her, but like Cinderella, she does not develop or undergo moral change through action in the plot; she is a charming character who becomes "seen" rather than one who grows. Similarly, Freckles learns about nature throughout the novel, but he too is unchanging, although, like Valancy, his worth becomes recognized. There is a scene early in *Freckles* in which McLean, the boss and later adoptive father of Freckles, "crouched among the bushes ... to see what mettle was in the boy";[28] he is observing how Freckles behaves in the same way that Freckles has been observing the birds and animals around him. Elnora and Valancy are also assessed and observed by the Bird Woman and by Barney/John Foster, respectively. The three protagonists' stories are stories of recognition in which other characters, particularly naturalists with observant eyes, realize and celebrate the sterling qualities of these overlooked people as they move about the natural world. These novels' narrative patterns mimic the task of nature writing: to foreground setting and to notice and appreciate overlooked or unobserved phenomena. Narratives of observation and recording do not lend themselves to a huge amount of plot-generating action. These books move out of bildungsroman or romance, but they do not quite move into nonfictional nature description. The unchanged yet unstable characters, their connection and recognition catalyzed by the naturalist, circle around the natural world, a space where nature and love mingle. A static world of love and nature, nearly plotless and embedded in a country setting, sounds suspiciously like a very old genre or classical mode: the pastoral. According to Terry Gifford, one general description of the pastoral is "any literature that describes the country with an implicit or explicit contrast to the urban,"[29] a significantly place-based or spatially defined literature.

Theories of spatial form or spatial poetics are worthwhile to look at in relation to the pastoral. Spatial form seems at first an unlikely aid to understand popular women's fiction of the early twentieth century, given that this theory was developed by United States critic Joseph Frank in 1948 in order to "read" difficult modernist texts like Djuana Barnes's *Nightwood*. Frank proposes that high modernist work "lacks a narrative structure in the ordinary sense" and that "it cannot be reduced to any sequence of action for the purposes of explanation"; in his view, time in particular "is no longer felt as an objective, causal progression with clearly marked-out differences between periods."[30] Frank's theory has been expanded upon since the 1940s, and he has continued to refine his ideas, most recently in a 1991 revision of his original essay, taking into account responses such as those by critic David Mickelsen who enlarges upon Frank's ideas and lists several qualities of spatial form writing that seem relevant to the Montgomery and Stratton-Porter texts: "a lack of development" or a work that "portrays someone already developed" and a conclusion to a novel that "is very often an arbitrary stopping rather than a summing up; a fatigue, rather than structural fulfillment." Although Mickelsen insists that "concern … with fictional renderings of physical space and its connotations" is an inappropriate context for "spatial form"[31] – in other words, he is thinking of textual space rather than setting or narrative locale – recent theorists, particularly postcolonial theorists, have revisited the primacy of physical space in narratives. Susan Stanford Friedman reminds us that a focus on temporal narratives at the expense of geographic ones makes it impossible to understand fully postcolonial texts that must deal with place and borders.[32] What she sees as a function of postcolonial discourse, ecocritics and geocritics see as a function of current ecopoetics and econarrative. Moslund argues for a "*topopoetic* mode of reading that revives the power of *platial* experiences in literature … [where there] is a reading not for plot but for the setting, where the setting of the story is not reduced to an expendable passive or ornamental backdrop for the story's action. Rather, place is experienced as one of the primary events of the story and any action is experienced as being shaped, at least partially, by the event of the place."[33] Similarly, David Mazel argues that in ecocritical critiques, the environment can be as significant and as full of potential agency as plot. He theorizes his ideas with reference to Soviet structuralist Jurij Lotman's theories of narrative, applying Lotman's work to the colonial and gender implications of the plot/place nexus.[34]

According to Lotman, the deep and prehistoric origins of plot arise out of a cyclical story or myth characterized by "the absence of the categories beginning and end: the text is thought of as a mechanism which constantly repeats itself, synchronized with the cyclical processes of nature." Over time, Lotman claims, a culture begins to extract various characters and linearizes the temporal strands of the story. Pastoral forms seem to be very ancient and only partially developed from this mythic narrative state. Lotman locates Shakespeare's pastoral play *As You Like It* as an example of a text full of vestigial pastoral elements, noting that another vestige of the cyclical myth is character doubles, who are not binaries or doppelgangers but the same character in a different form or in different situations:

> One might suggest that doubles represent only the most elementary and obvious product of the linear paraphrase of the hero of a cyclical text. In fact the very appearance of different characters is the result of the same process. It is not difficult to notice that characters can be divided into those who are mobile, who enjoy freedom with regard to plot-space, who can change their place in the structure of

> the artistic world and cross the frontier, the basic topological feature of this space, and those who are immobile, who represent, in fact, a function of the space.[35]

The doubled characters in the Stratton-Porter and Montgomery novels are "function[s] of space." Their name changes are not the result of personal development through temporality (plot) but rather where they are situated (place). The tendency of these characters is not towards mobility but towards becoming emplanted functions of space. Through the central catalyst of the naturalist/novelist, the characters are drawn into the woods, into the centre of the plot-stalled novel that is bolstered by or interwoven with nature writing and saturated in nature as lover/mother/divine presence. The land and the natural world are more than setting: they are the draw, the centrifuge that pulls all inward.

In Euro-western cultures, this enveloping environment is perceived as threatening or as a challenge to overcome, the immersive mother love that will kill and smother the hero. Typical heroes overcome or resist these so-called obstacles of space and cross boundaries separating different places, but they rarely enter into a relationship with the place itself. Montgomery and Stratton-Porter see that space/place as benign, healthy, and even egalitarian and certainly nature-focused. Montgomery and Stratton-Porter seem to be trying an alternate narrative, a refusal to resist envelopment, a returning to more cyclic narratives with characters whose doubling or even tripling reflects growing into a place rather than going on a journey. These are radical revisionings of the hero and the primacy of place or *topos* and closer to indigenous ideas of narrative in North America than most Euro-Western narrative where the hero moves through plot/space with mobility and unidirectionality. These revisionings are also similar to what Gifford describes as the "post-pastoral," where, to refer back to *As You Like It*, "we have as much interest in the welfare of Arden as in that of its exiled inhabitants, as much interest in their interaction with Arden as in what they take back from it, as much interest in how they represent their interaction with it as in how their representations of themselves as its inhabitants have changed."[36]

The typical hero's journey plot pattern has ecological and attachment consequences in North America. As environmental historian John Wadland observes of North Americans, particularly Canadians, "We have never really learned the true meaning of adaptation to place, and despite our fascination with exploration, we have never found home."[37] We are too busy on our hero's journey to notice where we are, and in North America, our busyness is wrapped up in commerce, commodity, and property. As Wes Jackson reports, the first European visitor, Christopher Columbus, noted how lovely the West Indies were but claimed he could not stay since he was looking for gold.[38] It is perhaps easy to see the pressure on Stratton-Porter and Montgomery to bring their narratives in line with prescribed temporal plot lines and their place-focus in line with the dominant capitalist system that needs to detach us from nature so it can be usefully exploited. *Freckles* ends with a ridiculous plot twist about being the long-lost child of aristocratic parents and gaining a life as a rich man with an aristocratic name. *The Blue Castle* has a similarly crazy plot twist of Valancy discovering that Barney is the son of a millionaire. In the end, Valancy and Barney, a rich, travelling married couple with family connections, reattach themselves to capitalism as they live off the proceeds of the Redfern patent medicines. Freckles takes on a capitalist role as the heir of an aristocratic estate and as the adopted son of a rich lumberman who is destroying the trees of the Limberlost for profit. Mrs Comstock becomes a conventional mother with her peeled skin and begins to sell her trees and set up oil wells on her Limberlost preserve, and Elnora, in the tourist resort of Mackinaw, ends up becoming a wife and mother instead of a nature teacher in the public schools.

It seems no accident that Elnora is caught in the web of convention in the O'More summer home, the heart of nature as tourist attraction or commodified summer cottage country or that Freckles is nearly destroyed but ultimately returned to his social status by the lumber industry or that Valancy and Barney are thrown back to their time-based senses by a train, that symbol of industrial capitalism and linear temporality. The narrative of North America that Montgomery and Stratton-Porter seem to want to resist is situated in the belief that the pastoral situation is only an interlude and that one cannot stay in it. As Leo Marx notes, the endings of pastoral fables are unsatisfactory: "How can [the protagonist] carry back into our complex social life the renewed sense of possibility and coherence that the pastoral interlude has given him [or her]?"[39] Gifford also notes that the essence of pastoral is "a movement of retreat [to the country] and return [to the court]."[40] In a narrative mode about mobility, the difficulty of affirming place-based stability is insurmountable. Interestingly, in Montgomery's and Stratton-Porter's novels, the pull back to "reality" (the plot or *chronos*) is narratively the most unreal, simplistic, and silly part of the novel. These two novelists undermine the view that the pastoral idyll is unreal, nostalgic, and sentimental. With their simplistic endings, the novels of Stratton-Porter and Montgomery hint that the non-pastoral world to which the characters return is the simple, single-fated one, contrasting the truly complex and diverse life of swamp and forest.

Stratton-Porter originally planned to end *Freckles* with tragedy, having Freckles killed by a falling tree as he saves the Angel.[41] Freckles would have been planted in the Limberlost and in the plot forever, which would likely have been the real spatial form or ecopastoral ending for this novel, but this ending was not acceptable to her publisher. Nevertheless, both Stratton-Porter and Montgomery have, through their naturalist characters, offered a submerged alternative to the endings they attached more obviously to their novels. Barney *did* earn his living in the wilderness. Elnora *could* have become an instructor in the public schools teaching children about owls. The Bird Woman *continues* to educate the public and work from her home without going anywhere except into a nearby swamp. These people stayed still and stayed home for a time. Their stories are latent in these novels, providing an economic, ecological, and narrative alternate.

However, in the end, staying home and a disinclination to "journey" continue to be pathologized in North American society (as in Montgomery's Pat novels, discussed in this volume by Catriona Sandilands). It *is* fearful to love a place in North America where place is real estate and where home is meant to be left behind or destroyed. These two novelists were attempting a new vision, one that we need to continue to imagine in this time of ecological crisis. They were not at the forefront of modernist literary experiments, but nevertheless they were on the cusp of a radical alteration of the relation of narrative and place, an experiment from which fiction writers today can learn as they attempt to write about nature, what Montgomery/John Foster calls "our most enduring kinship."[42]

CHAPTER FOUR

L.M. Montgomery's "Indoors and Out": Imagining an Organic Architecture

Rita Bode

In his account of his two year, two month, and two day sojourn in the woods on the shores of Walden Pond, Henry David Thoreau writes in *Walden*: "I went to the woods because I wished to live deliberately, to front only the essential facts of life … to live deep and suck out all the marrow of life."[1] To do this, he felt the need to turn his back on civilization, as represented by the nearby town of Concord, his usual place of residence. With the many familial responsibilities that L.M. Montgomery carried throughout her life, she perhaps never had Thoreau's opportunity to walk away from society and the demands of daily life into a pristine natural environment for any prolonged period of time. But it is not certain either that she would have wanted to. Although nature was a source of intense joy for Montgomery, and one of her aesthetic strengths is her ability to evoke a deep appreciation of and respect for the natural world, she never felt, as Thoreau did, the need to choose between civilization and wilderness.

Montgomery's outlook and desires encompassed both nature and culture. The beauty and wonder that she found in landscapes did not diminish her attraction to urbanscapes. Montgomery liked cities. One of the appeals of her Ontario residency was the easy access to Toronto and its cultural attractions that her homes in Leaskdale and Norval afforded her. Clarence Karr observes, "She was, as she pointed out to Ephraim Weber, equally at home in nature and in the sparkling city, and could 'slip from one to the other as easily as I can slip from one garment to another.'"[2] Her deep commitment to the nonhuman organic world did not detract from her abiding interest in and valuing of all aspects of human creativity. Like nature, built environments drew her attention. In a late chapter of *Anne of the Island*, pondering how to spend the leisurely afternoon ahead of her, Anne declares, "I'm contrasting the claims of indoors and out."[3] Perhaps not entirely surprisingly, Anne heads to the outdoors, but her decision-making recognizes unequivocally that human-built spaces, like the natural world, exert "claims."

Montgomery's choice of words significantly positions these claims as equal. Montgomery and her fictional creations alike value both "indoors and out," both built environments and natural settings. While a number of Montgomery's titles refer to place, some also invoke dwellings: New Moon, Silver Bush, Lantern Hill, Blue Castle. Subsequent book titles resituate her, but Anne is first and foremost Anne "of Green Gables." The "green" world that this association conjures up is constituted by a built structure created by humans and housing human experience. Montgomery's fictional houses provide a critical site for new understandings of and insights into the "matter of nature" in her writings. Her conception of houses embraces the significance of interior spaces but also the principles that create them. In her fiction, Montgomery articulates a dynamic architecture that looks to nature's presence and forms to create an environment in which the constructed is not only a shelter for its human inhabitants but is itself contained in harmony with and by the land on which it is situated.

For Montgomery, nature requires no human justification for its existence. She does not view nature as simply a resource for human needs, whether pleasurable, necessary, or exploitive, but at the same time, she is always searching for the importance and significance of the human element. Her perspective on the natural landscape includes the human presence within it. The introduction to this volume points out that Montgomery was influenced by North American naturalist thinkers and writers; she shared with them an awareness of what today we familiarly call ecosystems and biospheres in referring to the collective interactions among living organisms and their physical environments. As Elizabeth Rollins Epperly demonstrates in the next chapter, Montgomery shared Emerson's belief in the "kinship" between humans, nature, and things. Later in the volume, Lesley D. Clement invokes Frans de Waal's study of empathy to trace an ethic of care that embraces human and nonhuman life alike in Montgomery's work. In environmental theory terms more specifically, Montgomery's outlook on the sentient world and its habitations is perhaps closest to the perspective of early influential ecofeminists, like Donna Haraway, Val Plumwood, and Carolyn Merchant, all of whom, in different ways, look not to divisions among species and between the human and nonhuman but, rather, to continuities and connections. Perhaps most applicable to Montgomery's outlook is a variation on or modification of Carolyn Merchant's "partnership ethic," which Merchant, in *Reinventing Eden*, explains is "a synthesis between an ecological approach based on moral consideration for all living and nonliving things and a human-centered (or homocentric) approach based on the social good and the fulfillment of basic human needs."[4]

Montgomery's fiction contains multiple examples of the mediating potential in such an outlook. In her first and still most famous novel, Anne's perceptions make the rural world, which is Montgomery's usual creative focus, the site of bucolic pleasures, but Montgomery also makes evident that Avonlea is a working community of farmers. Montgomery frames Anne's story as an agricultural narrative. Jennifer Lister points out in an earlier chapter that "the daily tasks of farming life are but a murmur in the background of Montgomery's fiction," but it is a sustained murmur. Anne arrives at Green Gables by mistake, since the Cuthberts want "a boy to help Matthew on the farm," a situation of which we are reminded near the novel's end when Anne, seeing Matthew tired and ill, exclaims with regret, "If I had been the boy you sent for … I'd be able to help you so much now, and spare you in a hundred ways."[5] In his study of farm-centred texts in American literature, William Conlogue points out that one of the key components of the farm novel is its focus on the "*interrelationship between human work and nature*." Conlogue's literary criticism locates the potential of farm sites to practice the kind of balanced outlook proposed by Merchant's "partnership ethics": the "landscapes" of the "farm novel," Conlogue notes, "are not simply settings for human action but places where the human, animal, plant, and nonorganic worlds interact in interdependent relationships."[6] Similarly, environmental journalist Michael Pollan posits a garden ethic which rejects the idea that the human "impact on nature will always be negative."[7] From the "upside-down perspective" of "a plant's-eye view of the world," he recounts his surprise at the discovery that "all these plants, which I'd always regarded as the objects of my desire, were also ... subjects, acting on me."[8] Garden spaces, which appear throughout Montgomery's novels, offer reciprocal, dynamic possibilities for human engagements with nature for not only are they often sites that facilitate the fulfillment of human desires as in Anne's and Gilbert's declaration of love in Hester Gray's garden but they also continually assert their autonomy to balance human interventions, demanding work and effort on the part of gardeners. Again and again, we find in Montgomery's fiction that the human imagination does not impose on but elicits its full powers from the natural world, while nonhuman life enables human beings to strive more confidently toward the fulfillment of their potential. Farms and gardens draw the human, the organic, and their environs into the material intimacy of a shared common existence; even more firmly in the foreground than farms and gardens, however, as articulations of a balanced relationship between the human and nonhuman environment that answers to Merchant's "fulfillment of basic human needs," are Montgomery's human-built structures.

In their discussion of "reading the house," Kathy Mezei and Chiara Briganti suggest how houses offer a "semiotic system that signals status, class, and public display" as well as inviting "the exploration and expression of private and intimate relations and thoughts."[9] Both the exteriors and interiors of literary houses express the themes and intents of their fictions. Anne recognizes Green Gables at first glance – "just as soon as I saw it I felt it was home," she declares to Matthew in their buggy ride from the station – affirming not only her strong need to belong but also her conviction that she belongs to Green Gables and all that she intuitively knows it represents.[10] She is not proven wrong. Interior spaces, moreover, are also significant for Montgomery's fictional characters as they were for her own writing life. After leaving her Cavendish home when her grandmother died and she finally married the Rev. Macdonald, Montgomery thinks with profound sadness of "my dear old room where I shall never sit and hold pen more."[11] Ten years before Virginia Woolf's articulations, Montgomery affirms the importance of "a room of one's own" for female creativity. Drawing on the work of Gaston Bachelard, Margaret Steffler traces Montgomery's creative efforts as both contained in and overflowing the

Leaskdale manse interiors.[12] In her fiction, Montgomery provides writing spaces for her budding fictional writer, placing Emily in the New Moon garret to write the long letters to her father that help her psychic survival and are a preparation for the creative work that will confirm her vocation as a writer. Montgomery's interest, however, extended beyond exteriors and interiors to the house as the physical structure that encompasses these elements. While her fictional houses are the metaphorical and symbolical expressions of her story's meanings, they are also a pronounced physical, material presence, both objects and subjects in their own right. In building them, Montgomery envisions an architecture in which construction and design bring into creative interplay the indoors and out.

Houses, especially in their association with domestication, belong to civilization, but Montgomery's concepts of architecture aim to avoid the nature and culture binary. Domestication itself, as gardens indicate, offers mediating possibilities. In the emphasis on region, place, and domestic space, Montgomery's writing shares some similarities with the fiction of American female local colourists such as Mary Wilkins Freeman and Sarah Orne Jewett. Stacy Alaimo's discussion of these female writers holds relevance for Montgomery when Alaimo raises the possibility that the boundaries between "indoors and out" can be fluid. Her discussion identifies "hybrid spaces" where "nature takes root in the domestic and the domestic opens out into nature."[13] From the beginning of her career to its end, Montgomery's houses occupy an in-between, transboundary site that the structures themselves create. Anne's early creation of Idlewild as a child sets the pattern. In "a little ring of white birch trees," Anne and Diana have located their "playhouse," which she tells Marilla they have "fixed up elegantly."[14] Their efforts seem a worthy if inverted variation on modernist architect Louis Sullivan's well-known dictum that "*form ever follows function*"[15] as they make their playhouse's natural forms, "great big stone, all covered with moss," serve their required function of "seats" and create their shelving by placing "boards from tree to tree." Anne continues:

> And we have all our dishes on them ... There's a piece of a plate with a spray of red and yellow ivy on it that is especially beautiful. We keep it in the parlour and we have the fairy glass there, too. The fairy glass

> is as lovely as a dream. Diana found it out in the woods behind their chicken house. It's all full of rainbows – just little young rainbows that haven't grown big yet – and Diana's mother told her it was broken off a hanging lamp they once had. But it's nicer to imagine the fairies lost it one night when they had a ball, so we call it the fairy glass. Matthew is going to make us a table.[16]

Nature engages in the creation of this playhouse space through both beauty and practicality. "Red and yellow ivy" on a plate and a glass "full of rainbows" merge seamlessly to enhance nature and artefact alike. It is not even a question of inviting the forest in, for thresholds and boundaries between indoors and out do not exist here. In her comments in the next chapter on Washington Irving's architectural preferences and his influence on Montgomery, Epperly points to Irving's belief in bringing indoors and out into "meaningful, continuing dialogue." Similarly, in Idlewild, the natural world and the human presence contain no division between the "wild" and the civilized, but instead, they inhabit a shared and unique space in which neither absorbs the other.

Idlewild is a hard act to follow, but it is, after all, a playhouse that by necessity will be outgrown. Montgomery's sharper focus remains on the sturdier house of Green Gables, which modifies its boundary crossings through more traditional mediating activities like cooking and tea tables covered in "roses and ferns."[17] Montgomery's houses become mediating spaces in other ways as well, however, for attachment to place for her characters always involves both the natural and human-made environments. Anne's longing for Green Gables is not separate from her longing for the Island's natural environment. Houses, for Anne, are part of the Island setting and its many beauties. When in a later novel an adult Anne mourns her departure from the much beloved "little house of dreams," her descriptions of structure and nature run indiscriminately into each other:

> [S]he loved this little house of dreams so much. She loved *everything* about it – the garden she had tended, and which so many women had tended before her – the gleam and sparkle of the little brook that crept so roguishly across the corner – the gate between the creaking

> fir trees – the old red sandstone step – the stately Lombardies – the two tiny quaint glass cupboards over the chimneypiece in the living-room – the crooked windows upstairs – the little jog in the staircase – why, these things were a part of her! How could she leave them?[18]

While the interaction between houses and their natural environments can assume an intensity that results in imbalance, as Montgomery explores in her Pat books, houses and their natural environments most often create spaces in which culture and nature have the potential to interact creatively and seamlessly to transcend divisions.

Montgomery's interest in structures and the way in which they show the human and nonhuman in relation continues to the end of her career. In her late novel *Jane of Lantern Hill*, the growth of the young female protagonist invokes a traditional journey pattern through Jane's several moves: from city to country and back, from urban to island spaces, from mansions and chauffeured vehicles to seascapes and walks. Her journey, however, is also marked by a movement from one house to another, each tracing a different relationship to nature.

Jane of Lantern Hill is Montgomery's urban novel set partly in Toronto and partly in the rural scapes of Prince Edward Island. Throughout the novel, in both the city and the country, nature facilitates Jane's friendships with others, from Jody, who loves gardens, to Timothy Salt, who helps her learn to swim. But, like her creator, she also traverses the byways of culture with ease, finding materials in the urban Toronto environment for self-expression and self-definition: in the backyard of 58 Gay Street, next door to the "huge, castellated structure of brick" where she lives with her mother, her grandmother, and her aunt, she and her orphan friend, Jody, create an imaginary garden and a physical castle of tin cans. Before the collapse of the tin can structure, the "budding architect" who boards at 58 Gay sees it in the moonlight and whistles over it: "That's rather an amazing thing for those two kids to build." The links of this castle to nature may seem tenuous but it is a structure that is open to and "gleaming" in the moonlight, a direct participant in its environs. In contrast, Grandmother Kennedy's prison-like house seems determined to keep all natural flow outside its "high iron fence." The grass around it does not grow and the house, as passersby declare, is "a *dead* house." Nonetheless, "through her window," Jane establishes a relationship with the moon and finds solace for her dreary Gay Street life through this connection with nature. Since the moon can only peer at her from afar in the Gay Street house, she goes on "dream voyages" and moon sprees to it: "The dearest sight Jane knew was the thin crescent in the western sky that told her her friend was back."[19] Jane reaches out and invites in, refusing to recognize the boundaries that distinguish indoors from out.

Not only the promise of an attachment to place but a search for houses maps Jane's experience and growing sense of self-definition. In Aunt Irene's house on Prince Edward Island, Jane feels "as much at home as a sparrow alone on an alien housetop," her feelings reflecting the remote kinship between this Island house and the Gay Street mansion. Aunt Irene's house is "cosy and sleek" and, like its owner, comes with a veneer that lacks spontaneity and is all based on calculation, the realm of humankind. In their "jolly" house hunting, Jane and dad look at eight houses before finding in the ninth the one that not only satisfies but promises to nurture them. Their search for houses shows Jane's developing self-assurance: with dad's guidance and companionship, she trusts in her own assessment of the potential and limitations of each successive house. "The sixth house seemed to be all a house should be," but "new and white, with a red roof and dormer windows," it marks its borders as a "small bungalow" too strongly leaving no meeting space for structure and nature. It has a "wonderful view of the gulf," but it is "treeless" and in its model status lacks distinction. It elicits no associations by which to establish connections. In contrast, the house of the "Jimmy Johns … over on Lantern Hill[, t]he house their Aunt Matilda Jollie lived in," alerts Jane that "magic was in the offing."[20]

At Lantern Hill, Jane recognizes the "magic" of belonging to a house that is "*yours* before you buy it." Surveying the house and its environs on Lantern Hill, Jane realizes that "she had never been there before, but it seemed as if she had known it all her life. The song the sea-wind was singing was music native to her ears. She had always wanted to 'belong' somewhere and she belonged here. At last she had a feeling of home." She seeks a space that welcomes its inhabitants by affirming in some way what they value. At Lantern Hill, Jane recognizes a house that is inclusive. She likes "the pattern of this place," which includes the land, the sea, and the house that "squatted right against a little steep hill." As her father declares, "The house … and the pond … and the harbour … and the gulf! A good buy." The fences at Lantern Hill are "lichen-covered," with nature laying claim to the human-made barrier. "Indoors and out" flow into each other once again. Windows here are not barriers but entryways to engage with the natural world: "They could see the maple wood through the east window, the gulf and the pond and the dunes through the north, the harbour through the west. Winds of the salt seas were blowing in."[21] The outside is not remote or something to be admired and longed for at a distance but rather a proximate and intimate experience. This accepting, inclusive space allows for nature's autonomy as well as for Jane's growing independence. A mediating space itself, Lantern Hill encourages other intercessionary activities through which the raw materials of nature turn into cultural expressions: liberation comes in many forms, and, for Jane, to whom the kitchen's activities in the Gay Street mansion are forbidden, cooking and even cleaning are celebratory actions that meet her "basic needs" of both body and spirit.[22]

Jane's maturation is perhaps most evident in her realization that the flexibility of spirit and acceptance that she finds in Lantern Hill is transferable. The "Lakeside development on the banks of the Humber," when she visits there with her mother, comes as a "revelation" to Jane through her discovery that the country exists in the city: "she had never dreamed there were such lovely places in Toronto. Why, it was just like a pretty country village out here." Jane finds Lakeside Gardens "a friendly street. The houses did not look at each other with their noses in the air." She likes many of the houses that she passes on her walk, "but it was not until she was nearly at the end of the street, where it turned into a road winding down to the lake, that she saw *her* house … [S]he knew at first sight that it belonged to her … just as Lantern Hill did." From its front steps, she sees "misty pale green woods over the river," but she also notices that, "The banners of a city of night were being flaunted in the sunset sky behind the pines further down." Jane recognizes the house's transboundary potential as she peers in its windows imagining "curtains at the recessed window" of the breakfast nook "between gold and green that would look like sunshine on the darkest day." Like Lantern Hill, this Toronto house invites domestic intercession, and Jane sees "herself in it, hanging curtains, polishing the glass doors, making cookies in the kitchen."[23] Moreover, the small house in Lakeside Gardens also suggests a development in Montgomery's thinking on the creative relationship between the natural world and the structures that humankind places in it that she introduced with Emily's home with her father.

Idlewild and Lantern Hill share their openness to the natural forces outside their walls, letting the outdoors in and allowing it free passage through all their interiors to create shared, mediating spaces. In *Emily of New Moon*, among the several houses that Emily encounters, the dwelling's relationships to nature are a significant factor in determining their value. Emily finds pleasure in New Moon when her first sight of the "big house" has it "peering [at her] whitely through a veil of trees." In the novel's assessment of houses, some neglected houses are better than others because some, rather than disrupting, accommodate themselves to their surroundings. The Disappointed House puzzles Emily, for in its unfinished state it does not fit with its surroundings nor fulfil its role of sheltering human occupants. Lofty John's house, which his father in a peevish state plopped down where it stands, has only "a general air of indifference and neglect about it," but the dilapidated state of the Tansy Patch, the "little clap-boarded house" where Teddy and his mother live, signals an engagement with the natural world from the tansy aroma that engulfs both hill and home, through the "straggling rail fence, almost smothered in wild rosebushes," to the "stones … let into the side of the hill for steps up to the front door." But the *New Moon* dwelling that pushes Montgomery's architectural vision of a partnership between built structures and their environs beyond Idlewild and Lantern Hill toward a paradigm circumventing the threat of human domination of and imposition on the earth is the house that Emily shares with her father. Montgomery opens her novel with a description of the father and daughter's dwelling. It is a house that is conceived from the ground up:

> [T]he house in the hollow was … situated in a grassy little dale, looking as if it had never been built like other houses but had grown up there like a big, brown mushroom. It was reached by a long, green

> lane and almost hidden from view by an encircling growth of young birches. No other house could be seen from it, although the village was just over the hill.[24]

Montgomery's "house in the hollow" does not alter the natural landscape but rather emerges from and merges with its surroundings. It looks forward to the seamless connection between structure and natural surroundings in the Lakeside Gardens house in *Jane of Lantern Hill*.

The extent to which Montgomery was aware of contemporary directions in architecture remains uncertain, but with her intellectual curiosity and topical reading, it is likely that she knew about trends in social and cultural areas and beyond. Even more significant in a sense, however, is the possibility that her own ideas on human dwellings aligned with the leading modernist architects of her time. Idlewild's focus on function, as already mentioned, suggests one of the major dictums of renowned American architect, Louis Sullivan. Sullivan's main contribution to modern architecture was the skyscraper, but significantly, he embellished the exteriors with designs that often drew on organic forms. Working with Sullivan at an early stage in his career was Frank Lloyd Wright, who would go on to make arguably the most significant architectural statements of the twentieth century. Like Montgomery, both these modernist architects were influenced by the writings of Emerson and other American transcendentalists, such as Thoreau and Whitman. Mark Mumford points out that Sullivan "read Emerson deeply" and his influence on his younger protégée was significant, but he also confirms that Wright's involvement with the thinking of such authors on nature was firsthand. Edward H. Madden affirms that both architects read as well as acknowledged their indebtedness to Emerson, Thoreau, and the poet Walt Whitman. While he argues that Sullivan and Wright took different ideas from Emerson, his architectural analysis reads Emerson's influence into the buildings of both. Montgomery and these modernist architects all hold to a holistic vision of the kinship between human and nonhuman life in the built environments that they create.[25]

The confluence of Montgomery's architectural vision as reflected in her fictional dwellings with the modernist movement in architecture is particularly evident in relation to Wright. Born just seven years before her,

Wright and Montgomery were contemporaries. His influential work in architecture culminated in what he eventually designated "organic architecture," a process for building that privileges structures as an outgrowth of the surrounding land on which they stand.[26] Structures, in Wright's approach, should integrate with rather than impose on nature. Montgomery also arrived under similar influences at ideas that reflect Wright's architectural theories on the relationship between house and land, between human-made structures and the natural world.[27] One of Wright's most significant creations was Fallingwater, the spectacular house outside Pittsburgh, Pennsylvania that he built over a waterfall. Wright was working on it at the same time that Montgomery was writing *Jane of Lantern Hill*, and both house and book reached completion in 1937. Montgomery's description of the Lakeside Garden home speaks of the same kind of harmony and integration with setting that Wright was striving to achieve from early in his career. "A building should appear to grow easily from its site and be shaped to harmonize with its surroundings," he wrote in 1908, the year of the publication of *Anne of Green Gables*.[28] Lakeside Gardens is more consciously, and completely, part of its natural surroundings than any of Montgomery's previous houses: it "was built of grey stone and had casement windows ... some of them beautifully unexpected ... and a roof of shingles stained a very dark brown. It was built right on the edge of the ravine overlooking the tree tops, with five great pines just behind it." The house stands in harmony with the trees around it and takes its own colours from theirs. The gardens around the house follow the setting's directives – "At the back the ground was terraced right down to the floor of the ravine" – facilitating the human presence through "three flights of stone steps [that] went down the terraces, with the delicacy of birch shadows about them, and off to one side was a wild garden of slender young Lombardies." Even the wanderers in the garden, "robin" and "cat," saunter through in tolerable agreement.[29]

Jane's house in Lakeside Gardens seems to be the site where indoors and out, culture and nature, city and country can blend and coexist in dynamic relation. In *Through Lover's Lane: L.M. Montgomery's Photography and Visual Imagination* (2007), Epperly comments that "Montgomery's houses, natural settings, and characters' developing consciousness are all made to appear as parts of larger stories about beauty and belonging."[30]

Early in the novel, in a garden that does not really exist, Jane builds a tin castle that will not last, but her achievement here looks toward the novel's final house, the home in Lakeside Gardens on the banks of the Humber. At the novel's end, as dad tells Jane about his new job in Toronto, he comments that, "How you live is much more important than where you live," to which Jane responds as if she has not heard him: "I know the very house."[31] Father and daughter are both right. Jane knows that houses, in their relation to the natural world, facilitate the "how" about which dad speaks. Lakeside Gardens looks towards a more lasting fulfillment, offering the promise of enduring human bonds. It promises the "belonging" for which Montgomery and so many of her characters have longed, a belonging among the land, its houses, and its human inhabitants.

PART TWO

Nature's Embodiments

CHAPTER FIVE

Natural Bridge: L.M. Montgomery and the Architecture of Imaginative Landscapes

Elizabeth Rollins Epperly

L.M. Montgomery's concept of nature is key to her pattern of metaphors. This pattern, while as unique as a signature, may also, I suggest, be widely accessible and frequently transformative because of the way it involves nature in metaphor. In late Victorian rural Eastern Canada in a community of largely English and Scottish descent, Montgomery was schooled in interpreting nature through the Romanticism of (among others) William Wordsworth, Sir Walter Scott, and Washington Irving. As early as seventeen, she read Ralph Waldo Emerson (himself influenced by Wordsworth and Scott and influencing Irving), finding in Emerson's "Nature" a convincing description for the kind of power she experienced in and through her reading and her environment. She gives this experience of power to all of the heroines of her novels; it is the grounding for her metaphors as well as for theirs. This quality of nature experience Montgomery developed and reflected in her writing can best be described as a communion. The images I am going to develop through this essay to describe and explain this quality of communion are bridges and bridging. I am suggesting that Montgomery's lasting appeal may be found in the kinds of bridges and bridging she created: a pattern of metaphors dependent on, and reflecting, her ideas about nature and human interaction with "it."

All of Montgomery's (novel) heroines experience what can be called communion with nature – a reciprocal, animated interaction that renews the spirit or awakens it. Reciprocity is important in this imagined exchange; trees, flowers, lanes, shores know and care – in Montgomery's depicted world of nature – that they are observed and valued. Every part of a universal whole responds to and is affected by all other parts, no matter how small. "You, reader," Montgomery's writing seems to say, "matter to this nature; whatever your circumstances or frailties, you are needed because when you interact meaningfully with the natural world you help to increase harmony and intensify beauty for all entities." A red-haired orphan matters to this nature; she is blessed to the very extent that she perceives blessings. The pattern of metaphors surrounding each heroine, sustaining each novel, reinforces Montgomery's consistent underlying suggestion that nature is a conscious and responsive force.

In *The Song of the Earth*, Jonathan Bate reminds readers how the definitions of "nature" have changed in the last couple of hundred years in Western discussions and most especially since the publication of Rachel Carson's *Silent Spring* in 1962.[1] To acknowledge the necessary complexity of his own use of the term and to encapsulate much current ecocritical discussion, he adapts Kate Soper's useful three-part definition, which I summarize this way: (1) "a metaphysical concept" through which humanity distinguishes itself from what is nonhuman; (2) a "realist concept" that includes the "structures, processes and causal powers that are constantly operative within the physical world" and are not only the study of the natural sciences but inescapably govern all interactions within the physical world no matter how well humans may "harness" those powers; (3) a "lay concept" where "nature" is used as the observable everyday world, (the world opposed to the urban one – "this is the nature of immediate experience and aesthetic appreciation; the nature we have destroyed and polluted and are asked to conserve and preserve").[2] While these distinctions are helpful, Bate says "it is impossible to hold the three senses fully apart."[3] I would add, it is almost impossible to discuss "nature" or offer a depiction of it that involves cause and effect or consideration of interaction between humans and "it," without involving the first and third of these three dimensions, as did Wordsworth, Emerson, and Irving. Interestingly, the second distinction, involving science and the structure and causes within nature only seems to be foreign to the Romanticism of these three because their understanding of the laws of nature is more implicit than explicit; a keen and exact observation of the workings of the natural world is a hallmark of all three writers.

Montgomery, like Wordsworth, Emerson, and Irving, incorporated into her seeing and into the writing about her seeing not only a complex understanding of nature – where "human and nonhuman" are "equal participants" (as Bode and Mitchell's introduction to this collection suggests) – but also a belief in the kinship of all things in relation to each other. Wordsworth sums up this kinship in "Lines Written a Few Miles Above Tintern Abbey" this way: "I have felt/ A presence ... A motion and a spirit, that impels/All thinking things, all objects of all thought,/And rolls through all things."[4] The "presence" is nature seen and unseen. In this poem, not only does nature feel but it also is at one with the perceiver so that the "perceiving eye" becomes, as Bate suggests, "an ecologically connected organism."[5] The creative, inspiring kinship between the observable everyday world of nature and a larger force that "rolls through all things" is clearly though differently articulated in Emerson's 1836 essay "Nature," which Montgomery first recorded reading in 1892.[6] Montgomery continued to reread Emerson, quoting him in her journals and her fiction; his capitalized *Nature* (the creative force behind all life) and uncapitalized *nature* (the visible, everyday world)[7] are dual presences enriching her characters' interactions with the natural world. Emerson talks of the "plastic power of the human eye."[8] As I have discussed in *Through Lover's Lane: L.M. Montgomery's Photography and Visual Imagination*, Emerson's "eye" perceives according to its bent and creates according to its means: the laws of the universe are there to be read in Nature, and the glory of the individual is in finding a means to understand and to recreate from those laws.[9] Montgomery's fiction supports his neo-Platonic theories of the ideal harmony and unity of Nature behind nature (think of Emily's "flash") as well as his contention that language naturally reflects a lived kinship with Nature and nature.

Emerson describes "man" as an "analogist," one whose language embodies experience, who apprehends and also creates the world through metaphor. Further, he suggests a directness about picturing and understanding – supplying an image and understanding its immediate and larger applicability: "Every appearance in nature corresponds to some state of the mind, and that state of the mind can only be described by presenting that natural appearance as its picture."[10] In apprehending this "appearance in nature," and in rendering this "picture," we find, I think,

Montgomery's assumption about mind, metaphor, and nature. Emerson's essay anticipates today's neuroscience in how the mind perceives, if not in how it finds meaning. Cognitive linguists and some neuroscientists now tell us that the mind is hardwired to create images and to understand through metaphor. George Lakoff and Mark Johnson even define metaphor, in their groundbreaking book *Metaphors We Live By* (1980), as "imaginative rationality." We reason by analogy, Emerson says, to which Lakoff and Johnson add that we understand the world through "conceptual metaphors."[11] Montgomery's evident belief in a dialogue between nature and the human mind seems key to her "imaginative rationality." Neuroscience suggests that metaphors (conceptual metaphors, not only literary ones) – in encouraging the understanding of at least two things at once – mirror the architecture of the brain in its processing and the mind in its interpreting. Because Montgomery's metaphoric scheme relies on dialogue and communion, on parallels and connections, on nature *and* nurture, I am using the metaphors of bridges and bridging in this essay.

If metaphor is the bridge between brain and mind, as Jerome Feldman suggests in his book *From Molecule to Metaphor* (2006),[12] then looking at Montgomery's metaphoric scheme – which has appealed to readers for more than a century – may be a way of understanding something at once universal and also culturally constructed in our human metaphoric ability. Metaphor may be an ideal place to consider nature and nurture – or "natureculture" to borrow a term from anthropologist of science, Donna Haraway[13] – as one.

"The essence of metaphor," according to Lakoff and Johnson, "is understanding and experiencing one kind of thing in terms of another." Their scientific refinement of that simple explanation is: "In a metaphor, there are two domains: the target domain, which is constituted by the immediate subject matter, and the source domain, in which important metaphorical reasoning takes place and that provides the source concepts used in that reasoning." What is important is that when we are understanding two things at once, we are experiencing a neural firing that is linking those two things. "Metaphor is a neural phenomenon," they add, and "Neurons that fire together wire together." This means that metaphors not only act as bridges, but they also create new bridges that can last a lifetime if they are also linked to what are called primary metaphors, or metaphors that come from our deepest feelings as embodied in our deepest experiences. Conceptual metaphors come first; metaphors in language come later. As human beings, no matter what our culture or possibly even our time, we experience some things similarly, in terms of our brain mapping and the creation of conceptual metaphors. In short, Lakoff and Johnson argue, "There appear to be *both* universal metaphors *and* cultural variation."[14] In other words, as Feldman also claims[15] and as Paul Keen considers in a later chapter in this collection, there is no nature versus nurture: rather, there is only nature and nurture when we talk about how the brain works and how it perceives; our human ability is partly inherited and partly schooled.

The title of my chapter suggests at least three metaphoric schemes: "natural bridge" (an image from my own childhood and an example of a naturally occurring form reproduced in architecture), "architecture," and "landscape." I use the image of a bridge and the concept of bridging to explore what Montgomery creates *because* of her conception of nature, and what her work reflects about the neural basis for metaphor itself. I propose "bridge" and "bridging" as ways to think about Montgomery's dialogic treatment of opposing tensions and also about how she has inspired many readers to achieve a sense of wholeness, connection, and community. I am comparing Montgomery (that is, her writing and ability) to a phenomenon within the natural world (natural bridge) as a way to suggest her skill/gift for making effortless the understanding of at least two things simultaneously. For the purposes of this paper, and adapting the work of Lakoff and Johnson, Lakoff and Turner (*More than Cool Reason*), and their colleague Zoltán Kövecses (*Metaphor*), I am using bridges and bridging to suggest how Montgomery's writing relies on several basic conceptual metaphors about relationships and creativity that make her works particularly accessible: the conceptual source domains of architecture and building become ways of understanding the target domains of landscape, creativity, and relationships. By designing this essay to use "landscape is architecture" as a conceptual frame for the even larger conception of Montgomery as a natural bridge, I am suggesting that we can understand something about the acts of seeing and writing about constructed nature (landscape) by drawing from what we know about the practices and materials of architecture.[16] In framing and illustrating this essay, I am attempting to imitate and make visible what I discuss: bridges and bridging suggest the power of a process and of a proficient creator of metaphors.

I propose that Montgomery's writing creates a natural bridge across cultures and time because of the kinds of metaphoric bridges she consciously and unconsciously constructed as links and invitations within her imaginative terrain. A bridge spans a spatial or temporal gap; it may link states of mind, places, or both. It may provide a means of "crossing over" or simply of continuing. To many, it suggests a human presence and engagement. A bridge is a small part of a larger landscape – it is a means and a moment. Approaching, crossing, and leaving it are possibilities for ritual or recognition of change or exchange. A bridge suggests communication between at least two parts. It may be constructed to call attention to itself or to blend in; it may have formed accidentally, in a moment (as when a tree falls across a brook), or it may form through ages of accretion or erosion; it may be designed in various degrees of complexity and of materials appropriate or inappropriate to its environment. A bridge may also be a shape, one that has meaning because of the activities associated with it or that may be reproduced architecturally in many ways. It may involve arches, arcs, circles, curves, parallels, or straight lines, all of which are archetypal patterns themselves. Bridging may encourage us to think about parallels in person, place, idea, or process; bridging may be routine and automatic or transformative and generative.

Since Montgomery was a highly visual (metaphoric) thinker, at ease with pictures as well as words, I have developed my argument by using four pictures. I chose these four pictures to tell a story metaphorically, about seeing and imagining nature – my story about how I see and how I see Montgomery seeing. Together they are meant to suggest how reader and artist alike apprehend meaning and story in shape and give shape and meaning to story. The stories they tell may be literal or metaphoric and both. The first picture is of Natural Bridge in Virginia, whose arc has suggested power and meaning through oral and written history; the second is of one of the most famous arches in the world (the Wine Gate of the Alhambra in Spain), an architectural arch imitating a naturally formed arc, inspiring and featuring in the Romantic writing of Washington Irving, prized by Montgomery; the third is of Irving's home Sunnyside, designed with many arches to suggest a continuing dialogue with nature; and fourth is Montgomery's photograph of Lover's Lane in Cavendish, her favourite place in nature, a lane suggesting through its depicted bends, arches, and encircled vistas, Montgomery's conception of nature and of art.

Natural Bridge

All schoolchildren growing up in the foothills of the Blue Ridge Mountains of Virginia in the 1950s, as I did, made at least two field trips: one to Natural Bridge and the other to Monticello, the home of Thomas Jefferson. As schoolchildren, we were being given lessons in nature, history, patriotism, and myth. Formed over millions of years by the passing of water through a rock wall, Natural Bridge is 216 feet tall and has inspired human awe since stories began, starting with First Nations people who thought it was formed in answer to their prayer and including George Washington, who surveyed it when he was a young man, and Thomas Jefferson, who bought it to be part of a nature retreat. So famous was it as a tourist site that Herman Melville referred to it in *Moby Dick* (1851), confident that readers would understand through the comparison the awe-inspiring size of his white whale.[17] As young Virginians, we were encouraged to see Natural Bridge as our direct connection to "great men" such as Washington and Jefferson, our metonymic link to our illustrious past, and our image for the inevitably glorious future of the United States. Natural Bridge was nature's frozen rainbow, a stone promise that American patriotism could make us whole by connecting us with a mythical greatness of the equally mythical thing called the American community. We learned to read metaphor through landscape.

What else may this "picture in nature," as Emerson would call it, suggest? To me, at a conceptual metaphoric level, it suggests my rightful place – my home – in the scheme of things. Like current neuroscientists speaking of the automaticity of multimodal processes, Emerson claims that "[t]his imagery is spontaneous" because "the whole of nature is a metaphor of the human mind."[18] Everywhere he looked, Emerson found evidence of "the unity of Nature": "A leaf, a drop, a crystal, a moment of time, is related to the whole, and partakes of the perfection of the whole." Like Emerson's, Montgomery's descriptions are loaded with an imagery of

1
Natural Bridge (Virginia). Courtesy of http://www.naturalbridgeva.com/

nurturance and connection, reinforcing Emerson's claim that each particle "faithfully renders the likeness of the world."[19] In Emerson, and in Montgomery, the underlying law of nature is an affirmation of kinship with all things, states, beings – all is one. Looking at Natural Bridge, I understand something about archetypal shapes, symbols, linkages, and the making of meaning. Like Natural Bridge, I am part of that landscape. Like Natural Bridge, Montgomery connects me to that landscape.

The Alhambra Arch

In the late 1830s, when photography was first recognized as a means to capture images for international stories, the Wine Gate of the crumbling Moorish palace in Granada, Spain, became one of the most photographed places in Europe.[20] Engravings made it one of the most widely recognized images in the world. Photographers flocked to it largely because of Washington Irving's bestselling and highly influential book, *Tales of the Alhambra* (1832). The book was written while he was living in the partial ruins of the place as an invited diplomat, but also as a tourist looking for adventure and beauty, inspired by the Brothers Grimm in Germany and especially by Sir Walter Scott in Scotland to pursue history and to mine it for its romance and colour. Irving was captivated by the glory and mysterious otherworldliness that he read in the emblematic arches of the various parts of the palaces, arches that imitated above ground what the numerous legendary caves in the surrounding mountains had suggested throughout history: riches – and dangers – hidden and magically brought to light. This photograph was taken by Jessica Brookes-Parkhill in 2004 when we stood in front of the gate and lined up the shot to match a photograph from the 1850s that may have illustrated an edition of the *Alhambra* that Montgomery read and loved.[21] Inspired by his travels to England and encounters with Scott (who became his mentor and dear friend), Wordsworth, and Coleridge, Irving saw the past through British-American Romanticism and gave that Romanticism form in his most famous *Sketch Book* short stories, "The Story of Rip Van Winkle" and "The

Legend of Sleepy Hollow" as well as in *Tales of the Alhambra.* This archway, Montgomery's acknowledged portal to fairyland and inspiration for her *Blue Castle,*[22] may also suggest darker magic and the uncanny.

Inspired by natural shapes, architecture captures, imitates, and encourages patterns of relationships to be sites for patterns of events, or as architectural philosopher Christopher Alexander notes of a living building, "each pattern of relationships in space is congruent with some specific pattern in events." In creating living buildings, he adds, "To act as nature does is the most ordinary thing in the world."[23] Borrowed from nature, the arch "is the most familiar architectural form in the world," according to Francis Woodman, with some twenty-six kinds of arches commonly found across cultures.[24]

A bridge – often presented as an arch – is a span that can also be a portion of a circle. If bridging as an act also conjures the physical shapes associated with spanning and connecting, then the reverse or mirror image could also be true: a shape could conjure the enactment, the experience often associated with it. Using the computational metaphor preferred by neural theorists of language, I am suggesting that human beings may be "hardwired" with certain shapes in our source bank for memory and meaning. The shape or the concept of a bridge may be hardwired into human thinking in the same way that shapes are meaningfully part of what Carl Jung described as the collective unconscious. Jung certainly linked shapes to activities, as he states in his paper "Concerning Mandela Symbolism": "The term 'image' is intended to express not only the form of the activity taking place, but the typical situation in which the activity is released." Further, he warned those who were confused by his theories that the archetypal images he described were not full-blown myths ready formed in anyone's mind but were instead merely shapes that then had to be developed by an individual's experiences and relationships: "archetypes are not determined as regards their content, but only as regards their form and then only to a limited degree." He worked with patients to trace these shapes in mandalas because he realized over years of listening to, observing, and interacting with others that shapes were inevitably linked to archetypal patterns that connected the individual story with huge mythical stories. And what were those physical repeated shapes attached

2
The Wine Gate of the Alhambra (Granada, Spain).
Courtesy of Jessica Brookes-Parkhill.

to narrative threads and patterns? Squares, circles, triangles, arches, spirals, meanders. Archetypal patterns are evidenced in shapes and their relationships, Jung adds: "I could produce many more pictures from all parts of the world, and one would be astonished to see how these symbols are governed by the same fundamental laws that can be observed in individual mandalas."[25] As Jung and some neuroscientists differently suggest, we may be hardwired to interpret some shapes as powerfully metaphoric; this interpreting would then naturally link us to other human beings in the grounding of our images.

Anthropologist Angeles Arrien spent decades trying to trace recurring physical patterns in art and myth in hundreds of cultures across recorded time. In her book *Signs of Life: The Five Universal Shapes and How to Use Them* (1998), she presents these five shapes: square, circle, spiral, triangle, and equidistant cross. All five appear in every known culture, according to Arrien, and in all cultures they have similar meanings that are in turn represented in stories and art: square for stability and authenticity, circle for wholeness and completion, spiral for growth and change, triangle for goals and striving, the equidistant cross for relationships.[26] Arrien's work shows us that persistent patterns of shapes in an artist's work make that work accessible to viewers in astoundingly complex ways.

The arch – all on its own and as part of a circle – appealed deeply to Irving and partly through him to Montgomery. The arch links them to each other and to others as well as to larger patterns across time. I suggest that texts, which appeal to readers across time and cultures, as Montgomery's texts do, are ones that fire the neurons, despite changes in taste and time, and in so firing activate archetypal patterns that also support cultural meaning and relationships. If there are patterns in nature that lend themselves to an infinite variety of nurture, then there is no "or" in binary opposites unless there is always first an "and" bridging the two: nature and nurture; romance and realism; simplicity and complexity. The persistent appeal of the Alhambra arch suggests all of this; Montgomery's novels enact it.

Irving's Sunnyside

Consider another kind of bridging, with significant parallels, in the construction of Irving's home and career. Malcolm Bradbury credits Irving with inventing "transatlantic tourism itself," and Irving is said to have popularized the concepts of Old World and New World, building a bridge between European and American understanding.[27] Not only did Irving's writing bring tourists to the Alhambra, thereby ensuring its restoration and survival, but he also actively led others to identify his home and his village of Tarrytown, New York, as the originals for Sleepy Hollow. He encouraged tourists and tourism, and entertained in his home such celebrities as Martin Van Buren (the eighth US president and also a tourist of Natural Bridge in Virginia) and Charles Dickens. When Irving was five years old, he met George Washington (for whom he was named), and he ended his career with a five-volume biography of Washington.[28]

3
"Sunnyside," home of Washington Irving (Tarrytown, New York), November 2009. Courtesy of Jessica Brookes-Parkhill.

As a personal friend of Scott and an acquaintance of Wordsworth and Coleridge, Irving seems now to have spanned several Romanticisms as well. Like Montgomery, he was influenced by Emerson and by those who in turn had shaped Emerson. As a believer in Romanticism as a philosophy of nature, Irving valued Romantic architecture. He believed in bringing the outdoors and the indoors into meaningful, continuing dialogue, of a kind Rita Bode describes in this volume. In the designing of "Sunnyside" – his "three-dimensional autobiography," as Kathleen Johnson calls it[29] – he encouraged the illusion that natural life outside and appreciative, natural life within were reflections of each other. He bought an old Dutch two-room cottage and together with the designer George Harvey recreated it with three distinctly different architectural styles (Dutch Colonial, reflecting the world of Rip Van Winkle and of Sleepy Hollow; Scottish Gothic, in celebration of Sir Walter Scott's neo-Gothic Abbotsford, which Montgomery visited on her honeymoon; and Spanish, adding a tower with arches, to celebrate his early years in the Alhambra and his return from Spain as American ambassador). These three styles were held together by concepts of the picturesque and Romantic interactions with nature. Johnson notes that "Sunnyside was the creation of an amateur architect whose greater fame lay in his association with the 'Kindred Spirits,' a group of American artists and writers, including Thomas Cole, Asher B. Durand and William Cullen Bryant, who drew sustenance from the beauty of the Hudson River Valley and espoused the Romantic view of nature and art."[30] As Irene Gammel has suggested in *Looking for Anne,* this group is celebrated in the famous painting *Kindred Spirits,* depicting the nature-loving friendship of George Cole and William Cullen Bryant.[31] Irving preferred arches everywhere, just as he had experienced them and recreated them in his story of the Alhambra: in doorways, window seats, the curtained archway separating his writing desk from his reading sofa, and the windows of the Spanish tower he added to the house. A short train ride from downtown New York, "Sunnyside" became and still is a tourist destination as the real Sleepy Hollow. Its ten acres of surrounding gardens and orchards, bridged ponds and streams, create a small, self-contained world that reflects Romantic ecology.

Irving's and Montgomery's similar philosophies of nature are reflected in their written images, including depictions of landscape; these images, in turn, reflect and shape other imaginary and physical grounds. Whether or not Montgomery knew all the possible bridges connecting her life and work to Irving's, we can see how one bridging leads to another, perhaps richer still, and how a literary landscape can preserve and in turn reconfigure what is in a Cavendish or a Tarrytown, adding layers to interpretation and perception.

The Bridging Effect

This second bridge view shot of Lover's Lane was one of Montgomery's favourite images, capturing what she referred to as her "favorite object in Nature."[32] She had it colourized and hung it on the walls of the manse in Leaskdale and carried it with her to Norval and no doubt to Toronto. I featured this photograph in a 1999 Confederation Centre of the Arts exhibition on Montgomery's photography and visual imagination, discussed it at an international L.M. Montgomery Institute conference, and wrote about it at some length in my book *Through Lover's Lane* (2007) in trying to explain how certain metaphoric patterns – inspired by her reading and her informed communion with nature – are repeated within one book and echoed purposefully from book to book.[33] An arch and a keyhole, a circle, a bend in a road, a distant circle of light, all beckon the viewer forward. This arch over the small and almost invisible bridge is also a magic portal, a passageway like the Alhambra gate, like the romantic porches and windows at Sunnyside, like her window in the Macneill house in Cavendish, and like the framing of every lavishly coloured vista Montgomery saw or conjured. Lover's Lane, in Emersonian terms, is a place, a state of mind, and a conversation with ideas about the ideal of communion. What we see in the whole of Lover's Lane, Emerson would say, are "faint copies of an invisible archetype." Moreover, nature is "the organ through which the universal spirit speaks to the individual, and strives to lead back the individual to it."[34]

The bridging effect is an active force, I suggest, achieved on almost every page of Montgomery's fiction; sometimes she even conveniently punctuates the landscape with a literal bridge. Montgomery uses the bridge as a defining marker in Anne's first view, in *Anne of Green Gables*, of the Lake

4
"Lover's Lane," by L.M. Montgomery (Cavendish, Prince Edward Island), ca. 1900. Courtesy of the L.M. Montgomery Collection, Archival and Special Collections, University of Guelph Library.

of Shining Waters. A bridge and a dense palette of unusual colours highlight a moment of transition, when Anne enters fully into the emotional landscape of Avonlea: "A bridge spanned [the pond] midway and from there to its lower end, where an amber-hued belt of sand hills shut it in from the dark blue gulf beyond, the water was a glory of many shifting hues – the most spiritual shadings of crocus and rose and ethereal green, with other elusive tintings for which no name has ever been found."[35] Almost wordlessly Anne communes with a place peopled by the spirits of tiptoeing, white-clad trees, shy houses peering through screens of blossoms, and stars that shine brightly on purpose to guide her to the home waiting for her. Anne is searching for home, and this obliging Nature offers her lively imagination every possible expression of welcome. Montgomery's Prince Edward Island, what Elizabeth Waterston calls "Magic Island," is where every thing is conscious and capable of communicating with the right kind of person.

Anne's early encounters with Lover's Lane – before she names it – are also described, interestingly, in relation to the little log bridge below Green Gables, a bridge that, like the Lake of Shining Waters, has personality and agency, as does the pathway leading to it. The lane "*opened out* below the apple orchard and *ran up* through a belt of woodland," whereas the bridge "led Anne's dancing feet up over a wooded hill beyond."[36] Anne follows the paths and the bridge, finding all that she desires for beauty and wonder mirrored back to her. Anne's dialogue with nature is one the reader is invited to join; her mirroring of what she wants in what she sees is a habit of perception the reader is invited to imitate. Reinforcing the metaphorical concept of nature as nurturing companion and benevolent guide, the whole of the novel reinforces a firing and a binding of neural pathways that keep this imaging vital for those who are sympathetic to it and makes that firing portable to other nature experiences. What is always clear, as Nancy Holmes suggests in this volume, is that "the love of the natural world is imbued unequivocally with spiritual power and value." The pattern of images that are sustained by basic metaphorical patterns concerning nature and communion can be accessed wherever any one of the component elements – shape, colour, motion, and/or feeling – is triggered.

In *Anne's House of Dreams* (1917), colour is a bridge to heightened perception. Colour is significant in all Montgomery's books, but from the first page of this poetic antidote to war,[37] colour glows. Patterns of colour characterize place, state of mind, relationships, narrative turn, and human possibilities. Leslie Moore, who always wears a touch of red, suffers from "blood-red thoughts," including memories of her father's suicide and of her brother's face at his violent death. In the description of Leslie Moore's house, Montgomery uses coloured images to link several things at once, such as the colour red with beauty and with danger – with the sacred and the profane, a house with human consciousness, windows of a house with windows to the soul. Anne and Gilbert make their first walk to the lighthouse to see Captain Jim:

> The red light flamed on the white sails of a vessel gliding down the channel, bound to a southern port in a land of palms. Beyond her, it smote upon and incarnadined the shining, white, grassless faces of the sand-dunes. To the right, it fell on the old house among the willows up the brook, and gave it for a fleeting space casements more splendid than those of an old cathedral. They glowed out of its quiet and grayness like the throbbing, blood-red thoughts of a vivid soul imprisoned in a dull husk of environment.[38]

The active verbs in this passage ("flamed," "smote," "incarnadined," "glowed") show the red as a force as well as a reflection, a part of nature, and a part of metaphorical perception. Whereas the younger Anne perceived paths as welcoming her, the more mature Anne perceives hidden passion in the landscape. Colour surges in the book – as intense and kinetic as its unacknowledged backdrop of war; colour also shines steadfastly, as light, as a beacon for life even when it is a "baleful star" mourning the death of its keeper, Captain Jim.[39] Colour is a metaphorical bridge, a means of communing with and connecting with the vital forces – human and non-human – that are themselves reflected in the Four Winds landscape.

Montgomery's "nature" is not superficially, sweetly picturesque, or ornamentally painterly. There can be a wildness to it and deep mystery[40] – akin to the sinister in the Alhambra enchantment. In the Emily books, Emily spans barriers of time and place through the power of her artist's vision. Her Neoplatonic, Emersonian artist's "flash" connects her to unutterable beauty and also to the uncanny, sometimes to danger. Nature – in the form of a magnificent smoke-blue aster – lures her to the crumbling cliff edge where she, metaphorically and literally dangling above annihilation, crosses a psychic barrier to begin to solve the mystery of Ilse's mother's death.[41]

In each of Emily's psychic moments, Montgomery questions the supposed limits of the mind and the natural world, and what constitutes communication and the bonds that invisibly link one person to another. Emily must use magnifying lenses to search the heavens with Dean Priest, but for Teddy, she can cross the Atlantic in the blink of an eye. I have always loved the way Montgomery describes the psychic moment in *Emily's Quest* (1927) when Emily sits in the Disappointed House resigned to marrying Dean Priest. The miniaturizing and mirroring seem to imitate the processes of brain and mind and at the same time the objects (like the colour red in *Anne's House of Dreams*) take action. Pictures withdraw and candles mock:

> The walls of the shadowy room seemed slowly to fade from her vision. The pictures withdrew themselves. There seemed to be nothing before her but Great-aunt Nancy's gazing-ball hung from the old iron lantern – a big, silvery, gleaming globe. In it she saw the reflected room, like a shining doll's-house, with herself sitting in the old, low chair and the taper on the mantelpiece like a tiny, impish star. Emily looked at it as she leaned back in her chair – looked at it till she saw nothing but that tiny point of light in a great misty universe.

After she has saved Teddy, she returns to her body:

> still saw the station-room shrunk again to play-size – and that one figure running – still running – the cloud again – filling the ball – whitening – wavering – thinning – clearing. Emily was lying back in her chair staring fixedly into Aunt Nancy's gazing-ball, where the living-room was reflected calmly and silverly, with a dead-white spot that was her face and one solitary taper-light twinkling like an impish star.[42]

We follow Emily into the gazing ball and into the star and then we follow her out of the gazing ball and back to her chair, and we, too, are stranded, without Teddy, in a silent room beside a dead-white face and an "impish star" that mocks the boundaries we have crossed. The imitation of hypnotic gazing and breathless confusion and then deadly stillness makes the willing reader enact the sensations of forbidden seeing. Having crossed this barrier, Emily can never again be with Dean Priest. She may have crossed a bridge and recrossed it to return but her state of mind is permanently altered. In a moment, the text suggests, in a flash akin to Emily's own, we may be transformed.

Transformation may occur in a moment, and it may take years for the mind to catch up to, or to be able to live fully with, what it has perceived.[43] Montgomery's metaphoric patterns may mirror back to readers a generic and also an intensely personal wholeness that may change as the reader changes. In a paper given in 2009 at a conference at Uppsala University celebrating the centenary of the publication of *Anne of Green Gables* in Swedish, I mentioned the powerful healing effect of mirroring, also suggesting that Montgomery may have been synaesthetic, experiencing colour through several senses at once.[44] While investigating synaesthesia, and trying to trace through the heightened responses of synaesthetes a possible neural basis for metaphor, scientists discovered the healing power of the mirroring effect. Neuropsychologists have tested how the mind uses mirroring to heal the pain in limbs that no longer exist: as Cristina Cacciari reports in *The Cambridge Handbook of Metaphor and Thought* (2008), "arm amputees … reported vivid tactile sensations in the phantom arm when they saw the experimenter touching the mirror image of their normal arm." This is an important discovery, according to Cacciari, because "metaphorical language is pervaded by cross-modality references that mirror, at a linguistic level, our neural architecture."[45] This mirroring of "neural architecture" means that metaphors enter the mind with ease because they are structured as the mind itself is structured.

The phantom limb healed through mirroring may be like the feeling of home and belonging made real and whole through a reader's identification with character and place. People who identify with Montgomery's characters and places and reread her books repeatedly and over a lifetime may be supplying something missing from their own lives by experiencing a world that mirrors and then massages their healthy self and thus attends, indirectly, to the phantom limb that no longer works, that has been damaged or destroyed.

The images and metaphors we respond to most lastingly, that become part of our multiple dialogues with the world, are also ones grounded in brain circuitry, embodied in experience, and presented to us in a conceptual way so that we understand them effortlessly. The nature that Montgomery describes mirrors the spirit of the characters; by extension, the world of those characters is open to those who can realize and recreate the images. Montgomery's books have been healing generations of readers because she constructed images that mirror a place where, to return to Emerson's terminology, each particle "faithfully tenders" a whole that is shared. Montgomery's great gift to readers, I suggest, is this metaphoric richness and mirroring, where communion between place and state of mind is not only possible but also fundamental to the interconnectedness, the ongoing dialogue, of everything in the stories.

In "Reading to Heal: *Anne of Green Gables* as Bibliotherapy," Irene Gammel suggests that Anne, as a reader who has used books to survive trauma, "effectively models powerful strategies of bibliotherapy" including reading the same books repeatedly to enjoy a special kind of security and healing. Anne's personality – her exuberance – energizes readers, making them feel that Anne's ability to act can also be theirs since "Montgomery also depicts exuberance as an innate, irrepressible force, best seen in the blooming of nature and the regeneration of life in spring."[46] What better way to offer healing to readers, I ask, than to make Anne's personality and the natural world's energy seem one in the same?[47] This healing, metaphoric equating of Anne and nature, I add, is also another form of mirroring. The beautiful images in Montgomery, most of them of nature, also have the benefit of stimulating the part of the brain associated with intelligence (and the understanding of metaphor), foresight, and memory. Suggesting this benefit of picturing Montgomery's descriptions, Gammel quotes psychiatrist Kay Redfield Jamison: "clinical trials have shown that unpleasant pictures stimulate 'the primitive-subcortical' parts of the brain, while pleasant pictures 'activate' a phylogenetically much younger part of the brain, the prefrontal cortex."[48] In my opinion, Montgomery's "nature" is the means to create, amplify, and mirror positive energy and processes.

I suggest we can change our state of thought and we can enhance the brain's ability to create new thoughts by repeated, engaged entry into an imaginative landscape, into Montgomery's state and place of nature. Within this landscape, when we experience moments of heightened emotion, we may feel we have been changed by what we have felt. I say we have: we have crossed a bridge. We have experienced an arc, we have traveled through an arch, we have reached a point where we have squared our thoughts with our feelings, and perhaps we have come full circle or travelled to a new level on the spiral of understanding. I say we understand something new because our minds have compared it with something we already know, and we have incorporated this new knowledge almost effortlessly, naturally.[49]

Even my word "naturally" is itself suggesting at last two things at once: conveying the feeling of effortlessness and denoting a brain process. Feldman explains the inevitability of this simultaneity, the brain's metaphoric process, this way: what we apprehend almost instantaneously is a result of many slower parallel processes, synapses firing simultaneously in different parts of the mind, working through analogies that we are given as a result, not a process. In fact, this "massive parallelism"[50] is what has allowed our species to survive.

I will go one step further. It is this "massive parallelism" (which is the metaphoric process) that enables us to search for, to find, and possibly to create wholeness and comfort in our lived experiences and, if we are fortunate, to supply through a mirrored conception of wholeness what is missing, broken, or underdeveloped in ourselves. Not an "either/or" world of binary oppositions, but an "and" world of changes and connections. In Montgomery's vibrantly coloured, richly contoured landscapes,[51] many of us are able to experience reflections of emotion and meaning as we would choose to live with them. We appreciate, as Jennifer Litster describes it in this collection, Montgomery's ability to recreate the "natural world of her childhood" with "the soft focus of nostalgic recollections and a high-definition resolution." Sometimes, what is lost is restored when the mirror doubles creatively. Sometimes, we cross to a new way of thinking through a parallel or a repetition that lets us leap from the familiar to the unknown. Sometimes what we are able to picture makes us – partly through an empathy Lesley Clement describes in this volume – experience wholeness, connection, community.

Montgomery uses nature and descriptions of nature to give readers insight into a character's situations and states of mind partly as a kind of short-hand for multiple levels of understanding and partly because her conception of nature was inseparable from her own way of perceiving and feeling. Her interactions, and those of her characters, with the very colours and shapes of the natural world around her, picture and produce multiple connections of mind, metaphor, and nature. This connecting, I think, gives Montgomery's writing its continuing broad appeal and will make her work of increasing interest to those who study mind, metaphor, and ecological living. Walking repeatedly through Montgomery's landscapes teaches me – and the many like me – to want to create and to perceive my own eye/I in relationship to my environment, teaches me to want to know how to construct and to cross my own bridges when and where I need them, living with this fragile and magical planet.

CHAPTER SIX

L.M. Montgomery's Neurasthenia: Embodied Nature and the Matter of Nerves

Jean Mitchell

I could not realize any possible escape from suffering. It seemed to me that I must exist in that anguish forever. This is, I believe, a very common symptom of neurasthenia – and it is the hardest of all to bear.
– L.M. Montgomery, journal entry dated February 1910[1]

The worst is a fixed idea that I will never be better though my doctor laughs at this & says all victims of neurasthenia believe this.
– L.M. Montgomery, letter to G.B. MacMillan dated July 1940[2]

During the winter of 1910, on the north shore of Prince Edward Island, L.M. Montgomery suffered "an utter breakdown of body, soul, and spirit" immediately upon completing her third novel, *Kilmeny of the Orchard*.[3] In the journal entry detailing the three-week ordeal from which the first epigraph is drawn, Montgomery identified her suffering as symptomatic of neurasthenia, a nervous condition that had become the signature illness of the Victorian and early Edwardian eras. Neurasthenia was described in 1881 by American neurologist, Dr George Beard, as "the most frequent, the most important, the most interesting nervous disease of our time or of any time."[4] While Montgomery had previously experienced and recorded acute episodes of nervousness and despair, it was the first time in her journals that she authoritatively identified her condition. Neurasthenia, or weakness of the nerves, was a pervasive, somewhat vaguely defined chronic nervous condition that encompassed a wide range of symptoms.

Described in the United States as a disease of "modern civilization" and "brain-workers" that mainly afflicted the affluent and the educated,[5] neurasthenia included among its sufferers an elite group of intellectuals and writers. Montgomery certainly qualified as a modern "brain-worker," for by 1910 she was an international bestselling author facing pressure from her American publisher to continue producing novels with mass appeal. While her 1910 journal entry was written from the "snowy prison"[6] of the Prince Edward Island home that she shared with her elderly grandmother, Montgomery already inhabited imagined and international spaces. The diagnosis of neurasthenia firmly located the author as an artist within a cosmopolitan context.[7]

It is significant but not surprising that Montgomery was able to identify the specific condition of nerves that plagued her. Books, pamphlets, and magazines offering general information, advice or remedies for neurasthenia and related nervous illnesses "continued to pour off the presses" into the 1920s and its meaning was being negotiated into the 1930s.[8] As an avid reader, Montgomery paid attention to the medical discourses that proliferated during her lifetime. Not only does sickness play a pivotal role in the plots of her fiction but Montgomery also meticulously chronicled her own and her husband's experiences of illness over the course of her lifetime. Medical anthropologists Nancy Scheper-Hughes and Margaret M. Lock have argued that sickness is "not just an isolated event, nor an unfortunate brush with nature" but rather "a form of communication" through which "nature, society and culture speak simultaneously."[9] The nervous system was an important site for deciphering the language of sickness for it was a "double mediator" linking the mind with the body while connecting "the person, through his or her senses, with the outside world."[10] Neurasthenia drew attention to the environments in which people lived, providing an implicit critique of the excesses of modernity and their adverse effects on humans. At the same time, however, the nineteenth-century recognition of nature's therapeutic properties as a source of energy for depleted nerves, together with the need to preserve nature for the revitalization of humans, was profoundly human-centric.[11] Ultimately, this human-centric approach to nature, at the time of the emergence of neurasthenia, coincided with the massive destruction of the natural world that was fuelled by industrialization, a development that is noted in Nancy Holmes's chapter in this volume.

In this essay I draw on the insights of scholars who have explored the ways in which Montgomery articulated illness, health, and medicine in her fiction and journals. Janice Fiamengo provides an insightful analysis of how Montgomery's identity as a creative artist was crafted through the discourse of depression and sadness that she kept secret. Neurasthenia, according to Fiamengo, "undeniably played a major role in her self-conception" as a person with an "unusually sensitive temperament."[12] In a discussion of Montgomery's use of the Victorian sickroom, Kate Lawson argues that "[i]llness is a spur to both imagination and narrative" in her fiction.[13] Montgomery also drew on her personal life weaving fiction and realism, as Melissa Prycer notes, "to write out her preoccupation" with tuberculosis, the disease that claimed the life of her mother.[14] The anguish of mother loss, according to Rita Bode, "haunts" Montgomery's writing life.[15] Kylee-Anne Hingston in her analysis of *The Blue Castle* argues that Montgomery blurred the differences between health and illness as well as normality and deviance.[16] Montgomery, according to Susan Meyer, draws connections among health, creativity and the outdoors in her journals and in the *Emily* trilogy.[17] Holly Pike's exploration of the relationship between changing concepts of health and illness and the commodification of nature in *The Blue Castle* resonates with my discussion of neurasthenia.[18]

Mary Rubio and Elizabeth Waterston suggest that Montgomery's journals are "an important document on mental illness, in a period when no effective treatment was known and when the prescribed medications" often worsened matters.[19] While "mental illness" imposes a set of codified definitions of illness that now prevail, during Montgomery's lifetime symptoms of depression and anguish were not inevitably or solely located in the mind. One of the key features of neurasthenia was the idea that the illness was located in the body rather than the mind or, as Eric Caplan notes in *Mind Games*, it was about "*soma* not *psyche*."[20] The somatic framing of the nervous disorder provided a provocative reading of the mind-body relationship by stressing the materiality of nervousness and privileging the body.[21]

Neurasthenia was an important narrative in Montgomery's life – a diagnosis to which she would cling until the end of her life. It also marked an important chapter in medical history. Neurasthenia entailed a shift toward the consolidation of expert medical knowledge, a new kind of patient-doctor relationship, and the medicalization of individual bodies, while at the same time drawing attention to the effects of environmental stresses on the mind and body. The material focus shaped the understanding of neurasthenia's causes, symptoms, and treatment, appealing to both those who suffered from the disorder and those medical experts who treated them.

Neurasthenia offers insight into Montgomery's life, work, and the times in which she lived. This condition was the site of intersecting discourses of gender, class, race, medicine and nature, themes that are threaded throughout Montgomery's writing. Neurasthenia provided her with a vocabulary to express creative aspirations and artistic practices as well as her vulnerability and discontent. It also validated her life as a writer; however, over time the medicalization that accompanied this condition undermined her well-being.[22]

While the body as a "natural" and material phenomenon is privileged as a site of exhausted nerves under duress from modernity, neurasthenia also reveals the gendered sources of distress that, as I argue, were elided by medicine and accentuated by the erosion of social-ecological networks in Montgomery's life. The treatment of neurasthenia meant a simultaneous move away from the idea that illness, sickness, and healing were bound up with social-ecological relationships. I shall begin by outlining neurasthenia in the context of modernity and medicine and follow with a discussion delineating both the appeal that neurasthenia held for Montgomery and the liabilities that its treatment entailed. Montgomery's experience of neurasthenia, I argue, complicates and illuminates the entanglements of mind and body as well as nature and culture.

Modernity, Medicine, and Neurasthenia

From the 1870s until Freud's reconfiguration of the relationship between mind and body assumed ascendancy in the medical imagination in the middle decades of the twentieth century,[23] physicians increasingly believed that modern life placed excessive demands on nervous energy. The definition of neurasthenia was made possible by the late nineteenth-century belief that each individual possessed a fixed amount of nervous energy that acted as a messenger between various parts of the body. The idea of nervous debility has long been recognized. Prior to neurasthenia's introduction in Britain in the 1880s, medical practitioners had described what is currently known as depression as "shattered nerves or broken health."[24] By identifying specific etiology and symptoms, George Beard, as a pioneering neurologist, initiated "an expanding medical culture of nerve management" that was predicated on "a belief that modernization and civilization produced nervousness."[25] In *American Nervousness: Its Causes and Consequences*, he identified a number of specific causes of neurasthenia, most of which were related to social, economic, and technological developments including "steam power, the periodical press, the telegraph, the sciences and the mental activity of women."[26] Beard argued that women had their own forms of the disorder resulting from the overstimulation of their mental faculties through access to education and social opportunities that modernity afforded them.[27] From the outset, gender informed both the causes and treatment of neurasthenia. "Nervous women," according to Elaine Showalter, "received much more attention than nervous men, and were labeled as hysterical' or neurasthenic' in the contexts of a highly charged rhetoric about the dangers of higher education, women's suffrage, and female self-assertion in general."[28] Scholars have noted that nervous disorders among women expressed the conflict between their desire for agency and their assigned self-sacrificing roles of mother, wife, or caregiver in patriarchal contexts.[29] However, in *Neurasthenic Nation*, David A. Schuster argues that neurasthenia differed from other nervous disorders such as hysteria for it "allowed for more patient agency." In his view the story of neurasthenia is one of reciprocity, wherein "physicians, patients, and popular culture" all interacted to help shape the disease.[30] While Schuster underplays the gender dimensions of neurasthenia, it is important to recognize that Montgomery's identification with the condition did offer her agency, which, as I argue below, was constrained in the end.

Janet Oppenheim has identified the power of metaphors in shaping the ways in which scientists, medical practitioners, and the general public think about the human body and its relation to the social body.[31] The use of economic and technological metaphors in describing neurasthenia is striking. Beard defined neurasthenia as "impoverishment of nervous force" and a "deficiency of reserve"[32] that resulted when demand exceeded supply. The medical literature of the period frequently described the overtaxed nervous system as an overloaded electrical circuit. "The body-as-electrical-machine metaphor" resonated in an era of industrialization and emergent technologies.[33] Not only did this vocabulary reflect the growing importance of capitalism and technology that was transforming natural and human worlds, it also enhanced the legitimacy of the disorder. Capturing its hierarchies and restlessness, the nervous system and its management were emblematic of modernity. Neurasthenia offered new ways of understanding the body and of constituting social relations in a context of competition and rapid change. The human body, argues anthropologist Mary Douglas, is rife with symbolism about society: "just as it is true that everything symbolizes the body," she states, "so it is equally true that the body symbolizes everything else."[34] Catherine Gallagher and Thomas Laqueur, in *The Making of the Modern Body,* point to the ways in which the body itself has a history: "Not only has it been perceived, interpreted and represented differently in different epochs but it has also been lived differently."[35] This insight provides an important context for understanding Montgomery's embodied nervousness.

While neurasthenia was often considered an effect of modernity, scholar Brad Campbell argues that it was also integral to the ways in which modernity was constituted. Neurasthenia was not just an outmoded Victorian malady, argues Campbell, but rather a medical idiom through which class and race relations were regulated.[36] His contention shows how the afflicted body was intertwined with social and political relationships of class. Nervousness, for example, was linked to a refinement of class and culture that conferred an identity on its sufferers, who viewed it as a "badge of honour" and "a mark of superior sensibility."[37] Beard famously presented a portrait of a typical patient with specific and appealing qualities: "fine, soft hair, delicate skin, nicely chiselled features which distinguish the population of sufferers."[38] This characterization of nervousness, based on his own well-to-do patients, emphasized their sensitivity while avoiding the stigma of pathology. Construed as a product of over-civilization, neurasthenia was cast as a disease of the white, the educated, and the privileged, expressing ideologies about difference that were embedded in ideas of culture, class, race, and gender. These differences were also instrumental in sustaining and justifying particular social values and social relations. The preceding discussion suggests the efficacy of a relational view of the body that is never simply a "natural" phenomenon; as Mary Douglas argued, "there can be no natural way of considering the body that does not involve at the same time a social dimension."[39] Anthropologists Scheper-Hughes and Lock have expanded this insight by locating the body within a relational framework that includes the experience of being in the world as an embodied person: the social body or the domain of symbols and signs that shape and connect the body to society; and finally, the body politic where power and control operate on and through the body.[40] This approach suggests that the body is not just singular and natural.

The Matter of the Body and Medicalization

While Montgomery's identification with neurasthenia underlined her creative life as a writer, her affinity to modernity, however ambivalent, also served to set her apart from her husband and his nervous disorder with its metaphysical underpinnings. While it is clear that Montgomery and her husband both suffered intense mental anguish, their diagnoses were strikingly different at the outset. Ewan Macdonald's nervous condition, the full extent of which Montgomery had not known until 1919, was believed to have been rooted in religious melancholia. Her husband's suffering was a manifestation of his dread of predestination, an outmoded tenet of Presbyterianism that nonetheless "was firmly lodged in [his] mind" during his upbringing in Prince Edward Island.[41] Religious melancholia, at least initially, provided an authoritative Christian explanation of Macdonald's mental distress by contextualizing the causes and outcomes in religious terms. It also located him, following Maria H. Frawley, outside of "medicine's narrative of promise, a trajectory marked by diagnosis, treatment, and cure."[42] Montgomery's neurasthenia, conversely, provided a modern medical context within which to understand her mental distress. This is not altogether surprising since the medical languages available for explaining both health and illness from the late nineteenth century were increasingly displacing those of religion.[43]

The somatic characterization of neurasthenia was attractive to Montgomery. It offered an explanation for a wide range of conditions that had no other obvious organic cause such as lethargy, insomnia, headaches, body aches, fatigue, neuralgia, ennui, listlessness, depression, restlessness, fear, and digestive disorders.[44] As Barbara Sicherman argues, neurasthenia "provided the most respectable label for distressing, but not life-threatening, complaints," and it was "preferable to its nearest alternatives – hypochondria, hysteria, and insanity."[45] A diagnosis of neurasthenia could or would have reassured Montgomery that her nervous suffering was not due to mental illness but rather signalled a depletion of her nervous energy. Medical diagnoses such as neurasthenia, argues Nancy M. Theriot, created a "medicalized female subjectivity" with women patients often participating in the process of medicalization. As Theriot suggests, medical discourses such as neurasthenia are best read as a set of "multi-authored texts" in which gendered biomedical approaches to sickness and personal experiences of illness mutually shape each other.[46] While her perspective supports Schuster's point above by underlining agency, Theriot privileges gender.

A thriving economy developed around neurasthenia that included medical experts, treatments, pharmaceutical companies, and health resorts.[47] The treatment of neurasthenia translated into intense, long-term, and commodified relationships between doctors and patients, underlining the class-based nature of this condition and its treatment. Because neurasthenia was known to afflict large numbers of the bourgeoisie, elite artists, and other "brain-workers," doctors were particularly well paid for treating this incurable malady.[48] Montgomery's successful writing career facilitated her access to medical expertise throughout her lifetime and her reliance on doctors was a recurring motif in her journals. In her 1910 journal entry cited in the epigraph, Montgomery briefly described her first medical encounter after her neurasthenia was identified: "I went to Dr Simpson and told him I was suffering from insomnia and nervousness. He gave me some medicine which has already helped me a good deal."[49] Although many of the discourses concerning neurasthenia originated in the United States, Canadian doctors would have been acquainted with this phenomenon. The Canadian edition of the medical journal *Lancet* featured an article on neurasthenia in 1889 and, as noted, popular and medical print sources about it abounded.[50] In *The Nature of Their Bodies: Women and Their Doctors in Victorian Canada*, Wendy Mitchinson argues that "[p]hysicians and laymen alike saw women as more emotional and more prone to nervous disorders, and in need of control. Increasingly the medical profession became more involved in providing that control."[51]

The treatment of neurasthenia represented changes underway within the medical profession, including increasing specialization, the authoritative organization of medical knowledge, and the emergence of new patient-doctor relationships. These new relationships were integral to the development of modern medicine and characterized by what Michel Foucault called the medical "gaze," an increasingly intense relationship between patient and doctor.[52] Although medicine was becoming a specialized profession with growing claims to scientific knowledge, this process was not wholly linear or uncontested. Medical and popular views of health and illness overlapped and competed. Patent medicines, for example, that claimed to offer remedies for particular diseases were also crowding the market and were often sought after "among the less educated, rural and working classes."[53] Holly Pike points to the Stirling clan's reliance on a range of patented drugs, underlining the popularity of these remedies evident in Montgomery's novel *The Blue Castle*.[54] Lawson also aptly comments that in this novel, Doc Redfern "proves himself to be the ideal doctor" for "he recognizes the 'reality' of imaginary illness,"[55] underlining the idea that a person can experience illness without actually having a disease.[56] The changes in modern medicine increasingly focused attention on individual pathology, downplaying the significance of the social and gendered roots of distress. While Montgomery seemingly accepted – if not embraced – the expanding domain of modern medicine in her own life, she clearly queried its growing authority and its assumptions about society in her fiction and journals. Laura Robinson, in this volume, for instance, discusses the medical dilemmas that are raised in *Anne's House of Dreams*.

Treating Neurasthenia: Pharmaceuticals, Rest Cures, and Nature

While the diagnosis of neurasthenia was attractive to both patients and doctors, its actual treatment proved difficult and the effects of treatment had uncertain, if not deleterious, consequences. In enumerating some of the main drugs that Montgomery would have been given over the course of her life, Rubio notes the toxicity of bromides, which were designated useful in Canada around 1900.[57] Although often administered in tandem with other forms of therapy, medical practitioners typically relied upon drugs during some stage of a nervous patient's treatment. The drug therapies were related to the somatic interpretation of nervous illness, as drugs were understood to work on the materiality of the body. Victorian and Edwardian doctors used a range of pharmaceuticals when treating nervous disorders. According to Oppenheim, in the last half of the nineteenth century and into the twentieth, treatment options expanded beyond tonics, opiates, arsenic, and mercury "to include suphonal, chloral hydrate, barbiturates, the bromides – of potassium and ammonia, in particular – and much else that boasted either stimulant or narcotic effects."[58] Montgomery poignantly refers to their ubiquity and ineffectiveness: "[S]ometimes it seems to me as if my life now were little else than a search for anodynes. There is always some gnawing mental pain or anxiety to be temporarily obliterated by an opiate."[59] Following Montgomery's move to Toronto, her physician, Dr Lane, treated her neurasthenia with hypodermics "to tone up the nervous system," in response to Montgomery's quest for a treatment that "would control, if only for a short time, [her] unbearable indescribable restlessness."[60] While many physicians agreed that drugs had, at best, a limited role in the treatment of neurasthenia, few were willing to dismiss their use altogether, for administering drugs had become a central and expected aspect of medical practice. According to Caplan, abandoning the use of drugs would have undermined physicians' professional esteem and diminished their public appeal.[61]

In addition to pharmaceuticals, other remedies for neurasthenia were advocated. While Beard concentrated on neurasthenic diagnoses, the

American doctor, neurologist, and novelist, Silas Weir Mitchell, devised "the distinctive therapeutics" that included rest cure, dietary changes, recuperation at the seaside or a sanatorium, massage, and the cessation of mental stimulation, particularly for women.[62] While Mitchell originally devised bed rest for men, it was soon exclusively allocated for the treatment of women. For the most severe cases, he created a highly structured environment in which every aspect of the patient's life was under the doctor's control for at least a month. Weight gain and social isolation were imperative.[63] One of the goals of bed rest "was to discourage patients from dwelling on morbid thoughts or wallowing in self-pity, and to encourage an active, positive attitude."[64] In her famous short story, "The Yellow Wallpaper," Charlotte Perkins Gilman, who herself underwent the rest cure, depicts the treatment as detrimental, if not destructive.[65] Women, she suggested, needed social engagement and intellectual stimulation rather than isolation and confinement to sickrooms. The controversial rest cure, argues Elaine Showalter "asserted male medical domination over the nervous woman,"[66] underlining how gender shaped the treatment of neurasthenia. An incident from Montgomery's journal suggests the prevalence of the idea of the "rest cure" with its assumptions of gender-based susceptibility to overstimulation. In the months preceding the publication of *Anne of Green Gables*, Montgomery suffered extreme nervousness and physical misery. She noted in her journal entry of November 1908 that Ewan Macdonald, then her fiancé, felt "much concerned over [her] condition" and he "has insisted that I do no writing for a month. I have yielded to please him but I do not think it is a wise thing after all." Montgomery's response resonates with Gilman's insistence that creativity and social relations ensure well-being. Montgomery continues: "When I am writing I am happy for I forget all worries and cares. If I do not write I have all the more time for morbid brooding."[67]

By advocating the removal of women from their daily lives, Mitchell's rest cure paradoxically suggests that women's domestic environments may well be the source of their maladies. Oppenheim, commenting on the ambivalent nature of domesticity for women, writes: "In a culture that glorified domesticity, it is striking to note the Victorian medical acknowledgement that home could be detrimental to health."[68] Montgomery's situation was unique for she occupied both private and public domains.

She inhabited stimulating spaces in her domestic life where her writing took place, affording her both pleasure and creative expression. Homemaking activities also gave her pleasure and were a conduit for the aesthetic expression of the quotidian that permeated her fiction and journals. As a writer and as a minister's wife, Montgomery was a public figure whose life was also closely scrutinized. Montgomery, according to Helen M. Buss, "spent a great deal of her emotional energy, intelligence and time being a good preacher's wife," taking care of parish work and her husband.[69] Montgomery's "domestic disappointments," according to Kate Lawson, emerged early in her life and were characterized by "fraught relations" with her father, grandmother, and husband as well as anxiety about her two sons.[70]

Through her reading, Montgomery would have been aware that the rest cure was frequently prescribed for women suffering from neurasthenia,[71] but while available it was not widely advocated in Canada.[72] Montgomery often expressed her feeling of fatigue and a desire for respite from her domestic pressures.[73] According to Mary Rubio, Montgomery mentioned a longing for "a period of relaxation" to correct her depression just weeks before her death. Rubio suggests that these comments may have referenced Mitchell's rest cure.[74] Without the benefit of an extended rest from her relentless domestic and professional pressures, Montgomery concentrated on sleep to restore her nerve force. Her journals reveal an intense preoccupation with the duration and the quality of sleep, which she described in particular ways throughout the mid-1930s: "a veronal sleep," "a fair sleep," "a medinal sleep," and "a good normal sleep."[75] Her emphasis on sleep and sedation is consistent with the somatic nature of neurasthenia for "sleep, like rest, was viewed as enabling the patient to build up and store nerve force."[76]

The therapeutic aspects of nature were also emphasized as a corrective of nervousness. "The vital importance of nature," according to Schuster, "had been a theme in some of the earliest writing on nervousness."[77] Influenced by Thoreau and his declaration that health is a sound relation to nature or as he expressed it, "sympathy with nature is evidence of perfect health,"[78] environmentalists, artists and writers such as John Burroughs, John Muir, and Mary Austin advocated for strong relationships with nature.[79] John Burroughs, for example, as others in this volume point out, is a likely model for John Foster in *The Blue Castle*.[80] John Muir, who was also associated with influential American neurasthenic patients, used those contacts to effectively advocate for the establishment of national parks in the United States.[81] While Silas Weir Mitchell promoted the "rest cure" for women, he, too, became an advocate of the restorative power of nature. He wrote a romance novel located in the wilds of Canada linking mental health to engagement with the wilderness. However, as Patricia Jasen in *Wild Things: Nature, Culture and Tourism in Ontario* explains, his work represented a "very self-consciously masculine response to the modern predicament" of deficits of nervous energy. Men embraced the wilderness of nature to regain their strength, virility, and endurance to offset the detrimental effects of modernity.[82] The "wilderness" strategy for men stands in stark contrast to Mitchell's early prescriptions for the improvement of women's health. In Canada, as Jasen argues, concern with modernization's ill effects on the mental and physical health of people led to the development of nature preserves for restoration and recreation such as Algonquin Park and the Muskoka region of Ontario.[83] Some time after visiting Muskoka, Montgomery suggests that her husband's mental distress was rooted in neurasthenia or hysteria rather than melancholia.[84] Holly Pike astutely links this revised assessment of her husband's condition to Montgomery's holiday in Muskoka, which was marketed as a therapeutic location "to recover from neurasthenic symptoms."[85]

Montgomery also drew on her own vacation to Muskoka to write *The Blue Castle*. This novel is a testament to the restorative power of nature as the heroine, Valancy, is returned to health in the wilds of Muskoka. In this volume Holmes suggests that the natural world in this novel is depicted as therapeutic and invigorating while Robinson underlines how Valancy's health is connected to freedom from her dismal and oppressive domestic life. Drawing attention to the connection between a woman's place and her well-being, Buss argues that Montgomery's persistent exhaustion and ill health were "the result of her never having been allowed a place of her own, literally and figuratively as woman or as an artist."[86] In a similar vein, Catriona Sandilands, in this volume, draws attention to the importance of "a vibrant web of ecological and interpersonal relations" while at the same time pointing to the normalized expectation that women must leave their natal places upon marriage.

Montgomery exercised agency in identifying with neurasthenia; however, with its treatment, that agency was constrained. The process of medicalization that characterized neurasthenia subtly isolated patients. Montgomery recorded intense and recurring feelings of loneliness in her descriptions of neurasthenia. These feelings were accentuated by the sudden loss in 1919 of her cousin Frede (her confidante and intimate friend) the same year in which her husband suffered a debilitating nervous breakdown. These personal tragedies in the aftermath of the First World War were compounded by the ongoing pressures she faced being a prolific writer, a Presbyterian minister's wife, and a mother in rural communities far from her island home. The joy of companionship and the vibrancy of relationships were increasingly replaced by medicalization. The sense of isolation is evident in Montgomery's descriptions of her neurasthenic episodes. She describes intense feelings of worry and "aloneness" evident in the following excerpts from journal entries dated November and December 1934 that are associated with neurasthenia itself: "I have such a terrible feeling of despair and *aloneness*." "In the afternoon I had a very bad attack of neurasthenia but felt calmer this evening." "My loneliness was awful. I had a bad neurasthenic spell at 8 but feel better now." "The weather was cold and sunless and I got a little neurasthenic again about four."[87] During the increasingly difficult circumstances of her home and professional life as well as the escalation of her ill health and medicalization she continued to write, with the exception of two major hiatuses in her journal in the mid-1930s. In a journal entry in September 1938 she comments on the effort needed to write what would be the last novel published in her lifetime, *Anne of Ingleside*: "It is a year and nine months since I wrote a single line of creative work. But I can *still* write. I wrote a chapter. A burden rolled from my spirit. And I was suddenly *back in my own world* with all my dear Avonlea and Glen folks again. It was like going home."[88]

Conclusion

Neurasthenia demonstrates that the bodies are not just natural but cultural, maladies are not just discovered but created, and bodies are not just singular but multiple. Montgomery's accounts of neurasthenia spanned more than three decades and when she died in 1942, her death certificate recorded "a very high degree of neurasthenia" contributing to her death.[89] Her journal entry of 1910, cited at the outset, is arresting, for the first sentence is imbued with distress and immediacy, but the tone of the second sentence is dispassionate and distant. Anguish and analysis characterize Montgomery's approach to writing about her nervous condition. The diagnosis of neurasthenia provided Montgomery with a somatic explanation for her mental distress and helped dispel a fear of insanity while locating her within a modern cultural context of creative "brain-workers." The experience of neurasthenia encapsulated not only private anguish but also the stresses of embodied modernization. By generating a powerful set of discourses that privileged or disparaged people on the basis of class, race, and gender, neurasthenia suggests how modernity shaped individuals, nature, and social relationships in particular ways.

The somatic location of nervousness had important repercussions for Montgomery. The materiality of the body was conducive to interventions such as medicalization that shaped particular kinds of modern subjectivities. The treatment often emphasized the private realm of the individual whose care and well-being were increasingly crafted within the parameters of modern medicine. Neurasthenia was a gendered disease that assumed female susceptibility to nervousness and devised particular treatments for women that were categorically different from the treatment prescribed for men, which called for direct contact with nature. At the same time neurasthenia inadvertently drew attention to the detrimental effects of an oppressive domestic realm on women.

Montgomery's experience and writings draw attention to how sickness is a language through which "nature, society and culture speak simultaneously."[90] Neurasthenia, I have argued, is an important site for drawing attention to how the nervous system connects humans to their environments while revealing how society creates nervous disorders. The critique of human-centric approaches to the environment and the idea that human health and well-being must be located in a broad ecological context are now increasingly commonplace. In *Bodily Natures,* for instance, Stacy Alaimo argues that "individuals and collectives must contend not only with the materiality of their very selves but with the often invisibly hazardous landscapes of risk society."[91] Articulations of neurasthenia were innovative in underlining the adverse effects of the modern environments on humans as well as pointing to the therapeutic value of nature. However, neurasthenia was assigned to individual bodies neglecting the social and political relationships through which bodies are constituted and regulated. Nature, too, was rendered merely an instrument of good health compressing the broader social and ecological relationships fundamental to the well-being of humans and the more-than-human world.

Montgomery was a successful and modern writer with an international following who troubled the mind–body and material–discursive dualisms that construed nature and human nature. Her novels suggest the centrality of what Sandilands in this volume refers to as the "social-ecological and interpersonal" relationships. Through her novels, as Holmes tells us in her chapter, Montgomery led "countless readers, especially women, to an appreciation of the world outdoors" at a time when society and the treatment of neurasthenia often kept them indoors. She also contributed to the era's changing attitudes about nature and the relationship of human beings to the natural world. Her imaginative and innovative writing about nature and human nature has resonated for generations of readers. It also sustained Montgomery throughout her life as evident in her urgent declaration of agency: "But I can *still* write."

CHAPTER SEVEN

The Education of Emily: Tempering a Force of Nature through Lessons in Law

Kate Sutherland

In recent years, law and literature scholars have turned their attention to texts for young people in order to ask what lessons in law they might offer child readers. It is generally agreed that children's literature is an important vehicle for developing legal consciousness in children and in socializing them for citizenship. For example, John Morrison posits that, "children's literature is perhaps uniquely placed to help us understand how our concepts of right and wrong, of safety and dangerousness, of consensus or otherness are created, transmitted and policed." Sarah Hamilton asserts that, "the stories of classic children's literature play a formative and unparalleled role in the socialization of new legal citizens." In a similar vein, Desmond Manderson describes the bedtime story as a "contemporary instrument of … subtle, loving, but relentless socialization by which the child becomes fit and fitted out for adult life and law."[1]

There is no consensus on just what legal messages are embedded in children's literature broadly, however, or even in particular texts within the genre. Some scholars regard children's literature as primarily a didactic genre and identify its dominant message as one of unquestioning obedience to authority. "We expect children's stories to teach lessons and we are usually not disappointed," Katherine Roberts writes, articulating the content of those usual lessons through a contrast: "unlike literature for adults, in which subversion of social constraints is celebrated, children's literature stands in service of productive socialization." By way of example, she points to such canonical works as the fairy tales of Charles Perrault and the Brothers Grimm, noting that the former even went so far as to neatly sum up the moral at the end of each story.[2]

This simplified view is complicated by scholars who find space for subversion in children's literature, such as Sarah Hamilton, who asserts that Lewis Carroll's *Alice's Adventures in Wonderland* (1865) and L. Frank Baum's *The Wonderful Wizard of Oz* (1900) "promote a ... different jurisprudential lesson," that is, "that logic and independent thought are higher virtues than blind deference to authority," and Manderson, who finds in his detailed analysis of Maurice Sendak's classic picture book *Where the Wild Things Are* (1963) that "The relationship to law that the story develops problematizes rather than merely sustains a lesson in obedience. Instead, it invites children to begin to see themselves as actors in the play of legal interpretation, and to reflect on the purposes and meaning of law and not just on its force."[3] These insights parallel those of scholars who have made a compelling case for the radical potential of children's literature more broadly.[4]

Thomas C. Klein's contribution to the study of law and children's literature is of particular interest in connection with L.M. Montgomery because of its resonance with her legal philosophy as revealed in her accounts of the various legal battles in which she was engaged throughout her life. Klein highlights the distinction that legal and moral philosophers have long drawn between positive law, which is acknowledged to be a human construction, and natural law, which is conceptualized as a higher law based on universal ideals of justice and fairness. He asserts that, contrary to conventional expectations, children's literature may champion natural law at the expense of positive law.[5] In his analyses of a pair of children's novels, Kenneth Grahame's *The Wind in the Willows* (1908) and Phyllis Reynolds Naylor's *Shiloh* (1991), Klein finds representations of positive law and "its related institutions ... as complicated, sometimes corrupt and often arbitrary structures that prevent the protagonists from reaching their desired goals or resolving their difficulties." Instead, he notes, these novels embrace a form of natural law against which "positive law can and should be evaluated on moral grounds." Classic children's novels, he concludes, may depict child protagonists as not only being capable of but also having a responsibility to make moral decisions in accordance with natural law that "may conflict with the demands of ... positive law."[6] Rather than offer didactic lessons in law that shore up authority and reproduce the status quo, children's literature may actually open space for subversion.

The journal entries and letters in which L.M. Montgomery recounted her personal encounters with law can be characterized as expressing scepticism of positive law and a commitment to natural law. Montgomery pursued years of litigation against her first publisher out of a strong sense of justice yet all the while maintained a realistic sense of the limited capacity of courts to produce just results. This attitude to law is also reflected in Montgomery's fiction, and I will illustrate this point through an analysis of *Emily of New Moon* (1923), a novel that she wrote in the midst of her legal battles.

Natural Law Theory

The origins of natural law theory can be traced back to Cicero in the first century BCE and further to the Greek Stoic philosophers who influenced him. Natural law theory boasts among its adherents such notable figures as Thomas Aquinas (1225–1274) and John Locke (1632–1704).[7] Legal theorist J.W. Harris identifies three enduring tenets of the "classical doctrine of natural law": it is "universal and immutable … it is one conception of 'justice,' in the sense in which justice stands for the righting of wrongs, the proper distribution of burdens and benefits within a political community"; it is "a 'higher' law," with "a relationship of superiority towards laws promulgated by political authorities"; and it is "discoverable by reason" and, once we move from the classical period of Cicero on to Christian thinkers like Aquinas, by conscience.[8] This is the natural part of natural law, according to Brian Bix, in that it is purportedly based on "moral truths" that are "derived from truths about human nature."[9] Aquinas famously tried to reconcile natural and positive law by asserting that human laws derive their authority, "their power to bind in conscience, from natural law."[10] Following from that, however, he acknowledged that positive law that conflicts with natural law loses its moral authority and so may rightfully be disregarded. Although he did not necessarily counsel civil disobedience, he asserted instead that "a citizen is not bound to obey 'a law which imposes an unjust burden on its subjects' if the law 'can be resisted without scandal or greater harm.'"[11] John Locke, who focused on natural rights derived from natural law, asserted that "failure to protect [those natural rights] was a ground on which government could be changed."[12]

Natural law theory fell out of favour among legal theorists in the nineteenth century when it was superseded by legal positivism, a school of thought that draws a stark line between law and morality ("the separability thesis") and that regards the existence and content of law as dependent on social facts, not on its merits ("the social thesis").[13] This is not to say that legal positivists are entirely unconcerned with the morality of law but simply that they insist that it is one question to ask what law is and another to ask whether a law is good or bad.[14] The former is considered a legal question and the latter is not.

While natural law theory may have few contemporary adherents among legal theorists,[15] it is of continuing interest to moral philosophers and, according to Klein, to some authors of children's literature. Klein specifically notes that the rights of animals are "a prominent concern" in children's novels and that the ineffectiveness of positive law in protecting those rights often serves as a demonstration of its inadequacy and of the superiority of natural law.[16] This dovetails with some recent developments in natural law theory that posit it as a source of "an environmental ethic that generates human obligations to nonhuman animals, plants, and perhaps even ecosystems."[17] The link that I draw below between Emily, natural law, and nature thus also affords a link between this chapter and the environmental focus of other chapters.

It is at this point then that I turn my attention squarely to L.M. Montgomery, having noted that in the journal entries and letters in which she recounts her personal encounters with law, she evidences a skepticism of positive law and a commitment to natural law very much in line with what Klein found in his analyses of classic children's novels.[18]

L.M. Montgomery's Legal Battles

Montgomery's legal troubles, which extended from 1917 to 1928, involved a series of lawsuits against her first US publisher, L.C. Page and Company, and a personal injury lawsuit that was brought by a neighbour, Marshall Pickering, against her husband, Ewan Macdonald, alleging that the latter's negligence was responsible for a car accident between them. Montgomery's suits against Page were contractual: she initiated the first when Lewis Page attempted to cheat her out of royalties she was owed and the second in order to suppress an unauthorized version of her short story collection *Further Chronicles of Avonlea.* Although certainly she wanted those royalties and wanted *Further Chronicles* off the market, she was motivated to sue primarily by a strong sense of justice. On the eve of the second trial in April 1920, she wrote in her journal: "there is *something* in me that *will not* remain inactive under injustice and trickery and to satisfy that I am driven to this."[19]

Although Montgomery went to court seeking justice, she had little faith in the capacity of positive law to deliver it. She repeatedly expressed doubt about her chances of winning and made clear in so doing that she believed that the unscrupulous and dishonest are better served by the legal system than are upstanding people like herself: "I am dubious about the outcome," she wrote in a journal entry dated May 1917, "but I will not tamely sit down and let Page cheat me at pleasure."[20] In the aforementioned journal entry of April 1920, she added, "I fear my chance of winning is not good, considering the unscrupulous character of the men I have to deal with … I will likely lose and throw away a lot of money."[21] In January 1924, she elaborated on the iniquity of the Page brothers and of the law: "there is apparently no end to the devilry the Pages will attempt and no end to the kinks in the US law that enable them to do it."[22] This view of the co-optability of the law is perhaps never more apparent than when Montgomery compared her lawyer to the Pages' lawyer. She regarded her lawyer, Mr Rollins, as a good and honourable man, whereas she variously referred to the Pages' lawyer, Mr French, as "a cad," "a fiend," "a 'trick' lawyer," and as someone who would stop at nothing "if he thought he could get away with it." She nevertheless concluded that French was "the right sort of a lawyer to have if you want to win" and that Mr Rollins was not really a match for him.[23]

As it turns out Montgomery did win – eleven years, many suits and countersuits, and much worry and expense later. Whatever doubts she expressed about the capacity of positive law to do justice in connection with the Page litigation, however, were amply borne out in the Pickering-Macdonald lawsuit that was triggered by a 1921 car accident and was ultimately resolved in court in Toronto in 1922. Ewan Macdonald lost the case brought against him by Marshall Pickering in a judgment that was manifestly wrong, if not as to responsibility for the accident, then certainly on the question of the damages that flowed from it.[24]

Ultimately, however, Montgomery and Macdonald responded to this unjust decision simply by ignoring it. They refused to pay the damage award, court order notwithstanding. When the bailiff came to collect, Macdonald declared himself unable to pay, and Montgomery and Macdonald took steps to ensure that he would never have to do so. They arranged with the church treasurers to have his salary paid in advance so that it could not be garnisheed, and Montgomery made sure that their property was in her name. She even changed her will to ensure that Pickering could not get at their property after her death. Although Montgomery might be expected to be a law-abiding citizen, particularly given her conservative wife-of-the-minister guise, she was not so here. Where positive law conflicted with natural law, she felt justified in flouting the former.

Lessons in Law in *Emily of New Moon*

I contend that this attitude to law is also reflected in Montgomery's fiction, most prominently in *Emily of New Moon*, which was written and published in the middle of these legal battles. The novel does not address explicitly legal themes; there are no courtroom scenes in it, not even fantastical ones as in *Alice's Adventures in Wonderland* or *The Wind in the Willows*. That said, there is no shortage of rules and conventions within it to consider. Given Emily's transformation over the course of the book from something of a wild child to a respectable adolescent under the tutelage of a range of authority figures who could be said to personify positive law, it is nevertheless ripe for analysis through a legal lens.

Law and literature scholars tend to take a broad view of what constitutes law, borrowing the concepts of legal pluralism, unofficial law, and everyday law from legal anthropologists and from law and society scholars. In its initial anthropological incarnation, legal pluralism focused on the study of legal orders that existed alongside state law – Islamic communities practising Sharia law within secular states, for instance, or indigenous communities practising customary law in postcolonial states – and made the case for state recognition of them.[25] Critical legal pluralists and law and society scholars have taken a step further, however, asserting that regulations associated with less coherent and more dispersed communities, informal rules, and conventions that are operative in everyday life can also be analysed as law.[26]

As Roderick Macdonald states, "We enter on to law's terrain as soon as we orient our behaviour through tacit rules and informal decisions."[27] Morrison translates this idea into the context of children's literature when he argues that texts within the genre offer "another representation of the world and, particularly, ideas of right and wrong. Right and wrong may not be defined in terms of crime and punishment but in terms of doing the right thing, being good or bad (naughty), letting down friends, negotiating authority, and so on. These issues are often set within a framework that, while not necessarily realistic, will reflect the child's experience. The perplexing rules, relationships, and limitations of the wider world are previewed in children's literature."[28] Along similar lines, Manderson asserts explicitly in reference to children's books: "Since law exists in the everyday, it must be learned in the everyday, too."[29] Manifestations of such everyday law abound in *Emily of New Moon*. This is the sort of authority with which Emily must negotiate, and these are the sorts of lessons in law that she is called upon to learn.

Emily's identification with nature is clear from the very first sentence of the novel. The house in the hollow in which she lives is described as being "a mile from anywhere … looking as if it had never been built like other houses but had grown up there like a big, brown mushroom."[30] She is not exactly living in a state of nature. Her father is there with her, as is housekeeper Ellen Greene. She does not go to school, but there is mention of a Sunday school teacher. Yet her chief companions are animals, the wind, and the trees: her two cats, Mike and Saucy Sal, the "Wind Woman," "Adam-and-Eve," the "Rooster Pine," and "all the friendly lady birches."[31]

When Emily's father dies and her late mother's relatives arrive to determine what is to be done with her, it quickly becomes apparent that she is unschooled in some of the most basic social conventions, such as that it is impolite to eavesdrop. Aware that the Murrays are to decide her fate that evening and wanting to find out right away rather than in the morning, she thinks herself clever when it occurs to her to hide under the table around which they will shortly be convening and listen in to their deliberations. The plan goes awry when she cannot keep quiet in the face of criticism of her father and reveals herself. When asked by Aunt Ruth if she realizes "what a shameful thing [she's] been guilty of," Emily replies that she "didn't know it was such a dreadful thing to do." This is her first lesson at the hands of the Murrays and she proves herself not just willing but eager to learn: "'I didn't know – I didn't know,' she whispered. 'But I'll know after this,' she added with sudden vim, 'and I'll never, *never* do it again.'"[32]

It is decided that Emily is to take up residence at New Moon where she will be "cared for and educated properly" – an education, most often at the hands of Aunt Elizabeth, that will entail inculcation with a barrage of rules and conventions designed to fit her to take the place in society that is dictated by her gender, her class, and her family pedigree. In fact, the process does not wait for arrival at New Moon but begins immediately *en route* and continues until Aunt Elizabeth orders her to go to sleep: "Children should eat what is put before them and never turn up their noses at good, wholesome food." "[Y]ou are not to meddle with things that don't belong to you." "Don't contradict." "[Y]ou are to be grateful and obedient and show your appreciation for what's being done for you." "All we require of you is to be a good and contented child and to conduct yourself with becoming prudence and modesty."[33] This unrelenting stream of repressive directives sets Aunt Elizabeth up early as the primary personification of positive law in Emily's new life.

Initially, Emily is inclined to take the rules all too literally. "Don't ever let me see you kissing a cat again," Aunt Elizabeth tells her when she witnesses Emily kissing Saucy Sal. Emily agrees cheerfully: "I'll only kiss her when you don't see me after this." Gradually, however, Emily learns and begins to internalize the rules of New Moon. She might defy them, but she then feels guilty about it, such as when she smuggles Saucy Sal into the house against Aunt Elizabeth's orders when Aunt Elizabeth is away – "*But the next time I do it again*," she notes, a compulsion that she finds "very strange." Or she might choose to adhere to them, as later, when Aunt Elizabeth catches her reading *Rob Roy* and forbids her to read any more novels, and Emily refrains from taking up Aunt Laura's suggestion to do so on the sly because she has "a queer feeling about it."[34]

We can see Emily working her way through such conflicting impulses and achieving some resolution in the incident in which she defies Aunt Elizabeth by taking off her buttoned boots and stockings outside the gate, tucking them away, and walking to the store barefoot. Daydreaming on the way home, she forgets to put them back on, returns home without them, and is thereby caught. Aunt Laura once again counsels subterfuge, suggesting that in future, Emily should continue to leave her boots and stockings by the gate but always to remember to don them again before returning home. But Emily decides against this course of action: "That would be nice, but I don't mean to do it any more. I guess I must obey Aunt Elizabeth because she's the head of the family."[35]

Yet the novel does not depict a steady trajectory of socialization to conformity. Emily accepts some of the strictures placed upon her (sometimes, as above, for different reasons than those stated by Aunt Elizabeth) and rejects others, weighing each one against her internal sense of right and wrong. For example, returning to the matter of being caught going barefoot, Emily resolves not to do it again, but she evades her punishment – being locked in the spare room – without any pangs of conscience. She is terrified of the spare room, so when she discovers a ladder beneath the window, she makes her escape. "I hadn't been bad enough for *that* – it wasn't fair," she reasons.[36] The punishment does not fit the crime, so she rejects it.

This theme is amplified in subsequent episodes in the novel in which Emily moves beyond puzzling over the rights and wrongs of petty rules and confronts questions of principle that stir her deepest feelings. One such example involves the kitten given to her by Old Kelly. Aunt Elizabeth decrees that Emily cannot keep it and that it is to be drowned, and she is in such a temper that day that Cousin Jimmy does not dare to defy her. He secures the kitten in an old oat bag and dumps it in the creek. Emily walks down to the creek later and finds that the kitten has somehow escaped the oat bag and is stranded, bedraggled, on an islet of marsh grass. She acts on instinct, plunging into the creek to rescue it. The narrator tells us: "A suffering or tortured animal always filled her with such a surge of sympathy that it lifted her clean out of herself."[37]

Emily marches back to New Moon with the kitten and announces that she is keeping it and that it is not to be drowned again. As in an earlier moment of rebellion, Emily feels her face taking on the "Murray look" as she speaks, an uncanny process whereby her features take on the cast of those of her grandfather Archibald Murray, "the handsome, intolerant, autocratic old man who had ruled his family with a rod of iron" until he died, whom she otherwise does not resemble at all. Once again spooked by this, Aunt Elizabeth reluctantly accedes: "When Elizabeth Murray saw her father looking at her out of Emily's little white face, she surrendered without a struggle, rage at herself as she might afterwards for her weakness."[38]

All of the foregoing seems to demonstrate Klein's thesis about positive law versus natural law at work in Emily's continuing development. Emily embraces positive law to a certain extent, concluding that, as a matter of principle, Aunt Elizabeth as head of the family ought to be obeyed. But not so when Aunt Elizabeth's dictates conflict with what Emily perceives as moral imperatives – when wrongs like the infliction of suffering on the kitten impel her to obey a higher law than that of Aunt Elizabeth and take a defiant stand, thereby privileging natural law over positive law. In the second half of the novel, however, the depiction of Emily's battles with Aunt Elizabeth seems to complicate and perhaps extend Klein's thesis. For we begin to see Aunt Elizabeth not simply acceding in the face of the Murray look but shifting her views in response to Emily's, at first subtly and then more dramatically.

First, there is the incident of Miss Brownell and the poems. One afternoon at school, Emily is caught by her teacher composing a poem on her slate when she is supposed to be doing sums. Miss Brownell, pleased with this opportunity to take down her least favourite pupil, reads the poem aloud to the class in a mocking tone. This is excruciating enough for Emily, but it gets worse. Her former friend Rhoda Stuart, ever helpful, tells Miss Brownell that Emily has several more poems hidden in her desk. Miss Brownell retrieves them and makes sport of them until the end of class, at which point Emily realizes that she is about to burn them in the stove. Emily snatches them away and refuses to relinquish them: "They are mine. You have no right to them. I wrote them at recesses – I didn't break any rules ... You are an unjust, tyrannical *person*."[39]

Miss Brownell announces her intention to visit New Moon that evening to report Emily's disobedience, and Emily dreads her visit: "She would not have been afraid of justice; but she knew at the bar of Aunt Elizabeth and Miss Brownell she would not have justice."[40] Emily's fears are realized in that Aunt Elizabeth accepts Miss Brownell's account at face value and refuses to let Emily tell her side of the story. She instructs Emily to kneel down before Miss Brownell and ask her pardon.

Emily is weighing this terrible choice – to humble herself before the vindictive Miss Brownell or endure the consequences of refusing – when an intervention by Cousin Jimmy offers something of a reprieve. "A human being should not kneel to any one but God," he says and, wonder of wonders, Aunt Elizabeth reverses herself slightly: "I was wrong – I shall not ask you to kneel. But you must apologize to your teacher – and I shall punish you later on."[41] Aunt Elizabeth remains convinced that Emily's disobedience merits punishment, but she inches closer to Emily's conception of justice here, that the punishment must fit the crime. Further, in her acknowledgement of Cousin Jimmy's point, that one ought not to kneel before mere human authorities, she evokes the religious overtones of a natural law that trumps positive law.

We see Aunt Elizabeth bend still further in what, for me, is the climactic scene of the book, the confrontation between Emily and Aunt Elizabeth over the letters to her dead father that Emily has been writing on old letter bills throughout her tenure at New Moon. Emily is apprehensive when Aunt Elizabeth calls her into the parlour though she does not yet know why she has been summoned. The parlour is where Aunt Elizabeth deals with serious matters in what Emily terms "a trial in the parlour." When she sees the letters in Aunt Elizabeth's lap, she realizes immediately that Aunt Elizabeth has found them and read them. Emily's response is not what Aunt Elizabeth expects: "How dare you? … How dare you touch *my private papers*, Aunt Elizabeth?" Faced with this righteous indignation, Aunt Elizabeth, we are told by the narrator, for the first time in her life "wondered if she had done rightly."[42]

The lesson goes both ways here. Emily remains convinced of her right to privacy – Aunt Elizabeth ought not to have read the letters – but she nevertheless feels dreadful when she realizes how deeply Aunt Elizabeth has been hurt by the things that she wrote about her in them. This too runs counter to Emily's sense of right and wrong. She realizes that some of the things that she wrote about Aunt Elizabeth were unjust and that she ought not to have written them: "While she was under Aunt Elizabeth's roof – while she owed the food she ate and the clothes she wore to Aunt Elizabeth – she should not say, even to her father, harsh things of her. A Starr should not have done it." For her part, Aunt Elizabeth comes to realize that she has wronged Emily, and it is she who admits her wrongdoing and asks forgiveness first. The narrator sums it up thus: "Elizabeth Murray had learned an important lesson – that there was not one law of fairness for children and another for adults. She continued to be as autocratic as ever but she did not do or say to Emily anything that she would not have done or said to Laura had occasion called for it."[43] Given the way that Aunt Elizabeth customarily treats Aunt Laura, this may not yield a dramatic change in behaviour, but her embrace of a universal law of fairness suggests a profound shift in her thinking that once again moves her closer to Emily's conception of justice.

This brings me almost to my conclusion, but first I must return for a moment to the "Murray look" as it does not initially appear to fit into my thesis. It seems to me that it is in the moments when Emily stands up to Aunt Elizabeth to assert her own moral values that she is most herself, tapping into her deepest nature and thereby serving as an advocate of natural law. If this is so, however, why would she wear someone else's face while doing it? And why would natural law be thereby personified by Archibald Murray – a stern, autocratic patriarch who is surely, in fact, the epitome of positive law? This aspect of the tale would seem to throw a wrench into my analysis.

Ultimately, however, when it becomes apparent that the lessons in law run both ways – Aunt Elizabeth educates Emily who simultaneously educates Aunt Elizabeth – this factor can be reconciled. For if Emily is to challenge Aunt Elizabeth effectively, thereby teaching lessons in law as well as learning them, it makes sense that she would do so wearing a face that Aunt Elizabeth would recognize as having the authority of law, the patriarch who was "head of the family" before her.[44] And, of course, the Murray look also underscores the fact that Emily's deepest nature is Murray as well as Starr. Positive law and natural law intermingle in complex ways, the former sometimes conflicting with the latter, but the latter other times legitimizing the former.

Conclusion

In the course of her education at the hands of Aunt Elizabeth, Emily proves an eager student. Nevertheless, as I demonstrated above, Emily's transformation is not a straightforward matter of socialization to conformity. She evaluates all that she learns against her own sense of right and wrong, and responds accordingly. I use the word "temper" rather than "tame" in my title because, in my view, Emily emerges from this process changed but with her essential self intact.[45] As such, I would argue that *Emily of New Moon* exemplifies the phenomenon of a children's literature that champions natural rather than positive law. But it does not simply prove the thesis; it extends and complicates it, and in so doing expands its appeal to a broader audience. For Emily gives as well as receives lessons in law. As Emily is transformed, so too is Aunt Elizabeth.[46]

Thus Emily, the character, emerges from this analysis not simply as an advocate or an embodiment of natural law but as a reformer of positive law. She learns, embraces, and internalizes New Moon traditions, but she makes her mark on New Moon as well. And *Emily of New Moon*, the book, emerges as deserving of a place in the law and literature canon as a classic novel that has rich and complex lessons in law to teach both child and adult readers.

CHAPTER EIGHT

The Spirit of Inquiry: Nature Study and the Sense of Wonder in L.M. Montgomery's Anne Books

Tara K. Parmiter

On her drive with Matthew from the Bright River train station, Anne Shirley bursts with admiration for the natural world around her, bestowing new names such as the "White Way of Delight" and the "Lake of Shining Waters" on each detail of the landscape that strikes her fancy. But just as important as designating these romantic landmarks, Anne also seeks concrete information about the unfamiliar features of Prince Edward Island, revealing how the natural world inspires both her imagination and her intellectual curiosity. She is particularly struck by the red dirt roads and recounts to Matthew how they immediately seized her attention: "When we got into the train at Charlottetown and the red roads began to flash past I asked Mrs Spenser what makes them red and she said she didn't know and for pity's sake not to ask her any more questions. She said I must have asked her a thousand already. I suppose I had, too, but how are you going to find out about things if you don't ask questions?" Within this comical rambling, we not only hear how closely Anne observes the material world but also how intently she seeks to understand it by questioning everything she sees. Throughout L.M. Montgomery's Anne books we encounter many characters who share Anne's fascination with both the beauty and the workings of nature, characters who, like Anne, are prone to exclaim, "Isn't it splendid to think of all the things there are to find out about? It just makes me feel glad to be alive – it's such an interesting world."[1] This combined impulse to extol and understand the wonders of our "interesting world" is not unique to Montgomery's novels, of course; indeed, this attitude aptly describes the core philosophy of the nature study movement.

Although "nature study" would seem to apply generally to any study of natural phenomena, the term referred explicitly to a popular educational approach that was influencing teaching practices across North America at the turn of the twentieth century. By focusing on the direct observation of the natural world – such as asking, "what *does* make the roads red?"[2] – nature study instructors aimed not only to teach the fundamentals of science but to cultivate in students a greater love of nature through an increased awareness of their immediate surroundings. Many authors for young people embraced nature study philosophies, writing books that sought specifically to complement classroom teaching and broaden children's understanding of the world around them. Ernest Thompson Seton (1860–1946), founder of the Woodcraft Indians (a precursor to the Boy Scouts), delighted readers with his tales and drawings of *Wild Animals I Have Known* (1898) and offered outdoor guidance on building shelters, recognizing animal tracks, and identifying wild plants and animals in *Two Little Savages* (1903). Mabel Osgood Wright (1859–1934), president of the Connecticut Audubon Society and an influential leader in the formation of the larger Audubon organization, provided lessons in bird and animal identification in such works as *Citizen Bird* (1897) and *Four-Footed Americans and Their Kin* (1898) as well as lessons in sympathizing with the natural world in *Tommy-Anne and the Three Hearts* (1896). Bestselling author Gene Stratton-Porter (1863–1924), perhaps the most prominent of these writers, wove details about moth and insect identification into *Freckles* (1904) and *The Girl of the Limberlost* (1909), romances set in the swamps of Indiana and discussed in this volume by Nancy Holmes.[3] With their detailed descriptions and accurate illustrations, such texts could easily double as field guides, providing teachers and parents of this era with the tools necessary to engage children with life out of doors.

Despite her lush descriptions of natural landscapes, Montgomery does not initially seem to belong among this group of writers, who used storytelling explicitly as a means of teaching reverence for nonhuman nature. Like Anne Shirley in *Anne of Avonlea*, Montgomery strives "to add some beauty to life" through her writing; rather than aspiring to "make people *know* more," she seems more intent upon making them "have a pleasanter time" because of her influence.[4] Nevertheless, Montgomery's attention to the details of red roads, birch trees, and June lilies, as well as her enthusiastic sympathy with the "interesting world," promotes a nature study ethos in her readers; she encourages us to put down our books and open our eyes to the wonders around us. For Montgomery, then, the natural world is not only a site of wonder but of learning, where the matter of nature is also a matter of education. In this chapter, I examine Montgomery's fiction through the lens of the nature study movement to show how Montgomery's depictions of wild nature reflect and respond to these contemporary educational philosophies. Focusing particularly on five Anne books, four of which were published during the height of nature study's popularity, I argue that Montgomery models the intense connection to the natural world promoted by the primary philosophies of this educational movement.

The Nature Study Movement

Gaining popularity in the 1890s and flourishing throughout North America in the first two decades of the twentieth century, nature study built upon several progressive educational theories that aimed to bring children into direct contact with their environments. Nature study traces its influences to such figures as Heinrich Pestalozzi (1746–1827), the Swiss educational theorist who fought to replace rote memorization with child-centred experiential learning; Friedrich Froebel (1782–1852), the German innovator of the kindergarten movement, who encouraged teachers and parents to "Lead your child out into nature" but also to "let him [or her] be taught by nature rather than by you"; and Louis Agassiz (1807–1873), the Harvard naturalist who coined what would become a nature study mantra, "study nature, not books."[5] These theorists emphasized the need to tailor education to an individual child's development, and nature study teachers aimed to do just that by encouraging children to observe the natural world and to pose questions based on their observations, whether in a nearby field at a rural school or in a school garden in a more urban setting. Such lessons would become increasingly complicated as children advanced in the school system, but at its most basic, nature study for any age group relied on inductive learning and on students' active engagement with their surroundings. Instead of drilling facts into children's minds, nature study teachers sought to inspire wonder through direct interaction with nonhuman nature.

We see this innovative approach, for example, in our introduction to Miss Stacy in *Anne of Green Gables*. When Marilla expresses her concern that the new teacher allowed her students to climb "to the very tops of those big trees on Bell's hill after crows' nests," Anne explains matter-of-factly that the nests were for "nature study" and that they were on a "field afternoon" that day, studying nature rather than books, as Agassiz would have recommended.[6] This brief mention of nature study is one of many innovations that Miss Stacy brings to the Avonlea school, harkening back to Montgomery's own beloved teacher, Hattie Gordon, who "had the power of inspiring a love of study for its own sake and of making the dry bones of the school routine alive with interest."[7] In the words of Mattie Rose Crawford, author of the first nature study guide specifically designed for Canadian classrooms, teachers like Miss Stacy and Hattie Gordon understand that "Instead of telling children of wonders such as the giant trees of the tropics, or of glaciers, or of star fish, the aim to-day is to open their eyes to the wonders everywhere around them – to the maple, the beech, or the pine." These nature study teachers encourage students to embrace the beauties of their Canadian surroundings, favouring maples over mahogany as a subject for admiration and investigation. The adults of Avonlea may raise their eyebrows but the children respond enthusiastically to Miss Stacy's nature study classes, which encourage them, in Crawford's words, to "look at Nature with seeing eyes" and bring their own questions and interests into the educational process.[8]

More than simply an innovation to the school curriculum, nature study was one of the first concerted efforts to introduce science instruction into North American elementary schools. As historian Sally Gregory Kohlstedt explains, the amateur study of natural history had become increasingly popular in the United States and Canada throughout the nineteenth century, but by the 1880s educational leaders felt the lack of a "consistent or persistent commitment to teach the natural and physical sciences in the public school classrooms."[9] Educators saw in nature study a solution to two seemingly contradictory yet interrelated dilemmas: on the one hand, nature study could help prepare school children for the rigours of the sciences in the higher grades, a necessary goal in an increasingly industrialized, modern society; on the other, it could help revitalize the link between humans and the nonhuman world, addressing concerns that North Americans were becoming too urbanized and removed from the benefits of wild nature.[10] This second aspect was central to the nature study philosophy: Liberty Hyde Bailey, a professor of horticulture at Cornell University and a prominent leader of the movement, even distinguishes nature study from the hard sciences, not because it was not as valuable but because he believed that nature study provided something far more important than facts. "Nature-study, then, is not science," he explains in *The Nature-Study Idea* (1903). "It is spirit. It is an attitude of mind. It concerns itself with the child's outlook on the world."[11]

Bailey's distinction between nature study and science reveals an inherent tension in understandings of scientific study that was prevalent in this period and that in many ways persists today. Nature study advocates distrusted the work of professional scientists, fearing that the detached study of specimens in a lab would detract from a more holistic or sympathetic understanding of their subjects; as popular nature writer John Burroughs put it, the scientist "is so intent upon the bare fact that he [or she] does not see the spirit or the meaning of the whole."[12] Montgomery comments implicitly on these concerns in *Anne of Ingleside* (1939), which features several pointed jabs at the scientific establishment. When Gilbert jokingly quotes the "great Dr Von Bemburg" who has written in the *Medical Journal* that "Life is nothing more than delicately balanced organic chemistry," Anne retorts, "Don't quote that horrible Von Bemburg to me ... *He* may be a concatenation of atoms, but *I* am not."[13] Anne here rejects a narrow view of science that focuses only on facts – the concatenation of atoms – rather than on the wonder of life. When Bailey suggests that nature study is not science, then, he means that it is not the reductive, cold, disconnected work of the Dr Von Bemburgs of the world. Instead, Bailey seeks to complicate this limited view of science, reminding his readers that bringing nature study into the curriculum will develop not only a deeper understanding of biology, geology, physics, and astronomy but also a deeper sympathy and respect for nonhuman nature.

This emphasis on inspiring a love of nature became a hallmark of the nature study philosophy. In her classic *Handbook of Nature Study* (1911), Anna Botsford Comstock notes that while nature study "gives the child practical and helpful knowledge," its primary goal is to promote "a sense of companionship with life out-of-doors and an abiding love of nature." Comstock, a colleague of Bailey's at Cornell and an accomplished naturalist and scientific illustrator, saw nature study as a life-changing endeavour. Her *Handbook* invites readers out into the field, assuring them that engagement with nonhuman nature will transform their health, minds, and capacity for compassion. Insisting that a love of nature will best be inspired by regular companionship with the outdoors, she notes that, despite its length (over eight hundred pages), the *Handbook* is intended "to encourage investigation rather than give information." Even though each lesson opens with some background and a "leading thought" to direct the class, Comstock devotes most of her energy to framing questions to prompt students' observations. Most of these questions focus on specific sensory details of sight, sound, and touch but many explicitly elicit what Lesley D. Clement discusses in this volume as empathy with nature, as when Comstock asks how they could protect various birds or animals from abuse. Elsewhere, she reminds readers that nature study should never become a drill or the students would lose interest, but then again, she promptly wonders, "how could it ever be a task to see that the sky is blue, or the dandelion golden, or to listen to the oriole in the elm!"[14] That exultant exclamation point highlights Comstock's belief in the inherent appeal of the natural world and our innate affinity for blue skies and oriole songs, as though she cannot imagine anyone who would not enjoy the "companionship with life out-of-doors."

Nowhere do we see this sense of companionship more clearly in the Anne books than in the depictions of Jem Blythe and Carl Meredith in *Rainbow Valley* (1919). Although in all the novels Anne goes into raptures over birch trees and violets, Jem and Carl more clearly approach the matter of nature as young naturalists. We can easily imagine them tromping across the fields with a Comstock *Handbook*, presuming they felt the need to consult a book on their exploratory rambles. As Montgomery writes, Jem "never took things on faith; he always liked to investigate the truth of a statement for himself," investigations that prompt him to study the landscape of Glen St Mary and Rainbow Valley with a keen eye and ear. Montgomery enumerates his notable skills, emphasizing that he has developed them through "constant experiment and observation," the hallmarks of Comstock's nature study student. Montgomery tells us that,

> Jem always knew where the first and ripest berries grew, where the first pale violets shyly wakened from their winter's sleep, and how many blue eggs were in a given robin's nest in the maple grove ... He knew where the finest spruce gum was to be found, in pale amber knots on the lichened bark, he knew where the nuts grew thickest in the beechwoods around the Harbour Head, and where the best trouting places up the brooks were. He could mimic the call of any wild bird or beast in Four Winds and he knew the haunt of every wild flower from spring to autumn.[15]

Jem's skills reflect his attention to the natural world; he knows where to find such delights as spruce-gum and berries because he pays attention, gathering what Comstock calls "practical and helpful knowledge" to help him serve as nature guide to his siblings and friends.

Carl has also developed his powers of observation and his love of nature, particularly in regards to the insects and reptiles that frighten the other Glen children. Montgomery explains that Carl "knew the secrets of bugs and had a sort of freemasonry with bees and beetles," the terms "secrets" and "freemasonry" suggesting that Carl has been welcomed into the insect world and granted membership in their society. A true disciple of Comstock, Carl has earned this trust through his sympathy and attention. It is notable, furthermore, that after Walter makes his haunting prophesy about the Pied Piper at the end of the novel, Carl arrives on the scene "with a report of the doings in ant-land" and thus "brought them all back to the realm of facts."[16] We could even speculate that because of his fascination with the struggles of the natural world that are not softened with the fairy stories of Ingleside, Carl will later be better prepared to face the war than the romantic adventurer Jem or the prophetic poet Walter.

As Comstock reminds us, "Perhaps the most valuable and practical lesson the child gets from nature-study is a personal knowledge that nature's laws are not to be evaded."[17] Indeed, his penchant for insects and reptiles becomes his only real distinguishing characteristic: even as a young man and soldier in *Rilla of Ingleside*, Carl is still defined by his connection to the natural world. As Walter Blythe prepares to leave home to fight in Europe, he gazes around Rainbow Valley and remembers all his childhood friends, including a vision of "Carl, poring over ants and bugs." Mentioning one of Carl's letters from the front in which he tells her about a tame rat that "sleeps in his pocket at night," Rilla reflects in her diary that "Rats don't worry Carl as they do some people – he was always chummy with all little beasts." Later, when Carl has been wounded on the front, losing sight in one of his eyes, he cheerfully reminds his loved ones back home that "One eye is enough to watch bugs with."[18] In this joking remark, we sense that Carl's lifelong love of learning has not been trampled by the horrors of war. Instead, the fascination with nature instilled in him as a child has enabled him still to see beauty in a postwar world, even if he can only see it through one eye.

It is significant that Carl is still attuned to natural beauty after confronting the wastelands of the First World War, for even before the war, a number of initiatives in North America attempted to raise awareness of the devastation that humans had wrought on the land. In *Nature Study and the Child* (1900), Charles B. Scott observes that, "We have adapted ourselves to our physical environment by stripping our land of its forests, our air of its birds, our waters of their fish, by using in the most reckless manner our natural resources. Nature has been our slave, from whom we could take anything, to whom we owed nothing."[19] Teachers of nature study aimed to get children to question this recklessness. For example, in *Anne of Avonlea*, Anne recounts in a letter to a former classmate from Queen's Academy a comical response she received from a student "in nature study class." As Anne tells her friend, "when I asked them to give me a good reason why toads shouldn't be killed, Benjie Sloane gravely answered, 'Because it would rain the next day.'"[20] Anne's amusement with the anecdote stems from the superstition of Benjie's response, but her question to the class reveals a serious effort to have them consider their relationship with the nonhuman nature around them. Comstock suggests in her *Handbook* that, "through properly training the child, the man [*sic*] shall be enabled to enjoy nature through seeing how creatures live rather than watching them die,"[21] and in this brief exchange, we can see Anne as a teacher contributing to that conservationist ethic.

On the whole, as Comstock's words suggest, teachers of nature study avoided preaching environmental ethics but instead hoped to inspire this respect for nonhuman nature by making students better acquainted with their home environments. Perhaps the most prevalent means of providing this direct contact was through the "rolling year" curriculum, lessons designed around the changing seasons of the year, featuring field afternoons in the fall and spring and indoor experiments and observations in the winter months.[22] This curriculum was not only logical in its attempt to make use of the specific materials around the schools, but it drew on the literary influences of many naturalists, such as Henry David Thoreau (1817–1862) and Susan Fenimore Cooper (1813–1894), who shaped their respective narratives *Walden* (1854) and *Rural Hours* (1850) around the changing seasons.

Of the Anne books, *Anne of Ingleside* (published twenty years after but set earlier than *Rainbow Valley*) progresses most noticeably as a series of rolling years, framing human stories within details of the changing landscape around the home. In one chapter, the narrator breezes us through half a year with quick references to the world outside: in January and February, while "Anne sat up o' nights to pore over seed catalogues" for her flower garden, the Blythe children found a different use for seeds, feeding "seven blue-jays who came regularly to the orchard for their rations"; March blows with wild winds, then passes into April's rains, which bring, in turn, "pussywillows in the marsh," "the first robin," "the first mayflowers," and a Wordsworthian "show of daffodils."[23] Life for the Blythes similarly seems to blossom with the coming of spring in the year being described, thawing suddenly when Gilbert's gloomy Aunt Mary Maria, who had descended on the family like a never-ending winter, finally decamps to her own home. When Aunt Mary Maria leaves, the narrator records that "The first peony burst into bloom in the garden," as if the aunt's departure has provoked it, and young Walter enthuses to Anne, "The world is just full of poetry, isn't it, Mummy?"[24] Anne and her children recognize the day-to-day changes in the world outside and revel in them, acknowledging not simply an analytical understanding of the plants, birds, and weather but an appreciation of the "poetry" behind this knowledge.

It is notable, too, that Montgomery's seasonal descriptions focus on the very real details of a very real landscape. Many critics have rightfully observed that Montgomery does not emphasize the regional distinctions of Prince Edward Island in her writing. In *Making Avonlea: L.M. Montgomery and Popular Culture* (2002), Janice Fiamengo proposes that "Montgomery's landscape description is highly portable" and suggests that "Montgomery was far less interested in capturing the distinctiveness of Prince Edward Island than in conveying joyful affinity with the natural world." Nancy Holmes concurs in *Storm and Dissonance: L.M. Montgomery and Conflict* (2008), noting that, "little in the imagery underscores the current ecological appreciation for the specificity of place and a deep sense of localism."[25] While I agree on the larger scale that the descriptions of Anne's world could be easily adapted to other landscapes, I would also observe that Montgomery *is* very attuned to the specificity of place, this place being the backyard. In this respect, her depictions of the natural world are in sympathy with the aims of nature study, which, as Bailey explains, "is to set pupils at work informally and personally with the objects, the affairs and phenomena with which they are in daily contact." Or as Comstock puts it, "Nature-study is for the comprehension of the individual life of the bird, insect, or plant that is nearest at hand." Montgomery may not emphasize the distinctiveness of her *Canadian* landscapes but she does sing the details of the *home* landscape, of the poppies in the Ingleside garden, of Cock Robin, the bird who adopts the Blythe family, even of the toads Walter stashes in the basement because he "wanted to *study* them."[26]

Perhaps we should say, then, that it is not Montgomery's *landscapes* that are "highly portable" but her *relationship* to the landscape. That is, because she spends so much loving detail on the "nearest at hand," Montgomery models a relationship between humans and nonhuman nature that can be transported around the globe, as has been demonstrated by the tremendous international popularity of her novels. This, too, is in keeping with the nature study philosophy about the interrelatedness between love and knowledge: as Crawford notes, nature study practitioners believed that,

"By understanding the relation of the parts to the whole and the laws underlying them, the world, as the child looks out upon it, will be to him [or her] a related, living whole ... The more real love he [or she] has for Nature, the more interest he [or she] will take in it." In other words, the optimism of the nature study movement held that only by knowing and loving the "parts" of nature will we be moved to love and protect the "whole."[27] Situating Montgomery's work within the context of nature study therefore helps illuminate how attentive she was to the true matter of nature and how much the relationship with the *home* landscape matters.

Nature Study Beyond the First World War

As a defined movement, nature study flourished in the early twentieth century but faded from prominence after the First World War. Critics in the 1920s worried that the focus of nature study on sympathy and love for the natural landscape was too sentimental and that its curriculum, originally lauded for its attention to students' curiosity, lacked a systematic approach.[28] Nature study also suffered from a backlash against female teachers after the war, with critics marking a sharp divide between the masculine valour of quantitative science and the feminine softness of trying to create "sympathy" with nature. Like Montgomery's fiction, nature study was relegated to a greener, more romantic, more feminine prewar era.[29]

It is worthwhile, then, to look more closely at *Anne of Ingleside*, set before the war but published in 1939, for this novel both reveals why critics may have rejected nature study philosophies and offers a spirited defence of nature study's larger goals. One problem highlighted in this novel is that nature study aimed to promote both love *and* understanding of the natural environment: while Anne clearly loves the natural world, she often favours imagined narratives about the landscape over the actual details, siding with Paul Irving's Rock People and her son Walter's Tree Lovers over the facts of granite and birch. For example, when young Walter is saddened by the accurate knowledge that crickets don't literally sing but "just make that noise scraping their hind-legs," Anne comforts him at first by reminding him that "*that* is their way of singing," trying to soften the unromantic truth. When Walter is not consoled, Anne assures him that "You'll forget about the hind-legs in time and just think of their fairy chorus all over the harvest meadows and autumn hills." Anne here suggests that the facts about crickets are not as important to her as the impression they make on the listener; in trying to promote sympathy with nature, she seems overly willing to elide scientific realities, demonstrating the sentimentality that so concerned nature study's critics. Rather than insisting on an adherence to science, Anne as a mother seems more inclined, in Gilbert's words, to allow the children "to possess their heritage of fairyland as long as they can."[30]

At the same time, though, *Anne of Ingleside* offers some of Montgomery's most sustained descriptions of actual nature. With elements of both nature study and what we might call nature fancy, *Anne of Ingleside* reflects a more mature response to the natural world than Montgomery's jewel-toned writing of *Anne of Green Gables*; as Elizabeth Epperly notes, in the thirty-one years between these novels Montgomery "had changed with the times themselves to include more realistic and less idealized detail."[31] More important, though, in returning to Anne's life before the First World War on the eve of the Second, Montgomery constructs a world that allows nature study and nature fancy to coexist, refusing to dismiss either the facts of life or the power of the imagination.

Indeed, in *Anne of Ingleside* Montgomery celebrates the connection between imagination and knowledge, a connection that distinguished nature study as well. Instead of condemning an imaginative approach to the natural world, Bailey insists that "We have a right to a poetic interpretation of nature," and Comstock supplements the questions and illustrations in her *Handbook* with excerpts from stories, poems, and natural history, despite Agassiz's call to study nature, not books. Crawford even sounds like Anne when she insists, "Only in the natural world has the child's imagination free scope." For Bailey, Comstock, and Crawford, the imagination prompts questioning, which prompts observation and ultimately greater knowledge; Bailey even encourages such fanciful questions as "What does the flower think?" or "What is the brook saying as it rolls over the pebbles?" as ways to trigger the child's curiosity.[32] Elsewhere in *Anne of Ingleside* we hear Jem asking just such questions of his mother, ranging from the scientific ("Mummy, what do little birds do when it rains *hard*?") to the romantic ("Mummy, how far is it from here to sunset?") to the comical ("Mummy, is a widow really a woman whose dreams have come true? Wally Taylor said she was").[33] What is important here is less that his questions do not all focus on scientific phenomena and more that Jem has learned from Anne to cultivate his curiosity about the whole world around him. Encouraged to follow their flights of fancy, Jem and his siblings have learned that the imagination is integral to our investigations of the world. As Bailey points out, "Knowledge begins in wonder … it is the spirit of inquiry."[34] Nature fancy, as we see in the Anne books, is one way to access that sense of wonder.

Though published well after the height of nature study's initial popularity, *Anne of Ingleside* ultimately assures us that nature study did not disappear after the 1920s, despite its detractors. Although nature study lost its standing in the curriculum, its influence lived on not only in the science classroom but also in summer camp activities, boy and girl scouting, national park programs, 4-H clubs, the environmental movement, and other pastimes such as bird watching, which had concurrently risen in popularity around the turn of the twentieth century. Today, the interest in nature study has been revived by such figures as naturalist Edward O. Wilson, whose "biophilia hypothesis" proposes that humans have an "innate" affinity for nonhuman nature, and Richard Louv, whose call-to-arms, *Last Child in the Woods: Saving Our Children from Nature-Deficit Disorder*, has inspired parents and teachers across the United States to "Leave No Child Inside."[35] What was once a distinct progressive-era teaching philosophy has now, like Anne herself, influenced generations.

Almost twenty years after the publication of *Anne of Ingleside*, environmentalist Rachel Carson published "Help Your Child to Wonder," an article in *Woman's Home Companion* that shows both her indebtedness to the nature study learning of her childhood and her sympathy with the fanciful approach to nature we find in Montgomery's novels. Embracing both the imaginative and the scientific goals of nature study, Carson models an approach that focuses on "having fun together rather than teaching." She insists that "If a child is to keep alive his [or her] inborn sense of wonder … he [or she] needs the companionship of at least one adult who can share it, rediscovering with him [or her] the joy, excitement and mystery of the world we live in."[36] For many of us growing up, Anne was one of those adults who could share with us her sense of wonder, who could convince us that, as she exclaims in *Anne of Ingleside*, "there is no such thing as a common day. *Every* day has something about it no other day has. Haven't you noticed?"[37] Although Montgomery may not have aimed to teach nature study in her fiction as explicitly as did some of her peers, her novels have endured in popularity and continue to promote the philosophies of this movement, inspiring readers of the twenty-first century to rediscover the joys and mysteries of our world, one red road or robin's nest at a time.

PART THREE

Nature's Otherness

CHAPTER NINE

"No London street Arabs for me": The Unnatural Orphan in Anne of Green Gables

Paul Keen

Few scientific controversies trigger such strong opinions as what has become known as the "nature-versus-nurture" debate. As Mavis Reimer notes in her contribution on *Anne of Green Gables* to *The Oxford Handbook of Children's Literature* (2011), "questions of how the line between nature and culture is drawn have occupied critical theorists at least since the early decades of the twentieth century."[1] If, as Richard A. Lippa emphasizes in *Gender, Nature, and Nurture* (2002), "the nature-nurture debate has reverberated through the halls of academia" ever since Francis Galton coined the phrase in 1874, it is equally true that the debate has spilled over beyond these walls in ways that few scientific debates ever do.[2] Focusing on a "gathering tide of genetic claims for causes of human behavior," Gisela Kaplan and Lesley J. Rogers warn in their book *Gene Worship* (2003) that "we are surrounded today by contemporaries (and seemingly a growing number of them) who are convinced by the value of reductionist thinking and such reductionism in science, unfortunately, does not stay within the small select scientific community. It trickles out into the broader public, is often taken at its face value, and can do a great deal of harm."[3] The very familiarity of the phrase "nature-versus-nurture," which functions as an easy shorthand for what are actually highly complex scientific and sociological propositions, is a testament to the extraordinary extent to which this particular debate has ingrained itself within broader social thought. The handy simplicity of the phrase masks the real complexity of the issue, however. Nature offers the promise of a recourse to materialist foundations, but it ends up implying a range of meanings, many of them in contradiction with one another. Not only that, but nature and nurture usually overlap, given that the biological family is frequently cited as the primary force in terms of both genetic transmission and environmental conditioning, with inheritance blurring the line between the two. Regardless of these problems, and even though the one thing that most people *can* agree on is that these positions are not mutually exclusive, the debate tends to play itself out in terms of the opposition between the two: nature-versus-nurture rather than nature-and-nurture.

Behind both positions lies the dream of origins. Whether it is biology or social conditioning, the common assumption remains that there is some kind of observable identity whose origins we can uncover if we trace them back carefully enough, even if, as Freud argues, these origins lie in a network of repressions rather than overt influences. Either way, the dream remains the same: to follow some kind of diagnostic path back to the sources of who a person is, an urge that becomes all the stronger the more forceful a person's character seems to be. How to explain those extraordinary individuals whose personalities seem to triumph over circumstances? In *Anne of Green Gables*, for instance, Anne Shirley's childhood eccentricities appear to be as hardwired as they are memorable. From her buggy ride home from the train station, her character always seems to exceed the explanatory power of her circumstances. "There was no ciphering her out by the rules that worked with other children," Mrs Lynde eventually admits. "It's nothing short of wonderful how she's improved these three years, but especially in looks." But if Anne's capacity for unpredictable change bears witness to her inner resources – she develops in ways that cannot be reduced to the influence of her surroundings – the opposite is also true. Anne's reassuring comment to Marilla, that she has not really changed at all even though she has outgrown the "queer ways" of the little girl that Marilla has grown to miss, highlights this myth of the unchanging essence of the strong individual: "I'm not a bit changed – not really. I'm only just pruned down and branched out. The real *me* – back here – is just the same."[4] The "real" Anne is not the individual that everyone encounters in daily life but the private core that remains behind it.

Paradoxically, however, the allure of this promise of deep subjectivity – not the observable world of changeable surfaces but the inner essence, located somewhere "back here" – only intensifies other characters' interpretive desire to connect outward traits with underlying causes. Elizabeth Rollins Epperly has noted the extent to which the image of the stream in the opening paragraph of *Anne of Green Gables* serves as a metaphor for the development of Anne as a well-disciplined subject: the "quiet, well-conducted little stream" that knows better than to "run past Mrs Rachel Lynde's door without due regard for decency and decorum." Traced the other way, however, it also encodes a myth of origins and an economy of speculation: "it was reputed to be an intricate, headlong brook in its earlier course through those woods, with dark secrets of pool and cascade."[5] It is their very obscurity that ensures the appeal of these "dark secrets," which are, after all, only "reputed" to exist. To put it another way, the metaphor may say more about the world of small-town dynamics – the prying curiosity of nosy neighbours among whom these dark secrets are reputed to exist – than it does about the child whose fate it evokes.

Orphans might seem to be ideal test cases in the nature-versus-nurture debate: they occupy the subject position in which biological inheritance and social influence are most thoroughly divorced – genetics and environment remain at arm's length. Their development may well reflect both influences, but at least they can be distinguished, existing as wholly separate categories. What interests me, however, are the ways that L.M. Montgomery uses the figure of the orphan in *Anne of Green Gables* to challenge the binary limitations of the nature-versus-nurture debate about human psychology. In doing so she self-consciously performs the contradictions that lurk within any community's desire for coherent identity and offers a warning about the dangers implicit in the sorts of distinctions that this process necessarily implies. In scientific terms, orphans may have provided a valuable means for interrogating the respective roles of biology and social environment, but in social discourses, the spectre of the orphan circulated more often as a threat. As Beverly Crockett has argued, drawing on a history of nineteenth- and early- twentieth-century responses, people tended to view "children of unknown parentage and other 'alien' foreign creatures as potential threats ... All these children might be stereotyped as bastards, troublemakers, or even congenitally corrupt young criminals."[6]

At the heart of this reactionary disposition was a domestic ideology that stabilized self–other contrasts by celebrating the home and the natural (i.e., biological) child as mutually reinforcing positive influences. If the ideological power of this domestic ideal – "the happy home and the happy child" – helped to contain tensions *within* cultures, then Reimer is right to suggest that *Anne of Green Gables* played a role in naturalizing these ideas. Read on another level, however, Rosamond Bailey is correct in emphasizing the ways the novel deconstructs this position. Reading Anne alongside another graduate of the Hopetown orphanage, Mary Vance from Montgomery's *Rainbow Valley*, whose "slangy, ungrammatical, near profane" style marks her as Anne's antithesis, Bailey stresses the ways that Montgomery foregrounds these contrasts in order to question received ideas about the formative roles of both biology and the environment and, in doing so, to unsettle the prescriptive force of a domestic ideology grounded in narrowly conceived definitions of the happy home and the happy child.[7]

However different Anne may feel from those who live in the community that becomes her extended home, it is her lack of difference as well as her inability to reinforce the sorts of self-other distinctions that her mysterious background seems to promise, that make her most threatening. Orphans, as Mrs Lynde emphasizes, trouble the nature-versus-nurture distinction in fundamental ways: bereft of any identifiable ancestry, they defy efforts to read personality traits as biological determinism. "You don't know what you're getting. You're bringing a strange child into your house and home and you don't know a single thing about him nor what his disposition is like nor what sort of parents he had nor how he's likely to turn out." To know a child's parents is, in part, to know his or her future; lacking this history, an orphan's nature remains a mystery. Except, Mrs Lynde continues, in the absence of all of this, orphans tend to share a second-order nature *as orphans*. As Mrs Lynde's reported anecdotes show, to be an orphan is to behave unnaturally, to reject the home that he or she arrives at too late ever really to belong in: one "up west of the Island" set fire to his adopted parents' house at night, another "used to suck the eggs – they couldn't break him of it," and a third, "over in New Brunswick," put strychnine in the well "and the whole family died in fearful agonies."[8] Never having been nurtured enough, orphans become, seemingly by their very nature, unnaturally malicious. The surprise arrival of a girl only confirms Mrs Lynde's warning – "You don't know what you're getting" – which is important: to bring something strange into a home, to introduce the trace of the foreign into the heart of the domestic, would be to risk a moment of uncanny disruption at the very site of all that, conventionally speaking, should be most reliable. Mrs Lynde's diatribe, through its sheer extravagance, situates Anne's story within what Reimer describes as "an archive of discourses" about orphans as dangerous, alien figures.[9]

Mrs Lynde's distrust of foreigners or of whatever can be dismissed as foreign is a persistent theme in *Anne of Green Gables* and its sequels. In *Anne of Avonlea*, she voices her concern about their new neighbour, Mr Harrison: "I knew there'd be trouble when Robert Bell sold his place to a New Brunswick man … I don't know what Avonlea is coming to, with so many strange people rushing into it. It'll soon not be safe to sleep in our beds." Mrs Lynde feels justified in dismissing Mr Harrison as "a crank," the narrator explains, because "Mr Harrison was certainly different from other people … and that is the essential characteristic of a crank, as everybody knows."[10] Reinforced by the legitimating sense of collective identity, strange behaviour can be contained by reimagining it as the behaviour of a stranger, rewriting cultural differences as geographic distinctions. As Laura M. Robinson argues in her discussion of xenophobia and the communal identity in Montgomery's fiction, "In Avonlea, the foreign is always suspect and the suspect is always foreign."[11] Indeed, from Marilla's knee-jerk assumption about Italians when Anne admits that she bought her hair-dye from a peddler to derogatory comments about lazy French boys, the spectre of the foreigner, of those with affiliations elsewhere (even New Brunswick), circulates as the most readily available means of articulating a deeper fear about people's moral shortcomings. The arbitrariness of these judgmental postures is underscored by the mistaken nature of both – the peddler was not Italian nor can (or should) Acadians be dismissed as foreigners – but in some ways these sorts of mistakes are precisely Montgomery's point. Inaccuracy does not make these condemnations any less ideologically effective.

In her chapter in this volume, Robinson draws on Gabrielle Ceraldi's use of Edward Said's account of tensions between forms of affiliation (culture) and filiation (family) in the Modernist age in order to develop a similar argument about the ways that L.M. Montgomery unsettles the distinction between nature and nurture. In her earlier article, cited in the previous paragraph, Robinson rightly suggests that "much of the novel's satiric energy takes as its focus Anne's perceived foreignness,"[12] but as Benjamin Lefebvre has pointed out, Anne's foreignness is actually quite minimal, since her skin colour, her ethnic and religious heritage, and her language are all shared by the inhabitants of Avonlea: "while Anne as disruptive child is appealing precisely because she is an outsider to this homogenous community, her adoption into Avonlea seems possible only because she is not too significantly 'different' from its inhabitants."[13] However mistrustful locals such as Mrs Lynde, Marilla (after the brooch goes missing), and Mrs Barry (after Diana returns home drunk) might be, Anne is virtually indistinguishable from Avonlea locals. What makes her objectionable is not some form of social difference but her enigmatic status. If Anne is threatening, it is not because of her alterity but her capacity for mimicry. She is, to borrow Homi Bhabha's formulation, "almost the same but not quite" – a border phenomenon whose blend of identity and difference proves to be more troubling than any more clearly oppositional status. To adapt Bhabha's account of the centrality but also the complexity of self–other relations at the heart of colonial discourse, Anne's status as an orphan inscribes her "at the crossroads of what is known and permissible and that which though known must be concealed; a discourse uttered between the lines and as such both against the rules and within them."[14] Arriving from elsewhere but not noticeably different in terms of colour and background, Anne inscribes an absence at the heart of the dense web of signifying practices that ensure Avonlea's social coherence, a reminder of the ambiguity not just of orphans but also of communal identity generally. The irony that Mrs Lynde misses in her comment about Robert Bell, of course, is that by the time of *Anne of Avonlea*, she shares these concerns about foreigners with Anne, who was once a foreigner herself in both senses of the word (from elsewhere but also, as an orphan, fundamentally unknowable and potentially dangerous), but who has now become not only thoroughly local but also central in the community as schoolteacher. Anne has become *from there*, her origins retroactively assured.

Confronted by Mrs Lynde's suspicions early in *Anne of Green Gables*, Marilla falls back on a romantic nationalist theory of shared genetic inheritance. Anne may be an unknown entity as an individual, but at least she is part of a collective history whose lineage can be counted on. Mrs Lynde might question the wisdom of embracing this "imported orphan," but it is this very notion of importation – of foreign goods crossing borders – that Marilla is most eager to contend.[15] All orphans are, by definition, imports, in the sense of being an addition to domestic life from somewhere outside, but as Marilla insists, there are entirely different degrees of foreignness: "At first Matthew suggested getting a Barnado [*sic*] boy. But I said 'no' flat to that. 'They may be all right – I'm not saying they're not – but no London street Arabs for me,' I said. 'Give me a native born at least. There'll be a risk, no matter who we get. But I'll feel easier in my mind and sleep sounder at nights if we get a born Canadian.'"[16] Foreigners may be fine in their own distant contexts, Marilla insists – "I'm not saying they're not" – but not when they begin to stray across boundaries. The exception, of course, is found in her own example of "London street Arabs," which turns on a narrative of displacement that denies these orphans the possibility of any kind of national home ground. Always already alienated, these sorts of foreigners bring an almost ontological meaning to the term; they are the foreigners for whom home was never a real possibility. Not only are they estranged before they ever leave, but they carry their foreignness with them.

The term "street Arabs" did not refer to Arabs in any literal sense but, commonly in the nineteenth century, to homeless children especially those who survived by begging or stealing. In *Street Arabs and Gutter Snipes: The Pathetic and Humorous Side of Young Vagabond Life in the Great Cities, with Records of Work for Their Reclamation* (1884), well-known evangelist and writer George Needham (1840–1902) offered a typically Victorian mix of sensationalism, reformist zeal, and distrust. The point of the allusion to Arabs, Needham explained, was to emphasize these children's nomadic state, given that their rootlessness was antithetical to any sort of domestic attachment. Eager to refute the potential objection to "the term 'Arab' as applied to persons however outcast of christianized communities," in part because "it sounds rough, uncharitable, offensive, and degrading,"

Needham insisted that "nevertheless, the title 'Arab' is, in many respects, the most fitting that can be found. The 'street Arab' is a very Bedouin in the midst of the thronging city multitude, manifesting many of those selfsame traits which so uniquely distinguish the veritable 'child of the desert.'" Street Arabs, almost by nature, are vagabonds in the midst of a society that understands the importance of home. Ironically, Needham's preface described his book as a "plea on behalf of neglected and destitute children, found chiefly in our great cities, and too often educated in crime by unnatural parents or vicious guardians."[17]

If for social crusaders like Needham the term identified a precise social dynamic, a condition from which people must be saved in spite of themselves, on another level the term also encodes an Orientalist expression of distrust. It highlights the dangerous status of these children as outsiders, threats to the social order not through any revolutionary aspirations but as a result of their lack of any potential for integration into the harmonious world of respectable society. The ease with which this sense of class alterity became racially marked, however, illustrates both the magnitude of the anxieties toward this problem and the means that people in the Victorian period found of containing them. If social difference became threatening, it could be most easily negated, not by minimizing difference but by accentuating it, abjecting the problem by treating these children as wholly Other in order to reinforce the social order whose coherence their presence might otherwise threaten. "These nomadic tribes of the city are embryonic Ishmaelites," Needham continued, "with their own dialect, customs and traditions." Like the real Arabs after whom they are named, he explained, they were incapable of assimilation:

> Ishmaelites by descent, they are Ishmaelites in disposition also; their hand against every man, they trust no man thoroughly, save their own brotherhood. Uncertain, vindictive, and selfish, they are the source of apprehension to every traveler …
>
> And so, like the desert Bedouin, there is to be found in every large city a class of lads, whose aims, aspirations, habits, and methods, are the exact counterpart of these we have described.[18]

By contrast, as Marilla insists to Mrs Lynde, the boy that she and Matthew have requested will come from Nova Scotia, "right close to the Island. It isn't as if we were getting him from England or the States. He can't be much different from ourselves."[19] The comic effect of the novel's most famous mix-up – the girl that Matthew almost misses at the train station rather than the boy they expect – suggests just how misguided Marilla's logic could be. She has literally no idea whom she is getting nor, in some ways, could the child be much more different "from ourselves": "an odder, unexpecteder witch of a child there never was in this world," Mrs Lynde eventually recalls. Marilla and Matthew likewise cannot get over Anne's unusual personality and monologues: before knowing even her name, Matthew thinks of her on the drive home from the station as a "freckled witch." While he is immediately fond of this unusual child, Marilla does not share his sentiment: "There's something I don't understand about her," she tells him by way of an explanation of why Anne must be returned, and later, she recalls to Anne that "I did use to think you were possessed."[20] Repeatedly aligned with the supernatural, Anne is consistently identified as having transgressed Avonlea's most reliable cultural coordinates.

Not only does Anne's loquacity seem to be about as different as anyone can imagine but her real nature remains notoriously difficult to gauge. She is so adept at recreating herself (Anne with an "e," if not Cordelia) that she seems by her very nature to thwart speculation. Ironically, Anne may be far less interested in her origins than anyone she meets. "Oh, what I *know* about myself isn't really worth telling," Anne tells Marilla. "If you'll only let me tell you what I *imagine* about myself you'll think it ever so much more interesting."[21] In fact, we learn just enough about Anne's background to make the adoption scenario plausible. As Mary E. Doody Jones notes in her account of adoption practices in the period, Protestant orphanages were highly selective; they restricted their care to children of married or "legitimate" parents "as opposed to the 'unworthy' poor, the unemployed, the drunkard or the lazy."[22] Beyond these basic credentials, nothing else is known. In its place, Anne's faith in the primacy of the imagination undoes the opposition between what is known and what must remain a mystery and, therefore, between the familiar and the foreign.

Neither term retains its coherence within a world in which being interesting ranks above accuracy. Her proclivity for fiction outstrips the relevance of factual truths and lies. Subjectivity itself becomes nomadic, unpinned from any foundational recourse.

What the people who meet Anne have to learn is the way that orphans trouble assumptions about the nature of identity. Anne's "slyness and untruthfulness" about the missing brooch temporarily persuades Marilla that Mrs Lynde is right – "It's a fearful responsibility to have a child in your house you can't trust" – only to learn later that both are wrong in their judgments.[23] Like the saga of the brooch, the larger trajectory of the novel is a vindication of Matthew's initial optimism. What makes Anne deviant, among orphans at least, turns out to be her very lack of deviance; it is her good nature (rather than her Arab-like malice) that seems unnatural. Rather than any sort of mystery or lurking threat, this is what Marilla must learn to come to terms with, something that Matthew has insisted on all along.

Anne's development does not so much reverse as call into question the oppositions that structure the nature-versus-nurture debate, however. Her parallels with Marilla suggest a kind of phantom genetics that exceeds mere conditioning. The extent to which Anne seems always to have been intended for Green Gables and, having arrived there, to merge her own destiny with its future exposes the limitations of both nature and nurture. She is the orphan who arrives just in time at the home that she was always meant to have had, the daughter whose future seems to confirm an almost biological connection in ways that exceed both sides of the nature-versus-nurture divide. If Marilla's frustrated relationship with Gilbert Blythe's father repeats itself in Anne's own tortured mix of attraction and resistance to Gilbert, Anne's final recognition of the bankruptcy of her pride is implicitly offered as a compensatory sequel to Marilla's earlier mistake. Anne was always already Marilla's daughter, predisposed to renew and to redeem Marilla's most fundamental traits: as Gilbert states late in the novel, "You've thwarted destiny long enough. I know we can help each other in many ways." Anne's destiny, in the absence of any sort of history worth knowing about, bears witness to this unnatural sense of affiliation: a spiritual bond that runs against the grain of the arbitrariness of her history. Not only is Anne more like Marilla than Marilla ever allowed herself to be but being close to Anne inevitably enables – or forces – Marilla to understand more about herself than she had ever allowed herself to do. Listening to Anne's moral indignation at having been insulted by Mrs Lynde, Marilla experiences an unsettling déjà vu: "An old remembrance suddenly rose up before Marilla. She had been a very small child when she had heard one aunt say of her to another, 'What a pity she is such a dark, homely little thing.'"[24] Anne's moral indignation triggers a very unhomely moment for Marilla, resituating long-held memories in the uncanny light of her unexpected affiliation with this stranger whose arrival was itself famously accidental.

As the final chapters of the novel turn to Anne's maturation, it is not Anne but the people around her who begin to seem like orphans. "The velvet carpet with the pink roses and the pink silk curtains of Anne's early visions had certainly never materialized, but her dreams had kept pace with her growth, and it is not probable she lamented them." For Marilla, on the other hand, change amounts to loss: the night that Anne leaves for Queen's,

> when Marilla went to bed, acutely and miserably conscious that the little gable room at the end of the hall was untenanted by any vivid young life and unstirred by any soft breathing, she buried her face in her pillow, and wept for her girl in a passion of sobs that appalled her when she grew calm enough to reflect how very wicked it must be to take on so about a sinful fellow creature.

The scene bookends and recalls Anne's first night, when "in the east gable, a lonely, heart-hungry friendless child cried herself to sleep."[25] Marilla's stern religiosity marks the differences between them, but her grief highlights a shared frustration with the difficulty of making a sense of home stay in place.

Anne's development throughout the novel seems to suggest that the problem with all questions of identity (and therefore of origins) is the extent to which the desire for it is mediated by underlying tensions that can best be resolved by insisting on the difference between a collective self and those others who are not from around here. If Edward Said's *Orientalism* dramatically highlighted a Eurocentric history in which social coherence could be assured through derogatory accounts of Arabic Others, Julia Kristeva's more psychoanalytically inflected *Strangers to Ourselves* emphasized the uncanny continuity between social repression (the Other within) and abjection (those Others whose foreignness must always be insisted on). Being sure of "how the line between nature and culture is drawn," as Mavis Reimer puts it, turns out to be inseparable from the struggle to stabilize the line between self and other, or all that can be embraced as local, native, or domestic, and therefore trustworthy, and all that must be rejected as foreign, unassimilable, and therefore dangerously unnatural.[26] To look more closely at a phrase from the novel that I have already spent some time on, however, this may have been Montgomery's point all along. After all, what Marilla insists that she wants nothing to do with is not merely street Arabs, but *London* street Arabs, a phrase that had, by 1907, become a touchstone for a number of often conflicting ideas about self and other, nature and nurture, the local and everything that could be dismissed by insisting on the equation between foreign and unnatural. The well-known Victorian artist Dorothy Stanley had published in 1890 a book by the same name – *London Street Arabs* – with an introductory essay that questioned many of Needham's judgments. Recalling her life-long affection for London's "ragamuffin[s]," Stanley took exception to the distortions that characterized most accounts of these sorts of people.

> Most of the pictures I had seen of ragged life appeared to me to be false and made up. They were all so deplorably piteous – pale, whining children with sunken eyes … dying match girls, sorrowful watercress girls, emaciated mothers clasping weeping babies. How was it, I asked myself, that the other side is so seldom represented? The merry, reckless, happy-go-lucky urchin; the tomboy girl … No ragamuffin is ever vulgar or common. If the pictures render him so, it is the artist's fault, since he always puts himself into his work.

Stanley's essay bears witness to the importance but also to the difficulties implicit in this sort of redemptive gesture. Eager to coach others on how they too might position themselves to paint these sorts of more appreciative portraits of ragamuffins, Stanley offered some practical advice: "You must first walk about little back streets and alleys towards sunset … Then look, and look without troubling your mind to remember; take it all in – the movements, the groups, the attitudes – without troubling yourself much as to detail." Having waited until a particular image "takes your fancy," readers are invited to proceed more methodically, in part by hiring some of these homeless children as models. "Perhaps the necessary ingredients of your picture are a red-headed boy, and a fair curly-headed boy, a small girl and a big baby, and an old hamper. All these have to be found and brought home." She adds that, "One must not be too exacting about the colour and style of hair and dress, etc." These sorts of inaccuracies can be compensated for through a variety of secondary strategies. "The best thing is to keep your properties in the studio. A good supply of rags is essential (carefully fumigated, camphored, and peppered), and you can then dress up your too respectable ragamuffin till he looks as disreputable as you can wish." Or, "if you have no rags to start with, and shrink from keeping them *by* you," there is an alternative strategy: "find an average boy, win his confidence, give him six pence, and promise him another six pence if he will bring you a boy more ragged than himself." Continue to do this with each new and more ragged boy and very soon you can "get down to a very fine specimen." Such an approach has its advantages – one need not keep a supply of rags in one's studio – but it is not without dangers of its own. "The drawback is the loss of time caused by the cajoling, the difficulty of explaining what you want and why you want it, and the great probability of failure after all your time, energy, and sixpences."[27]

These more dubious aspects of Lady Stanley's advice were almost certainly intended to be read ironically as a satirical critique in the social hypocrisies of her contemporaries, but her subsequent reflection on the need to keep these children adequately entertained reflects the difficulties that the spectre of orphans presented to even the more progressive observers. Her piano was one of their favourite attractions, she explained, though allowing the children to use it rendered it "prematurely old": "Not so long ago it was quite a smart well-toned piano, now its pedals are irresponsive. The ivory has dropped or been picked off the notes, and the white keys are smudged over by small black finger marks." Even more frustrating, however, was the task of trying to teach them to play. "You take the ragamuffin's fore-finger, which is unduly stiffened, and direct it to each note with a thump ... I do not know which is worse – to teach him or to hear him hammer it out for himself."[28]

In writing fiction, Montgomery was immune to these sorts of inconveniences, her representation of Anne was not burdened with the same kind of contradictions. On the contrary, her depiction of Anne is animated, not merely by Anne's own recognition of the fundamentally theatrical nature of social relations (the need to make a proper apology or to avoid seeming unconventional) but also by Montgomery's use of free indirect discourse to juxtapose Anne's moral earnestness with the bigotry of the Avonlea locals who respond to her as an orphan. *Anne of Green Gables* offers not just a salutary correction to the Orientalizing tendency to insist on a "false and made up" picture that Lady Stanley objected to but it also offers a critique of the social dynamics which underlie this tendency – the "dark secrets" which must be "reputed" to exist if the coherence of a shared identity is to be maintained. Montgomery may well have heard of Lady Stanley, who was well-known for her depictions of London street life, some of which are still exhibited in the Tate. But whether she had heard of Stanley or not, her own deliberate reference to "London street Arabs" registered her familiarity with a discourse that had crystallized in the decades before *Anne* appeared and highlighted her understanding of the power dynamics that informed its distrust of those whose uncertain background seemed to defy late Victorian efforts to consolidate a domestic ideology. Scrambling the distinction between lines of affiliation and filiation, L.M. Montgomery not only blurs the line between nature and nurture but, more fundamentally, unsettles the ways that these divisions reinforce the lines that get drawn between self and other. It may be the novel's most optimistic insight, and perhaps its most valuable political observation, that as the citizens of Avonlea become less interested in the origins and identity of this "imported orphan" so too do they also become increasingly less strangers to themselves.

CHAPTER TEN

Kindred Spirits: Kinship and the Nature of Nature in Anne's House of Dreams *and* The Blue Castle

Laura M. Robinson

> "… You're young and I'm old, but our souls are about the same age, I reckon. We both belong to the race that knows Joseph, as Cornelia Bryant would say."
>
> "The race that knows Joseph?" puzzled Anne.
>
> "Yes. Cornelia divides all the folks in the world into two kinds – the race that knows Joseph and the race that don't. If a person sorter sees eye to eye with you, and has pretty much the same ideas about things, and the same taste in jokes – why, then he belongs to the race that knows Joseph."
>
> "Oh, I understand," exclaimed Anne, light breaking in upon her. "It's what I used to call – and still call in quotation marks – 'kindred spirits.'"
>
> – *Anne's House of Dreams*[1]

When L.M. Montgomery's fictional characters experience a deep connection with another person, as Anne and Captain Jim do in *Anne's House of Dreams*, they understand that friendship with reference to biological and physical connections, using phrases such as "the race that knows Joseph," "kindred spirits," and "bosom friends."[2] Through these sayings, Montgomery's texts naturalize friendship by emphasizing a belief that deep connection must be based on racial or natural similarity, and yet she also represents these kinship connections as deeply contradictory. In her journals as well as in her fiction, Montgomery's insistence on clan qualities being bred into people constructs a kinship identity that is essential and unchanging. At the same time, her fiction also suggests that individuals can transcend the biological to forge their own kinship relations. Paul Keen's discussion of *Anne of Green Gables* in this volume makes a similar argument that Montgomery's orphan tale blurs the line between nature and nurture, with the result that affiliation is privileged over filiation. In two later novels, *Anne's House of Dreams* and *The Blue Castle*, Montgomery also scripts heroines who are in thrall to the notion of the natural, which works to uphold the patriarchal family and heterosexual marriage. In the former, Leslie Moore is married to an abuser turned invalid as a result of pressure from the last surviving member of her biological family of origin, while in the latter novel, Valancy Stirling languishes in the bosom of an abusive extended family. By having these women escape their familial prisons, Montgomery's texts argue that the "natural" is in some cases most unnatural by undermining the belief that family must be a specifically biologically determined entity. As I show in this chapter, the challenge in these texts to family and kinship ultimately serves not only to disturb but also to overturn traditional and restrictive gender roles for her female characters. In doing so, Montgomery highlights the extent to which the "natural" has often been a social construct used to justify women in subservient roles. By challenging this discourse of the "natural," Montgomery allows space for nature to appear.

My focus in this chapter is on how Montgomery situates the human being as part of nature. Nature is not simply landscape or the nonhuman but is also the human in its environment and, in the case of this article, in its social environment. Many material feminists have recently sought to redress the largely poststructuralist feminist drive to distance itself from the discourse of nature and, thus, problematic essentialism. While the discourse of nature has worked for years to position women as naturally subjugated to men, material feminists argue that attempting to create a false dichotomy between nature and culture by suggesting that all identity is a result of discourse and language is not effective or desirable. Similarly, nature is not separate from culture. In the volume, *Material Feminisms*, the theorists each attempt to develop "a new way of understanding the relationship between discourse and matter that does not privilege the former to the exclusion of the latter," as Stacy Alaimo and Susan Hekman explain in their Introduction. Nancy Tuana discusses her use of the phrase "viscous porosity" in order to understand nature and particularly the human in nature. "*Viscosity* is neither fluid nor solid, but intermediate between them. Attention to the *porosity* of interactions helps to undermine the notion that distinctions, as important as they might be in particular contexts, signify a natural or unchanging boundary, a natural kind." This type of blurriness or fluidity is similar to what Stacy Alaimo calls "trans-corporeality": "the time-space where human corporeality, in all its material fleshiness is inseparable from 'nature' or 'environment.'"[3] To return to Montgomery, then, these theorists lay a framework for examining how Montgomery conceives of nature. Rather than uphold the traditional, discourse-driven construct of biological family and kinship, Montgomery's novels challenge this tradition, and they do so in order to unleash their heroines from oppressive regimes. Moreover, by revealing the operations of the traditional understanding of nature, Montgomery opens up the space for the characters' actual natures to blossom. Counterintuitively, by dismantling the discourse of nature, Montgomery allows a glimpse of transcorporeality, of the human in its environment.

In order to understand how Montgomery's novels challenge traditional constructions of nature, it is important to examine how Montgomery represents the family, usually regarded as a natural entity. My discussion of these two novels draws on the work of past critics who have pointed out that the families in Montgomery's fiction can be conflicted at best, downright abusive at worst. Discussing the "emotional incest" that runs throughout Montgomery's novels, Margaret Doody argues that, for Montgomery's characters, "Too much happiness in family life, too high a valuation of familial claims, may be dangerous" because the families they belong to can be either "a stale site of torment and fixity" or "a place of incestuous stoppage, of poisonously sweet waylaying." My own work on family pedigree in *Anne of Green Gables* and *A Tangled Web* looks at how establishing connections over "blood identity, [over] genealogy and lineage" is necessary in these novels "for the creation of a cohesive community bond." In other words, characters in these two novels create a sense of family by shutting out those with perceived racial difference.

Diana Arlene Chlebek suggests that a subplot in *Jane of Lantern Hill* carries with it a subversive message when the orphan Jody is adopted by two spinster sisters: "within the family structure an emotional kinship comes to replace bonds of consanguity, which stress hierarchy and possession." Chlebek concludes that Montgomery is "wrenching away from an old order, struggling with new alternatives" by contrasting the creation of Jody's nontraditional family with the restoring of Jane's biological family of origin.[4] In this way, Montgomery's texts offer a criticism of familial kinship structures at the very moment that they seem to reentrench them.

Gabrielle Ceraldi similarly explores the complex representation of family in Montgomery's Emily books of the 1920s, tying the "startling dearth of families" to postwar modernity. Drawing on Edward Said's distinction between filiation and affiliation, Ceraldi demonstrates a clear tension between a nostalgia for postwar filiation and the reality of modernist affiliation in Montgomery's Emily books: "For Said, 'filiation' refers to the generational, hierarchical bonds of family, nationality, class, and culture. If the modernist age marks a breakdown in those bonds, it also involves a transition towards affiliative relationships, which are forged voluntarily to compensate for the loss of family and community." Indeed, as Said argues in *The World, the Text, and the Critic* (1983): "Childless couples, orphaned children, aborted childbirths, and unregenerately celibate men and women populate the world of high modernism with remarkable insistence, all of them suggesting the difficulties of filiation."[5] Both Ceraldi and Said overlook the degree to which affiliative relationships appear in prewar works of fiction as well; one might simply gesture to the many orphan novels of the nineteenth century, for instance, to trouble their claims. In Montgomery's fiction, specifically, affiliation occurs in several of her prewar novels: a brother and sister adopt an orphan in *Anne of Green Gables* (1908); another brother and sister, Thomas and Janet Gordon, adopt an Italian baby and their niece Kilmeny in *Kilmeny of the Orchard* (1910); and two unmarried women, an aunt and her niece, keep house together (as do Marilla and Mrs Lynde) and rent their home to four co-eds in *Anne of the Island* (1915).

While I would agree that Montgomery's later fiction highlights a nostalgia for a prewar simplicity, all her works betray a similar distrust of the ease and naturalness of filiation, even where she most appears to support it. Her works thus disrupt the discourse of nature that operates to uphold the patriarchal family. As Benjamin Lefebvre has suggested in his reading of *A Tangled Web* as a modernist text, this later novel represents "an explicit expression of Montgomery's own 'irresolvable ambivalences' about marriage, patriarchy, and feminism."[6] Thus, Montgomery's support for affiliative over filiative relations might be another example of her tentative embrace of modernism. If so, then Montgomery's contradictory depiction of families in her fiction begins earlier than the modernist period. Indeed, Rita Bode's argument earlier in this volume concerning the "mediating spaces" between nature and culture throughout Montgomery's fiction would support my position that most of Montgomery's novels reveal ambivalences about what constitutes the natural. *Anne's House of Dreams* and *The Blue Castle* are no exception in their insistence that filiation is necessarily a construct, one that is always under contestation under the guise of the natural. By exposing that construct, Montgomery clears a space for her female characters to behave more naturally.

The Bonds of Kinship

For anthropologists, kinship might be considered synonymous with the family: genealogical connections based on biological roots and the binding ties of legal marriage. However, kinship studies in anthropology have undergone much change in the past few decades. In their introduction to *Relative Values: Reconfiguring Kinship Studies* (2001), Sarah Franklin and Susan McKinnon point out the ongoing debate over the role of nature and biology in kinship studies. Many anthropologists have come to understand an expanded definition of kinship tied not to biological descent but to alliance. As Franklin and McKinnon suggest, "Since relations of power are central to the articulation of such classificatory boundaries and movements, kinship is also utilized to articulate the possibilities for social relations of equality, hierarchy, amity, ambivalence, and violence. In so doing, it becomes evident that kinship's classificatory manoeuvres can be mobilized to bring into being other categories of relationality – including genders, sexualities, races, species, machines, nature, and culture."[7] Furthermore, Janet Carsten suggests that, while formerly "a domain popularly conceived as resulting from ties based in nature," kinship as a concept has necessarily changed due to "reconstituted families" and changes in technologies such as in vitro fertilization.[8]

Following the lead of these recent anthropologists, poststructuralist feminist theorist Judith Butler yanks the understanding of kinship connection away from the biological family. In *Undoing Gender* (2004), she argues that, rather than a static, knowable, cross-cultural entity, "kinship is itself a kind of doing, a practice that enacts that assemblage of significations as it takes place." What Butler imagines, then – and what many cultural anthropologists have recently come to embrace – is a more open and fluid understanding of kinship that is not structured on blood lines. She argues that an attempt to define kinship necessarily breaks down its very own definition: "the relations of kinship arrive at boundaries that call into question the distinguishability of kinship from community."[9] Rather than the assumption that kinship based on blood ties is somehow more natural than other types of relationships, the inevitable breakdown of kinship's boundaries points out that *all* kinship is constructed.

With great prescience given her time period, which valued clan connections above all else, Montgomery in her fiction frequently establishes kinship relations along ostensibly nonbiological lines, connecting like-minded folk rather than showing that families are necessarily like-minded. While Montgomery's novels deal with locating and maintaining family, her critique of traditional kinship emerges through the sense that friendship, rather than families, is where emotional kin reside. For instance, eleven-year-old Anne rather famously declares her feelings about Matthew Cuthbert: "I felt that he was a kindred spirit as soon as ever I saw him."[10] Montgomery herself agonized over the prospect of losing her first cousin and dear friend Frederica Campbell, who coined the term "the race that knows Joseph," by promoting her kinship status when she was critically ill in 1915: "Frede, my more than sister."[11] These and the earlier examples I cited of the language of kinship applied to intense friendship show the limitations of the discourse available. The necessity of using the metaphor of kin to describe deep feelings for another person demonstrates the ideological primacy of kinship and family in Montgomery's society and imagined worlds. Nonfamilial relationships are necessarily devalued, unless characterized as being like kin. Montgomery's language also thus works to naturalize friendship by equating comradeship with biology. Most importantly, however, this strategy uses the language of family and kinship to expand the limited definitions of those connections, effectively overturning the notion of the biological by exposing the constructedness of what we take to be natural in the first place.

At the same time, Montgomery's writings also expose a deep-seated belief that "blood is thicker than water," as Valancy's cousin Georgiana says.[12] Montgomery's depiction of clans and families suggests that biological roots determine character and are essentially inescapable. The hierarchical clan politics emerge clearly in *A Tangled Web*, for instance, as members of the Dark–Penhallow clan compete for the inheritance of the matriarch's beloved heirloom. Throughout the Anne books, certain families evince specific inherited traits. In *Anne of Avonlea*, Diana comments on Ruby's flirtatiousness as an unavoidable biological trait: "It's the Gillis coming out in her … she can't help it."[13] Similarly, in *Anne of the Island*, Mrs Rachel reveals a prejudice against the Sloanes when discussing Charlie's feelings for Anne: "Charlie Sloane is wild about her, too, but I'd never advise her to marry a Sloane. The Sloanes are good, honest, respectable people, of course. But when all's said and done, they're *Sloanes*."[14] In *Anne's House of Dreams*, Anne cites Mrs Lynde's pronouncement about one of the most maligned families in Avonlea: "Mrs Rachel says, 'Pyes they always were and Pyes they always will be, world without end, amen.'"[15] Montgomery expressed similar feelings of clannishness in her journals. Her response to her son Stuart's girlfriend, Joy Laird, reveals her inability to consider the girl apart from her kin: "The thought that one day he might ask me to accept that bootlegger's spawn as a daughter was something I could not bear. If she had been of a decent family – if she had been a nice girl herself – I would not have minded."[16]

While a central concern in all of Montgomery's *oeuvre*, kin or clan allegiance determines characters' choices and behaviour perhaps most clearly in *Anne's House of Dreams* and *The Blue Castle*. Significantly, Montgomery presents a more negative view of family structures in these novels than she does elsewhere, notably in the Kings of *The Story Girl* and its sequel, the Murrays of *Emily of New Moon* and its sequels, the Lesleys of *Magic for Marigold*, the Darks and Penhallows of *A Tangled Web*, and the Gardiners of *Pat of Silver Bush* and its sequel. In *Anne's House of Dreams*, Leslie's family life has yielded few benefits for her: Miss Cornelia informs Anne that Leslie witnessed her brother's violent death, found her father after his suicide, and had to comfort and care for her selfish mother, who coerced Leslie into marrying the abusive Dick Moore in order to save their mortgaged farm. Miss Cornelia explains Leslie's acquiescence: "Leslie is clannish – her own could never do wrong in her eyes." Soon after their marriage, Dick Moore and his cousin left for their ill-fated adventure to Havana in a boat significantly named the Four Sisters, highlighting the central role that kinship plays. Since Dick's return as an invalid, Miss Cornelia points out that Leslie is "tied to that imbecile for life" because Leslie is almost blindly committed to family duty.[17] Leslie's sense of familial responsibility is also endorsed by Gilbert when he states: "Shirking responsibilities is the curse of our modern life – the secret of all the unrest and discontent that is seething in the world."[18]

In *The Blue Castle*, on the other hand, Valancy has a much larger and more demanding family structure to live up to. Terrified of upsetting members of her clan who keep close watch over her life, Valancy's existence is a remarkably small one: "there were so many things Valancy never dared to do," the narrator observes, because she is afraid of "offending the whole clan's opinions and prejudices – afraid of not keeping up appearances – afraid to say what she really thought of anything."[19] As Gabriella Åhmansson points out, even Valancy's nickname – Doss – highlights her docility, whereas Elizabeth Waterston suggests that the nickname resonates with dross.[20] The family certainly does treat her as if she were trash or commonplace. One of the myriad traditions in the Stirling clan, and one that keeps Valancy in check, is the belief that Valancy has a delicate nature and is prone to colds,[21] a tradition that sets her up for accepting the doctor's misdiagnosis about her impending death.

While Montgomery's texts suggest, on one hand, that biological family determines an individual's identity, they also emphasize that traditional kinship is not necessarily natural or inescapable. In *Anne's House of Dreams*, Leslie chains herself to caring for a man whom she believes is her husband, however, after his operation, he reveals that he is actually George

Moore, Dick's lookalike cousin. That the two men's identities could so easily be interchanged suggests that biological truth is not necessarily self-evident. In *The Blue Castle*, not only is Valancy obviously not emotionally kin with her clan but she also differs from members of her clan in a distinctly racialized manner. From the first pages onwards, Valancy's skin is sallow and her eyes are described as odd, queer, and slanted, the latter in a way that is "almost Oriental."[22] When Valancy marries Barney Snaith, Uncle Benjamin implies that she must have been exchanged at birth. When Aunt Wellington protests, he adds: "She was the oddest-looking baby I ever saw, anyway."[23] Although these bodily markers are noted by the narrator from the very beginning of the novel, it is only once Valancy proves rebellious that her uncle denies the validity of the bloodlines based on her racialized appearance.

Both women escape their oppressive familial roles through medical diagnoses and cures, highlighting a strategy for change. That these medical interventions are highly improbable serves to underscore the fictional quality of the two women's imprisonment and liberation. Moreover, the illnesses that require intervention indicate how nature is always agentic; bodies will be disruptive, regardless of cultural discourse. Leslie's "husband" is cured by an operation that Gilbert recommends and that represents the central ethical dilemma of the novel. Anne and Gilbert disagree over whether or not he should tell Leslie that her husband can be cured: Anne believes that Leslie will be worse off if the abusive Dick is restored to health and does not want Gilbert to meddle in another family's business, but Gilbert prevails, his perceived duty as a doctor trumping all other considerations. Leslie's chosen family comes to her aid when she decides to travel to Montreal for the operation: Captain Jim loans her the money and Miss Cornelia vows to devote her "energies to comforting and sustaining Leslie."[24] As Elizabeth Rollins Epperly points out, *Anne's House of Dreams* is primarily about friendship rather than Anne's marriage,[25] despite the book's title, therefore subtly privileging affiliation over kinship connections or marriage.

Similarly, Valancy is ironically freed from her familial chains the moment she receives a diagnosis of heart disease, which means she will have less than a year to live. Kylee-Anne Hingston argues that "Valancy takes control of her medical diagnosis and thus rebels against social readings of her body" in her refusal to see other doctors or to tell anyone about her illness,[26] suggesting that the disease gives Valancy permission to become deviant. The diagnosis alters the course of her life by provoking her to leave the Stirling clan and to establish her own surrogate family with the invalid Cissy, her father Abel, and their frequent visitor, Barney Snaith. When she later discovers that the doctor's diagnosis was actually intended for a "Miss Sterling" who was not related to her and who, significantly, has no family of her own, she leaves her husband Barney in an attempt to return to the clan and her former submissiveness. Even though Valancy prepares to succumb to her former existence as "Doss" the moment she discovers the diagnostic error, her rebellious behaviour has already necessarily and irrevocably altered her role in the family. As E. Holly Pike argues, Valancy's clan regards her rebellion as a symptom of disease.[27] By having doctors play key roles in the plot twists, Montgomery's novels suggest that an individual does not necessarily need to submit to a supposedly biological circumstance: a cure might be possible. It is worth noting here, however, that these two novels offer up a critique of the medical profession at the same time they deploy medicine as a metaphor for a cure. Anne accuses Gilbert of toying with Leslie in his desire to find a cure for her husband: "I believe myself that you modern doctors are entirely too fond of making experiments with human flesh and blood."[28] Even though Anne is proven wrong in this instance, her exclamation sets the tone for this novel and for *The Blue Castle* as well. In the later novel, Barney is as much an exile from his family as Valancy is, having fled his father's embarrassing enterprise of creating tonics and pills for numerous ailments, all of which are "harmless" and "do people whole heaps of good when they believe in them."[29] Placed alongside Valancy's doctor's typographical error which results in a mistaken diagnosis, Dr Redfern's "cures" might suggest Montgomery's negative take on the medical profession, but these medical interventions actually do cure what ails, if not directly. Valancy finally begins to live because of her diagnosis, and the Stirling clan embraces the couple because of the money behind Dr Redfern's son and heir. Montgomery's novels emphasize that the refusal to accept what is passing as natural – a sick husband, one's sick place in one's family – is the cure. Moreover, the novels then reveal a possibility more natural.

Destabilizing Gender and the Discourse of Nature

Montgomery's critique of traditional kinship structures predicated on nature ultimately empowers her heroines. In *Antigone's Claim* (2000), Butler argues that, "the disturbance of kinship appears to destabilize gender." Clearly, in *The Blue Castle*, Valancy troubles traditional gender roles the moment she walks away from her biological family. The clan's rector, Dr Stalling, attempts to reason with the young woman, to no avail. The narrator relates his incredulity: "A girl who cared nothing for public opinion! Over whom sacred family ties had no restraining influence!"[30] Åhmansson suggests that *The Blue Castle* is primarily about exposing society's attempt to control female sexuality,[31] shown in Valancy's mother's pleading question – "Won't you try to remember you're a lady?" – in response to Valancy's stated opinion about her uncle's ostentatious house.[32] Indeed, after her diagnosis, Valancy takes great pleasure in acting against the "restraining influence" that has ensnared her for her entire life. Her transgressions continue the list of medical parallels, such as when she announces her intention to "have a little fun" (which, to her mother, sounds "as if Valancy had said she was going to have a little tuberculosis") or when she cuts her hair (which, in the time period "before the day of bobs," is "regarded as a wild, unheard-of proceeding – unless you had typhoid"). That her misbehaviour is identified with illness reveals the agency of nature; bodies, like fictional heroines, will behave in inexplicable or rebellious ways, get ill, fail, die. Most notably, Valancy is the one who asks Barney Snaith to marry her, a shocking reversal of the patriarchal norms that are upheld by the characters as natural and normal. Even at the end of the novel, when Valancy has been restored to the bosom of the clan, she reminds the reader of her gender transgressions at the very moment she appears to be restoring the status quo. The final words she speaks in the novel place her firmly in the active subject position: "You are never, under any circumstances or under any provocation, to cast it up to me that I asked you to marry me."[33]

In *Anne's House of Dreams*, Leslie appears to maintain appropriate gendered behaviour in her steadfast duty to Dick, and yet she emerges as the most empowered when kinship relations are most disrupted and is silenced and acquiescent when traditional kinship is restored. Her tenure of care for the invalided man represents a disturbance of traditional kinship, and not only because the man is not actually her husband but because Leslie also seeks "family" outside her legal family in the characters of Anne, Gilbert, Miss Cornelia, and Captain Jim, even asking Anne to "*mother* [her] a bit."[34] When caring for Dick, Leslie is actually quite independent, despite being described as chained to her ill husband: she oversees the finances (as meagre as they are), runs the household, makes all the decisions, and takes in a boarder. The descriptions of her highlight her nature as being one of vitality and passion. Anne is surprised to find Leslie is married as "there seemed nothing of the wife about her," a comment that remains unexplained but presumably means that Leslie does not fulfil docile, wifely expectations. Leslie speaks with "an odd passion" upon their first meeting, and later, when she dances to the "wild, sweet abandon of the music" at a New Year's Eve gathering, "[a]ll the innate richness and colour and charm of her nature seemed to have broken loose and overflowed in crimson cheek and glowing eye and grace of motion." Leslie herself describes her conundrum when faced with curing the man she believes to be her husband: "It seemed to me that I had once been a prisoner in a hideous cage of torture, and then the door had been opened and I could get out. I was still chained to the cage but I was not in it." Leslie's metaphor demonstrates that her life with the invalid is more liberating than her previous existence with the abusive husband. Anne points out that the discovery that Dick is George means that, "there is no cage."[35] Leslie, presumably, is now completely free.

This is where it gets complicated. Leslie's "freedom" means that Owen Ford, her former boarder, can now court her, but when he proposes, Leslie's voice gets silenced. Owen demands to hear her response to his declaration of love: "And I *know* you love me – I don't need to ask you. But I want to hear you say it – my darling – my darling!" The narrator then adds: "Leslie said something in a very low and tremulous voice."[36] Waterston suggests that the ending of this novel strikes false notes in part due to Owen's overly saccharine verbosity, but it is Leslie's shift in character here from the passionate and strong to the "low and tremulous" that is equally off-putting.[37] The final piece of information about the newly engaged couple is that Owen has decided to purchase the "House of Dreams" for his and Leslie's summer home. While this ending is presented as emotionally satisfying, Leslie moves from being Owen's landlady to hearing by letter of his unilateral decision to purchase the house in which she is presently living. Arguably, Leslie's position has shifted from economically self-reliant to economically dependent on her husband-to-be, and her passion is squelched. Traditional gender roles, predicated on nature, trump Leslie's actual nature.

Ultimately, through this disruption of kinship relations, Montgomery's texts demonstrate how the operations of the traditional biological family work to reinforce gender roles under the guise of a static, knowable nature. Her heroines experience the most freedom and act with the most authenticity when they either outright reject or cannot fulfil the expectations of the clan. Most telling is the emotional draw of kinship, which is why Montgomery uses the language of race and family to describe close friendships. In both novels, the heroines find themselves nestled comfortably back in the bosom of family by the end. Valancy's clan accepts her because Barney turns out to be a wealthy, successful man, and Valancy's marriage also establishes her at the centre of her own kinship structure. Similarly, Leslie's engagement to Owen, replete with the House of Dreams where Anne and Gilbert began their married life and which led to the birth of Jem, establishes Leslie as having a family of her own. The novels lead readers hungrily to these conclusions where the heroines receive love and acceptance and security – as Åhmansson adds, these firm resolutions prevent readers "from drawing any uncomfortable conclusions from Leslie's story as it stands before the happy end."[38]

Because of the endings that reestablish marriage and family as central, Montgomery's novels appear simply to reentrench kinship relations, the discourse of nature, and the belief that blood is thicker than water. However, the challenge to the patriarchal family whose existence is justified through the discourse of nature remains the central story of each novel. While Montgomery presents her readers with a satisfying if too easy "happy ending," she disturbs that ending with the troubled tale that precedes it. Epperly suggests that *The Blue Castle* presents a traditional and conservative ending, but reminds us that, "With Montgomery, conventional expectations triumph, but not completely."[39] As Valancy's cousin and rival complains in a letter at the very end of *The Blue Castle*: "Well, I think I'll run away, too, and disgrace myself. It seems to pay."[40] Indeed, Montgomery's quiet message just might be that it does.

CHAPTER ELEVEN

The Empathic Poetic Sensibility: Discerning and Embodying Nature's Secrets

Lesley D. Clement

In *The Age of Empathy: Nature's Lessons for a Kinder Society* (2009), biologist and primatologist Frans de Waal draws from his decades of research on primate behaviour to demonstrate that empathy, "commonly presented as an illusion," especially by the scientific community, is a very real trait which humans share with many other species. De Waal describes empathy variously as our "'inner ape' that is not nearly as callous and nasty as advertised"; "the bedrock upon which everything else is constructed"; a multilayered Russian doll whose inner core is "the ancient tendency to match another's emotional state" and whose outer layers, through evolution, have "built ever more sophisticated capacities, such as feeling concern for others and adopting their viewpoint"; and "a second invisible hand, one that reaches out to others." All these metaphors suggest that empathy is well hidden and difficult to discern, factors that are primarily a result of western society's denial of the existence of empathy as a natural – as opposed to nurtured – quality. "What we need," de Waal declares, "is a complete overhaul of assumptions about human nature."[1]

L.M. Montgomery would concur with de Waal's argument that nature both holds and hides the secret of humanity's propensity for empathy, but whereas for de Waal empathy is a trait inherited from our primate ancestors and honed through the evolutionary processes of natural selection that the scientific observer can study and analyze, for Montgomery empathy is a trait that has been buried so deeply within both nature and human nature that its emergence and transmission demand certain prerequisites of the poetic temperament and of a receptive society. To protect itself "from curious or indifferent eyes," Montgomery writes in *Anne's*

House of Dreams, to remain "inviolate," nature conceals its "secrets in its recesses, – secrets whose charm is only to be won by entering in and patiently seeking" the guidance that an understanding of these secrets might afford.[2] How is it possible to enter into nature with all its varied moods and manifestations and discern nature's secrets? How can the artist give body to – even assume the body of – nature and become a conduit for nature's secrets? In a late chapter in *The Golden Road* entitled "The Path to Arcady," Beverley King retells one of the Story Girl's tales that begins to answer these questions. The tale is, Bev writes, "a very simple little story, that of the slender brown reed which grew by the forest pool and always was sad and sighing because it could not utter music like the brook and the birds and the winds" until a beautiful youth fashions the reed "according to his liking" and releases the music that has long been shut up in the sighing reed's soul and is "set free at last through its pain and suffering." The Story Girl's fable builds on an observation that her father has made earlier in the day: "it is the by-ways that lead to the heart of the woods and we must follow them if we would know the forest and be known of it. When we can really feel its wild heart beating against ours its subtle life will steal into our veins and make us its own for ever, so that no matter where we go or how wide we wander … we shall yet be drawn back to the forest to find our most enduring kinship."[3] With its emphasis on autumn and the passing of childhood, this episode reinforces themes threaded throughout the two books featuring the Story Girl – that mutability is the lot of humankind and that there is a force linking us with everything in nature. If we are responsive to its "wild heart," which may very well include elements of "pain and suffering," we will discover, through empathy, both "our most enduring kinship" with nature and the secret to releasing and even embodying nature's "music."

Montgomery's characters who are endowed with poetic sensibility have the capacity to develop an intimate relationship with nature and, through close observation, to discern and embody nature's secrets, including that of empathy. In Wordsworthian fashion, current or remembered perceptions engage the imagination, but this imagination must be complemented by empathy if nature's varied moods and manifestations are to be transmuted into artistic form. The stages of the creative process, then – perception through imaginative engagement to expression – are dependent on progressive stages of a relationship that develops through intimacy (which requires a high degree of familiarity) to empathy. Empathy is usually conceptualized as a relationship between humans, as "fellow feeling," an imaginative placement of oneself in the situation and perhaps even the very body of another, "becom[ing] in some measure the same person" as this other, according to mid-eighteenth-century author Adam Smith,[4] well before psychologist Edward Titchener, translating the German *Einfühlung*, introduced the word *empathy* into English in 1909. Psychologists today generally view empathy as "a total response" to another person's situation, "sparked by a deep emotional sharing of that other person's state, [and] accompanied by a cognitive assessment" of the other person's "present condition."[5] For Montgomery, however, it can also be a reciprocal relationship between humans and nature. For *I* to engage with *you* and become *we*, the sense of self must merge completely with the sense of other. It is not simply a matter of "our head getting into the other's head," observes de Waal; "it's our body that maps the other's," emotionally and physically. From this core emanates more "advanced empathy," which "requires both mental mirroring and mental separation." If only mental mirroring occurs, then *I* just mimics or imitates *you*, but with mental separation, "we parse our own state from the other's" and a full empathic relationship develops.[6]

Anne Shirley possesses a poetic sensibility, but she never moves from intimacy to empathy, and therefore, her creative potential never fully matures. In this respect, she differs from other artist figures such as Emily Byrd Starr and Walter Blythe, who succeed in negotiating the threshold not only between perception and imaginative engagement but also between imagination and creative expression by "writing themselves out" to attain the empathy required to understand nature on its own terms. This negotiation to acquire empathy is all the more challenging when the landscapes are unfamiliar and less accessible than the gardens, orchards, groves, brooks, and ponds of a more tamed nature because what Martin L. Hoffman refers to as the "familiarity bias" – the fact that "most people empathize to a greater degree" with those "who are family members, members of their primary group, close friends, and people whose personal needs and concerns are similar to their own" – must be surmounted.[7] If he "could change one thing" about "the human condition," de Waal reflects, "it would be to expand the range of fellow feeling."[8] Montgomery's vision of empathic relationships extends to all forms of sentient life, including the domesticated animals discussed in the next chapter of this volume by Idette Noomé. Moreover, the artistic creations of those who have realized their poetic sensibility have the power to take their audiences into an actively empathic engagement with this life. Empathy thus becomes an indispensable component of the subject-artist-audience triad.

Anne's periscopic perspective and visualizing imagination, which enable her to pierce through the seen to the unseen and give her access to the secret recesses of nature, bode well for her developing an empathic relationship with nature; however, her responsiveness to nature is always marked by her need to transform it into something that she can experience at a personal level.[9] In this respect, Anne's privileging of imagined landscape narratives over the details of actual landscape is very much in the style of contemporary nature study advocates, as described by Tara Parmiter earlier in this collection. In Anne's first dialogue, with Matthew at Bright River station, she imagines the wild cherry tree as a grand marble hall, her ideal accommodation should no one come to collect her.[10] Anne's connection with nature consistently suggests more of an intimacy rather than true empathy – the capacity to feel, physically and emotionally, and to think herself into the inner life of nature. In other words, Anne goes to nature not as the artist to discover perspectives distinct from her own but for the companionship that nature can offer her. As a child and later as a young adult, Anne imposes human form and emotions on nature – personifies it – in order to befriend it: she names flowers to make them "seem more like people"; she makes "friends with the spring down in the hollow" and with the varied colours and moods of the winds, all of which she claims as friends or sisters; she imagines herself as the wind caressing her beloved trees, flowers, and lakes; she listens to the whispers of the "sociable" maple trees in Lover's Lane; she kisses a white birch, another of her sisters; and she trusts that pines could provide comfort in times of sorrow.[11] Anne's powers of perception and imaginative engagement with nature are constants throughout her life, as is her propensity to filter nature through her "beauty-loving eyes" and optimistic temperament.[12] When Anne captures her ecstatic responses to nature on paper, the results are predictable. Stuck on the duck-house roof at the home of a neighbour, she imagines a "most interesting dialogue between the asters and the sweet peas and the wild canaries in the lilac bush and the guardian spirit of the garden." Several years later, when *Youth's Friend* publishes this sketch, Anne's "literary ambitions sprout[] and bud[] in her brain," more auspicious metaphors had they referred to her creative process rather than "her budding literary dreams."[13] Ultimately, Anne's anthropomorphic engagement with nature is of the senses – touching and hearing and seeing – and never pierces, and perhaps even prevents piercing, the epidermal layers for the experience to flow in her veins or beat in her heart.

Not all elements of nature are so open to human converse or readily adaptable to human form as the more easily sensed and domesticated birds, flowers, and trees.[14] The sea, the winds, and the stars all conceal their secrets more deeply, darkly, and irretrievably, often making them inaccessible. Her intimate relationship with nature is challenged when, in *Anne's House of Dreams*, the recently married Anne is confronted with a landscape very different from that to which she is accustomed. Despite Anne's having "lived in sight of the sea, it ha[s] not entered intimately into her life. In Four Winds it surround[s] her and call[s] to her constantly."[15] Whereas in Avonlea "a duet of brook and wind" inspires an imagined journey "with the evening star for pilot, to the land of Heart's Desire," in Four Winds the winds are "of change" and the sea's call is of "unrest and mystery."[16] Against such forces, Anne's house of dreams, with its "grove of fir trees behind it, two rows of Lombardy poplars down the lane, and a ring of white birches around a very delightful garden," and Captain Jim's light, which "flashes like a magnificent star through the twilights," "a trembling, quivering star of good hope,"[17] intensify Anne's psychological barrier against gaining access to the spirit or body of a wilder nature:

> The woods are never solitary – they are full of whispering, beckoning, friendly life. But the sea is a mighty soul, forever moaning of some great, unshareable sorrow, which shuts it up into itself for all eternity. We can never pierce its infinite mystery – we may only wander, awed and spell-bound, on the outer fringe of it. The woods call to us with a hundred voices, but the sea has one only – a mighty voice that drowns our souls in its majestic music. The woods are human, but the sea is of the company of the archangels.[18]

Given her life experiences, Leslie Moore, who appears to be "the spirit of the sea personified – all its mystery, all its passion, all its elusive charm," prefers "the struggle – and the crash – and the noise" of the sea better than "when it's calm and quiet."[19] Rather than embrace the sea's "infinite mystery," Anne likens the sea to something with which she is familiar: "The sea at Four Winds is to me what Lover's Lane was at home. Tonight it seemed so free – so untamed – something broke loose in me, too, out of sympathy," Anne comments to explain her dancing "along the shore in that wild way."[20] There is a difference between sympathy and empathy, however, between simply feeling and feeling with a demand for an understanding and even embodiment, which Anne fails to experience. When the shadow of Venus, the evening star, reneges on its New Year's promise to herald in "life's most wonderful gift," which Anne interprets as the pending birth of her first child, her heartbreak is severe and convalescence long as she questions the justice of undeserved pain, "the riddle of the universe."[21] Prior to the death of her first child, the adult Anne – despite her early childhood experiences as an unwanted orphan – does not understand the darkness in life so is unprepared to query the soundness of Captain Jim's dichotomous reasoning: "I reckon when the darkness is close to us, it is a friend. But when we sorter push it away from us – divorce ourselves from it, so to speak, with lantern light – it becomes an enemy."[22] There is, however, a compromise position between intimacy and hostility – that of empathy, which Anne, described in *Anne of Avonlea* as "one of the children of light by birthright,"[23] never achieves because she is unable to abandon her tendency to seek intimacy with nature as she sees it – beautiful, familiar, accessible. While this may result in her literary output being no more than "pretty, fanciful little sketches that children love and editors send welcome cheques for" and poems to which only her family are privy, her humanity endears her to family, friends, and readers alike.[24] She has not given up writing entirely, she says near the end of *Anne of Ingleside*. She is truly a writer of "living epistles," and as de Waal argues, the maternal bond "provides the evolutionary template for all other attachments."[25]

As with Anne, everything seems conducive for ten-year-old Emily Byrd Starr to develop through intimacy to empathy with nature. She initially lives in a house that appears to have sprouted "like a big, brown mushroom" in a secluded dale with her ailing father, her cats, the trees – Adam and Eve, the Rooster Pine, and the friendly lady-birches – and her best friend, the Wind Woman.[26] Emily's intimacy with the Wind Woman is one of identification, permitting her soul to escape social restrictions, and is often accompanied by an inspirational "flash" when her "soul seem[s] to cast aside the bonds of flesh and spring upward to the stars."[27] Excerpts from her juvenilia include the line that "shape[s] itself in her mind" after she has experienced a "flash" – "The hill called to me and something in me called back to it" – as well as her apostrophes to the buttercup, "And you shall always, buttercup, / Be a flower dear to me," and to the blue-eyed-grass flower, "But the poor talent I possess / Shall laurel thee my flower of blue."[28] At this stage of her growth, Emily's imagination is ungrounded, disembodied, and while nature provides inspiration for her poetic outbursts, examples such as these reveal a young girl in thrall to her own responsiveness to nature rather than the mature seeker of guidance and insight from nature.

As the trilogy continues, Emily's changing relationship with the Wind Woman, in particular a series of events at the heart of *Emily Climbs*, marks her adolescent transition from intimacy to empathy as she strives to grasp humanity's "enduring kinship" with the natural world. The writing of the poem "The Wind Woman" during her first year in Shrewsbury heralds the beginning of these changes. For the past several years, Emily has been practising "writing herself out" in the sense of both giving voice to self and exorcising self.[29] Only by exorcising self – albeit intermittently – can she embody another self. Several weeks before the publication of "The Wind Woman," an incident occurs that suggests that, with Emily's having "written out" her intimate friendship with the wind woman, the relationship has evolved. In the chapter "The Madness of an Hour," Emily has walked from Shrewsbury to New Moon and back again following an argument with Aunt Ruth. A journey that begins in bitterness, anger, and rebellion is "transmuted into a thing of beauty," Emily being (the narrator continues) "one of 'the eternal slaves of beauty,' of whom [Bliss] Carman sings"; however, this is a different kind of beauty than she has previously experienced. As "a certain wild, lawless strain hidden deep in Emily's nature" is unleashed by the "wild, lawless charm" of the night, Emily hears the Wind Woman "whistling eerily in the reeds of the swamp" and imaginatively enters a world "not mortal or human. She [has] always lived on the edge of fairyland and now she step[s] right over it."[30] Rather than recreate the scene and the wind in her own image – in fact, there is no mention of her recording this moment at all – Emily opens herself to the less familiar, often hidden elements of nature that can widen and deepen her sense of self and of the world. As an emerging artist, she can now tap into unexplored poetic reservoirs of her soul as she understands more fully and profoundly the density and subtlety of nature. On the evening Emily spends under the stars on the haystack, which occurs several months after "The Madness of an Hour" and the publication of "The Wind Woman," Emily describes the Wind Woman as a multifaceted personality: "a shrew when she blows from the north – a lonely seeker when she blows from the east – a laughing girl when she comes from the west – and … from the south a little grey fairy." Emily's fall from the haystack at the end of this scene confirms that this evening has been, as she states on several occasions, a "milestone" in her growing understanding that, even as she commits herself to serve at the altar of "flawless beauty," ultimately she must humbly serve a much more complex and demanding mistress.[31]

But what happens when Emily not simply experiences imaginatively what she beholds – mentally and emotionally – but is "possessed" bodily by natural forces perceived to be alien to her? What happens when she has a full empathic encounter with the "wild heart" of nature? Will she avail herself of the kind of freedom that Montgomery's contemporary Charles G.D. Roberts claims that the animal story fosters in the reader – freedom "from the mean tenement of self" that "leads us back to the old kinship of earth" without a "return to barbarism"?[32] A year after the publication of "The Wind Woman," Emily composes two poems on the same evening. Emily climbs the hill in the Land of Uprightness, the grove of firs behind Aunt Ruth's, and lets "the loveliness of the evening flow through [her] like music." The world speaks to her of beauty and freedom and youth, inspired by the Wind Woman "singing in the bits of birchland," a new silver moon over the harbour, and "rippled grey-satin seas." She tries to "put those moments of delicate happiness into a poem," but although she is able to catch "the shape of them fairly well," their "soul" escapes her. As she descends the hill, however, Emily is inspired by an "eerie – almost sinister" encounter with nature to compose another poem. The trees, her "old well-known friends," are "strange and aloof." Nor are the sounds "companionable" or "friendly": they are "creeping and weird, as if the life of the woods ha[s] suddenly developed something almost hostile to [her] – something at least that [i]s furtive and alien and unacquainted." Emily records in her journal the "hurt" that this scene has inspired: "It was that little fascinating whisper of something unholy. I was afraid of it – and yet I loved it." Writing the second poem, Emily alleges, "exorcised something out of my soul and Emily-in-the-Glass seemed no longer a stranger to me."[33] Later, Mr Carpenter tears up this poem because it is, he says, "sheer Paganism" with "a streak of diabolism," even though "from the point of view of literature it's worth a thousand of your pretty songs. All the same, that way danger lies. Better stick to your own age. You're part of it and can possess it without its possessing you."[34] Although Mr Carpenter recognizes the distinction that Charles Roberts makes between poetry that "deals with pure description, and that which treats of nature in some one of its many relations with humanity," achieved only when nature "is passed through the alembic of [the poet's] heart,"[35] he advises against her nurturing Roberts's "old kinship of earth." Unlike Roberts's scientifically evolutionary perception that Janice Fiamengo describes as "the possibility of return without regression, a revisiting of origin that is not also a relinquishing of development,"[36] Mr Carpenter's perception, which reinforces those of two other mentors of Emily, Father Cassidy and Dean Priest, enshrines Emily in a mythical time before the Golden Age as an elf or a fairy but chivalrously protects her from being its poet. All three male mentors insist on keeping her in a fantasyland where the self is prominent and advise her to avoid "possession" by elements they believe – and which Emily ends up believing – are alien to her nature.[37] The irony is that, as Emily has recognized, writing generated through empathy enables her to exorcize the pagan or barbaric from her soul.

The title of the chapter in which Emily records these experiences, "'Airy Voices,'" alludes to three lines from John Keats's *Endymion* that Emily cites: "He ne'er is crowned / With immortality who fears to follow / Where airy voices lead."[38] But what if these "airy voices" demand a more prolonged commitment to a complete empathic engagement with nature's mysterious and hidden forces of darkness than Emily's flashes inspire? Will Emily fear to follow? At the end of the novel, as Emily prepares to leave Shrewsbury, she expresses in her journal the hurt she feels because she will "never again hear the night wind in the Land of Uprightness" but consoles herself with the thought that she will have her "night wind in Lofty John's Bush." Several details from this final scene are suggestive of the direction that Emily's writing career will take. Emily's thoughts on the night wind trigger her gratitude to Aunt Elizabeth for giving permission for a lamp to write by, revealing that Emily is still very much bound to and by society's control of when and how she will write, which the names "uprightness" and "lofty" also indicate. Emily then records that her final moments in the Land of Uprightness are spent by the pool, always "a witching spot" for her to linger near, but this final evening the Wind Woman is notably absent. Gazing at the still pool, "unruffled by a breath" and with "every leaf and branch and fern and blade of grass" mirrored on its surface, Emily sees her own face, an image distorted "by an odd twist of reflection from a bending bough" that gives the impression that she is wearing a laurel crown.[39] Emily's reflection imposes itself on the images of nature. "Mental mirroring" has occurred but not "mental separation" as Emily's aspirations for recognition inhibit a humble encounter with nature. Unlike the Story Girl's fable in which the music of the reed – the other – plays through the instrument fashioned by the youth, this image is much more focused on self and what art can do for self rather than what the artist and art can accomplish for nature.

A year later, at the beginning of *Emily's Quest*, Emily's apprenticeship as writer continues, and it is clear that she is engaged with both the beauty and ugliness, "the comedy and tragedy of life": "A world of lost but immortal dreams, lying just beyond the drop-curtain of the real, called to her for embodiment and interpretation – called with a voice she could not – dared not – disobey."[40] And what of Emily's Wind Woman? She has become less humanized, less anthropomorphic, more abstract, more metaphoric – "A thought swayed [Emily] like a strong wind. An emotion shook her as a tempest shakes a rose" – but Emily still has reunions with her old friend when her soul needs renewal.[41] Furthermore, although Emily will never look at life solely through the eyes of prose, storytelling that is more focused on human nature than on nature itself becomes her preferred medium. "Oh, there was beauty in life still – always would be," we hear near the end of this final Emily book, after Emily has won praise for her first published novel. "Immortal, indestructible beauty beyond all the stain and blur of mortal passion. She had some very glorious hours of inspiration and achievement. But mere beauty which had once satisfied her soul could not wholly satisfy it now."[42] While Emily has had several empathic experiences in which she embodies the "stain and blur" of the mysterious darkness of nature, not just of human nature, she no longer seems committed to write of these elements. As Elizabeth Epperly concludes about Montgomery's own "reworking poetry" into the prose medium, "the repeated images and allusions that failed her in poetry helped to create atmosphere, enrich character, and generally modulate the tone of her prose."[43] By "writing herself out," Emily has eschewed the anthropomorphism that hinders a truly empathic relationship with nature and experienced a more mature empathy with all aspects of sentient life than Anne; nevertheless, Emily's world seems too sheltered for her to commit herself unreservedly to the pursuit of understanding and embodying the full extent of nature's empathic opportunities.

One final character, one of Anne's "living epistles," rounds out the roster of characters with a potentially empathic poetic sensibility: Walter Blythe, in whom "the music of the immortals" is "woven into his growing soul," according to the narrator of *Rainbow Valley*, and through whom, like Emily, some voice seems to speak.[44] Is he a throwback to the past, writing poems that, as Gertrude Oliver observes in *Rilla of Ingleside* of prewar poems such as those of Wordsworth, seem "so far away now," poems whose "classic calm and repose and the beauty of the lines seem to belong to another planet, and to have as little to do with the present world-welter as the evening star"?[45] The evening star, of course, is Venus, goddess of love and beauty, the values to which Walter is committed. As early as age six, we are told in *Anne of Ingleside*, a book set before but published two decades after *Rainbow Valley*, Walter had "the remote, detached look of a soul from another star. Earth was not his habitat."[46] But Walter has had to adopt Earth as his habitat to produce "The Piper," a poem that is described in *Rilla of Ingleside* as "an epitome of all the pain and hope and pity and purpose of the mighty conflict" of his world. "*Realities* never scared him – only his imagination could do that," Jem tells Rilla after Walter's death.[47] Walter not only writes of those who follow the piper's music through the "hideous welter of filth and blood" that has temporarily obscured the beauties of nature[48] but eventually becomes one of those about whom he writes.

The full text of the "three brief immortal verses" of "The Piper" is never given in *Rilla of Ingleside*; however, the *The Blythes Are Quoted* opens with a poem of that name, written by Montgomery retrospectively during the Second World War, one that Epperly calls "a lacklustre lyric, … a tepid endorsement of war" that contrasts with the final poem in the book.[49] In the final scene in *The Blythes Are Quoted*, set in the midst of the Second World War, Anne shows Jem "The Aftermath," a poem that Walter has written from the perspective of a soldier who "waved [his] bayonet aloft in glee" after killing "a stripling boy," the memory of which now obliterates the promise of spring and dawn. "Walter never bayonetted anyone," Jem informs his mother. "But he saw … he saw …"[50] Like the reed in the Story Girl's fable, the music released is produced through the pain and suffering of humankind and of nature. Works of "great literature or great art," Montgomery states in a 1928 journal entry, "are growths that have to be fertilized with blood."[51] To create poems such as "The Piper," deemed "a classic from its first printing," and, more pertinently, "The Aftermath," which adopts the communal voice of those who have experienced "the pits of hell" and who "shall not sleep as we have slept before,"[52] Walter assumes the body of that which suffers – he fully empathizes with it – and then one of Anne's "living epistles" dies. Has he died in vain? Discussing the sacrifices that Walter has made, Jem acknowledges that a better world in which wars cannot happen is still in its infancy.[53] Scientists such as de Waal now argue that warfare, contrary to those who see it as "inevitable," "the product of an aggressive drive," is "more a product of hierarchy and following orders than of aggression and lack of mercy" and therefore "conflicts at the deepest level with our humanity." Because "empathy with their fellow human beings" makes it difficult for most people to take the life of another, a better world is not simply a futile dream: "Ideologies come and go," those "whims of politics, culture, or religion," contends de Waal, but the empathy at the core of "human nature is here to stay."[54] Jeremy Rifkin would concur, opening *The Empathic Civilization* (2009) with a chapter entitled "The Hidden Paradox of Human History" and an anecdote of a "surreal 'Christmas truce'" that occurred in Flanders on 24 December 1914, when German and English soldiers "broke ranks, not only from their commands but from their allegiances to country, to show their common humanity. Thrown together to maim and kill, they courageously stepped outside of their institutional duties to commiserate with one another and to celebrate each other's lives."[55] Although Walter has the intensified capacity for "advanced empathy" of the poet, his sensitivity to and abhorrence of the bodily harm inflicted during war are not anomalies; these qualities can be found even in those who, like Jem, consider themselves to be "a tougher brand than Walter"[56] or, as Parmiter's chapter in this collection discusses, the naturalist Carl Meredith who retains his childhood fascination with nature even after he is blinded in one eye in the war.

Rilla of Ingleside explores various forms of empathy. With the advent of war, "the whole face of the world seemed changed," alien and unrecognizable, but this novel celebrates our unchanging kinship with one another and with nature: Rilla's decision to take on Jims when she empathizes with his mother's lonely death and her outburst of love for him when she empathizes with his loneliness; Dog Monday's empathy for Jem, many miles away, and, on the night Walter dies, for Walter; and Walter's empathy with those he envisions killing, which first prevents him from enlisting, and then with the women and children who have drowned when the *Lusitania* was torpedoed, which inspires him to enlist.[57] The novel also celebrates, in more symbolic form, nature's empathy with humanity not only in Gertrude's dreams of the ebbing and flowing waves of the sea but also in those occurrences when nature participates in the vicissitudes of the human condition: "the low moan of the gulf – the presage of a storm already on its way up the Atlantic" on the night the outbreak of war is announced; the lunar eclipse on the night of Vimy Ridge; "the whole planet … agroan with universal convulsion" on "Black Sunday," reflecting "searing human agony"; and a new star entering the firmament – a star that had its birth thousands of years ago – when the tide begins to turn.[58] Most important, however, is Walter's embodiment of "the Idea" – before, during, and after he and his compatriots have gazed into "the pits of hell." This is his legacy to the ultimate kinship humankind can feel with one another that exorcizes the fear to make the sacrifice for "a generation later, when the seed sown now shall have had time to germinate and grow," and with nature when the reed becomes the instrument and the poet releases its music, as shown in the final quatrain of "The Aftermath": "The wind has voices that may not be stilled."[59] In the sacrifice of his bodily existence for the Idea, Walter ensures that these voices will resonate through the memory of heroic deeds and the body of his and future art.

Montgomery understood the importance of developing empathy, not simply intimacy, with nature in all its manifestations and the dangers that our ignoring and even losing empathy could accrue when she wrote in a 1901 journal entry, "Two and three thousand years ago men wrote immortal poems. Today they create marvellous inventions and bend the erstwhile undreamed-of forces of nature to their will … have we not lost as much as we have gained?"[60] For the generations immediately succeeding Walter's, the new order was one that had faith that science will – or even has – turned all mysteries into solvable problems. Empathy, one of nature's secrets nurturing a kinder society, has only recently been "taken seriously by science … It was considered an absurd, laughable topic," writes de Waal, "classed with supernatural phenomena."[61] Fortunately, those possessed of a poetic sensibility – of the powers of observation, imagination, and empathy – have never dismissed nature's well-kept secret, of our enduring kinship with even the most menacing face of nature, and, on the contrary, have devoted their lives to affirming that nature matters.

CHAPTER TWELVE

The Nature of the Beast: Pets and People in L.M. Montgomery's Fiction

Idette Noomé

In a journal entry dated 10 June 1932, L.M. Montgomery writes: "Lucky is purring on the table as I write and looking at me with bright round eyes. How dreadful it would be *not* to love a cat! How much one would miss out on life."[1] This entry raises a number of issues. First, it obviously shows Montgomery's *love* (not mere affection) for her favourite cat – according to Elizabeth Waterston, Montgomery was "cat-crazy."[2] This tells us something about Montgomery, both as a private person and as an empathic being. Second, it reveals a particular attitude to pets, partially conditioned by discourses about animals in her time and partially a personal choice that is in dialogue with those discourses – she appears consciously to prioritize the human perception of the interrelationship between humans and animals and its value but allows for a parallel awareness of the animal as a sensate, intelligent, affectionate, and companionable being. Third, it focuses on a pet, which is a different class of animal from wild animals or even animals domesticated for utilitarian and commercial purposes. The comment also invites an exploration of Montgomery's use of animals in some of her writing, particularly in her fiction.

In *The Blue Castle*, Valancy's favourite author, John Foster, writes about "the woods and birds and bugs and things like that," urging his readers to explore their "enduring kinship" with nature,[3] as discussed especially in the chapters by Nancy Holmes and Tara K. Parmiter in this volume. However, other than mention of a wolfskin and bearskin rug,[4] there is little explicit evidence of wild animals (dead or alive) in Montgomery's imagined world. Hers is a tamed world in which "nature" does not include much wildlife.[5] By the time she wrote, the moose, caribou, wolves, and bears featured in some realistic Canadian animal stories, like those discussed in Janice Fiamengo's collection of essays, *Other Selves*,[6] were no longer found on Prince Edward Island, and the beavers, skunks, and foxes that remained were more likely to be regarded as vermin than as boons by the farming community. Animals in Montgomery's works are therefore mainly domestic, but, even though most of her protagonists live in a farming community, these characters are not depicted as connecting intimately with farm animals, which remain on the periphery of her stories, "a murmur in the background of Montgomery's fiction," as Jennifer H. Litster points out in her chapter in this volume. Matters are very different with household pets, however, particularly cats and dogs. The affection of many of Montgomery's protagonists for their pets often mirrors her own lifelong attachment to her beloved cats, but not all human–animal relationships in her texts are positive. Montgomery uses pets in her fiction to depict a variety of relationships, introducing animals in a range of ways, but mainly to explore, first and foremost, what the treatment of nonhuman animals reveals about humans themselves. Not only does Montgomery's fiction use relationships between pets and people as indicators of moral worth and the potential for empathy but it also reveals a changing discourse about human–animal relations and the place of animals in the world at the time when she was writing.

In Western cultures, a dualist view of the human world versus the animal world dominated for centuries. In *What Animals Mean in the Fiction of Modernity* (2008), Philip Armstrong argues that in "medieval Europe the security of the division between human and animal rested upon theological and moral qualities. Christian dogma, exemplified by Augustine and Aquinas, saw human nature as a conflict between the animal passions of the mortal body and the divine aspirations of the immortal soul." This discourse propounded a hierarchy placing "animals below humans, and angels above … Theology licensed, indeed demanded, the subjugation … of the human's own animality, but also of the nonhuman animals over whom Adam and Eve were granted dominion." According to Armstrong, humanism and the Enlightenment led to a more anthropocentric but equally dualistic vision, fed by Cartesian ideas that humans are capable of thought, as opposed to animals that operate like mere machines and cannot think at all.[7] Industrialization of the Western world, and the concomitant alienation from nature, compounded the artificiality of human–animal relations, denying animals agency in the world, often making them mere objects of and for science.[8]

While it is generally accepted that human–animal relations prior to the eighteenth century operated primarily in the realm of hunters versus prey, which contributed to the increasing commodification of animals as sources of food or beasts of burden, the dimension of pet keeping took a new form in the Western consciousness of the human–animal interface in the eighteenth century. This trend was promoted by the rise of capitalism, the "ascendancy of the bourgeois nuclear family," and urbanization.[9] As Keith Thomas has noted, proximity to pets in this period "encouraged the middle classes to form optimistic conclusions about animal intelligence; it gave rise to innumerable anecdotes about animal sagacity [anticipating science in some ways[10]]; it stimulated the notion that animals could have character and individual personality; and it created the psychological foundation for the view that some animals at least were entitled to moral consideration."[11] In short, according to Armstrong, this shift allowed for "a heightening of the potential for sympathetic identification between human and non-human."[12] Thus the dualist Cartesian view continued to be contested throughout the nineteenth century, particularly in the work of Charles Darwin.[13] However, traces of it survived: in January 1845, twelve-year-old Louisa May Alcott lists a "*Love of Cats*" in her journal among such vices as "idleness" and "selfishness" that she was obliged to overcome.[14] For both Alcott and Montgomery, their love of cats was met with disapproval and suspicion by surrounding adults: looking back on her childhood fondness for cats, Montgomery writes in her journal in 1910: "I do not know how I came by the taste. Father hated cats, mother did not like them, and grandfather and grandmother detested them."[15]

Although loving cats was met with disapproval in her childhood, her fiction introduces cats (and some dogs), engaging with the hierarchies inherent in human–animal relationships by creating narrative worlds in which humane or inhumane treatment of animals becomes an indicator of a human's moral worth. This vision suggests that Montgomery was aware of shifts in the diverse discourses surrounding human–animal relations that persisted throughout the nineteenth century. Some of the older discourses were contested, for example, by new animal rights legislation and the founding in Britain in 1824 of the Royal Society for the Prevention of Cruelty to Animals. Sister societies formed in the United States and in Canada by 1870. Montgomery's awareness of the organisation is demonstrated by her reference to it in "Penelope Struts Her Theories."[16] The Society's views about animal rights are also reflected in the disgust with which Captain Jim, in *Anne's House of Dreams*, speaks of people who keep pets in the summer holidays and then abandon them. He sees these people as committing "the worst kind of cruelty – the thoughtless kind ... They keep cats there in the summer, and feed and pet 'em, and doll 'em up with ribbons and collars. And then in the fall they go off and leave 'em to starve or freeze." He goes on to describe a dead mother cat and her kittens, and his own cat, the First Mate, whom he found abandoned and choking on a ribbon collar.[17] Montgomery felt strongly enough on this matter to repeat this description almost verbatim in "Abel and His Great Adventure," a short story first published in *The Canadian Magazine* the same year as *Anne's House of Dreams*, when Abel tells of how he found his cat, Captain.[18]

Against this background of changing views, Montgomery records her fondness for pets in her life writing and depicts in her fiction (although rarely in her poems) a rich connection between her human characters and the animals they clearly love.[19] Even nonliving cats and dogs, such as the oddly named china dogs Gog and Magog loved by Anne Shirley and the china cat with green shining eyes treasured by Andrew Stuart, are tangible reminders of the affection in which Montgomery's kindred spirits hold pets as companion animals and of people's interconnection to animals and to the living human and nonhuman world around them.[20]

Montgomery's treatment of animals remains strictly subordinate to her interest in humans. She does not go so far as to anthropomorphize animals in her books, despite her enjoyment of books that do so, such as Kenneth Grahame's *The Wind in the Willows* (1908). She was probably aware of Anna Sewell's *Black Beauty* (1877) and certainly knew Marshall Saunders's work, including the bestselling *Beautiful Joe* (1893),[21] both texts which use animals as first person narrators in "animal autobiography" to advocate animal rights and adopt a didactic stance against cruelty to animals. As Jennifer Mason argues in *Civilized Creatures: Urban Animals, Sentimental Culture and American Literature, 1850–1900*, the middle-class home regarded "the proper keeping of companion animals [as] a reliable indicator of good moral character and, in particular, a person's ability to care well for others," adding that pet keeping "came to assume an important place in the discourse of child development."[22] In the light of texts such as *Black Beauty* and *Beautiful Joe* and the reports of the SPCA, by the mid-Victorian period a literate person was expected "to develop [his or her] sensibility and sympathy through the vicarious experience of reading narratives of animal suffering,"[23] and Montgomery could assume that many of her twentieth-century readers shared this discourse. In *Anne of Ingleside*, Montgomery's last novel published in her lifetime, Jem Blythe most clearly articulates the principle underlying her depiction of affectionate relations between pets and their owners. After returning Bruno to Roddy Crawford because the little dog was pining to death for his previous owner and seeing the dog perk up at the sight of Roddy,[24] Jem expresses his anxieties to Anne: "*why* wouldn't Bruno love me when I loved him so much? Am I … do you think I am the kind of boy dogs don't like?"[25] Jem's concern reflects the tacit assumption that animals know what people are trustworthy and bestow their affections accordingly, which guides the depiction of pets in all of Montgomery's works.

Cats and Dogs: Affection for Animals, Kindred Spirits and Boundaries

Given the desire of Montgomery's protagonists for connectedness, including connection with nature in general, sympathetic connection to pets is a strong marker for a protagonist's capacity for sympathy and empathy. In *Imagining Anne: The Island Scrapbooks of L.M. Montgomery* (2008), Elizabeth Rollins Epperly points out that it is "a puzzle that cats play so small a part in young Anne's life," especially compared to Montgomery's later protagonists. Indeed, as the narrator states rather bluntly in *Anne of the Island*, Anne is "*not* especially fond of cats,"[26] an observation that supports the conclusions about Anne's capacity for empathy by Lesley D. Clement in her chapter in this volume. By contrast, later protagonists such as Emily Byrd Starr and Jane Stuart are deeply attached to their cats, an attachment met with incomprehension and suspicion by narrow-minded adults. Of all Montgomery's books, the ones most imbued with cats are *Pat of Silver Bush* and *Mistress Pat*, whose protagonist Montgomery describes in her journal as "more myself than any of my heroines" and who is lent the ink blot cat that is part of Montgomery's trademark signature – one of Pat's letters has "a border of dinky little black cats inked in all around it."[27] Cats abound in these two novels – Judy Plum, who keeps the Gardiner house, owns (or is owned by) a cat named Gentleman Tom. Similarly, there are many images of cats: a "big, dark-red rug with three black cats hooked in it" lies in the Gardiner kitchen, and after the fire that destroys the Gardiner home, the fact that Judy's picture of white kittens survives the fire is, to Pat, "The only thing that seemed to be the least bit of comfort." Moreover, with some self-irony, Judy describes herself as "grey as a cat" and alters an idiom to characterize herself as someone who has the ability to "talk the hind-leg off a cat."[28]

Montgomery uses a liking for pets as an authorial strategy, a kind of shorthand between herself and her readers, to establish secondary characters as kindred spirits, including Aunt Jamesina in *Anne of the Island*, Captain Jim in *Anne's House of Dreams*, Aunt Laura and Father Cassidy in *Emily of New Moon*, and Mrs Meade in *Jane of Lantern Hill*.[29] In a possible self-parody of this rhetorical strategy, in *Mistress Pat*, Montgomery shows how Tillytuck's liking for a cat named Bold-and-Bad cements his position at Silver Bush: "I have a feeling for cats, Miss Plum. When I wandered in here the other morning I thought I'd like the people here because there was a cat on the window sill. It's a kind of instink [*sic*] with me."[30] Some characters overcome a dislike for cats: Susan Baker claims in *Anne's House of Dreams* that cats suck babies' breath and cannot be convinced otherwise, and she links the schizophrenic behaviour of Dr Jekyll-and-Mr Hyde in *Rilla of Ingleside* to the German successes in the First World War, but in *Anne of Ingleside* she becomes fond of Shrimp, the Blythes' pet cat. Even Emily's Aunt Elizabeth becomes more lenient over time. Characters' growth in sympathy may thus manifest in their gradual acceptance of animals. In some stories, animals are linked to human relationships and intentionality, marked by animals as living gifts: in *Jane of Lantern Hill*, Jane adores the pets given to her by her friends, the Snowbeams, the

Jimmy Johns, and Ding Dong Bell. However, although she dutifully takes care of the pricy Persian imposed on her in Toronto by her icy grandmother, she is unable to love it.[31]

In contrast to the variety of cats, dogs in Montgomery's books tend to be rather stereotyped, as loving and faithful. They range from Joe Gardiner's Snicklefritz and Hilary Gordon's McGinty in the Pat books, to the most faithful of all, Dog Monday, who in *Rilla of Ingleside* waits for four years at the Glen St Mary railway station for Jem Blythe to return from the War, a parallel to the faithful women who wait for their menfolk. It is Dog Monday who voices the anguish and pain all the humans strive to repress in the face of human loss and absence. Although Montgomery does not go so far as to humanize animals in her fiction, two dogs in the Anne books reveal Montgomery's admiration of the sagacity of dogs. First, Dog Monday knows his master is leaving and senses the ominous future at the beginning of the war; he senses Walter's death before the news reaches the family, howling all night long; and knows that Jem is alive. Second, in *Anne's House of Dreams* the dog Carlo knows that the man purported to be Dick Moore is in fact not Dick. Overall, however, these dogs do not evoke the same intense emotion in the protagonists (or arguably the author) that cats do. Perhaps, like Emily, Montgomery is "not so learned in lore of dogs as in lore of cats."[32]

A curious limitation in Montgomery's affection for animals is revealed in her language when people are compared to pets, suggesting what Joan Dunayer might regard as a remnant of speciesist thinking:[33] Montgomery's characters frequently express disapproval of others by comparing them to dogs, cats, or other animals. For example, in *Anne of the Island*, Alec Ward cryptically comments on old Mrs Douglas, who prevented her son from marrying his long-time sweetheart for twenty years: "I like cats as *is* cats. I don't like cats as is women." Anne suggests reservations about Philippa Gordon's lack of seriousness when Anne teasingly calls her "a dear, sweet, adorable, velvety, clawless, little – kitten."[34] Such remarks reveal speciesist thinking, in that they label both cats and women who behave "cattily" as inferior or, in the case of "kittenish" Philippa, frivolous. Language referring to human "cats" becomes more complex in later books. Aunt Irene, described as "sleek" in *Jane of Lantern Hill*, "purr[s] over [her brother Andrew] … actually purr[s]." In *A Tangled Web*, Pennycuik Dark's being "as well-groomed as a cat" adds to the negative impression he makes; Aunt Becky comments that Nan Penhallow, who deliberately ruins her cousin Gay's romance, is "switching [her] tail;" her true nature is described as "sleek and self-indulgent and cruel as a little tiger." Readers should thus be alerted that disaster is about to strike when Gay lies in the sun in her bed and uncharacteristically "stretche[s] herself in it like a little lazy golden cat."[35]

Animal Cruelty and Abuse

In contrast to the protagonists and their kindred spirits who love animals, Montgomery also portrays people who do not share this love or whom animals do not love. Some characters fail to connect with animals from ignorance of human or any other kinds of warmth, an emptiness of soul reflected by their lack of sympathy for animals. As a shorthand to a character's nature, this motif is adopted to typify Roy Gardner's mother in *Anne of the Island* and Aunt Mary Maria in *Anne of Ingleside*, neither of whom can stand cats, and Aunt Elizabeth in *Emily of New Moon*, who "would as soon touch a snake" as a cat. Similarly, in *The Blue Castle*, the narrow-mindedness of Valancy's relatives is underlined by the horror expressed by Second Cousin Sarah Taylor and Aunt Isabel at the rumour that Barney Snaith keeps "dozens of cats" on his island. By contrast, the idea of cats "in the plural" sounds "quite alluring to Valancy." In *Pat of Silver Bush*, Jingle's mother refers laughingly to McGinty as "an ugly little dog," adding to the negative impression she makes on Jingle (and the reader) on the only occasion when she ever visits him.[36] However, Montgomery also depicts incidents that go beyond dislike or neglect of animals: the books show far more active ways of hurting animals – animal abuse arising from custom, ignorance, and deliberate manipulative cruelty in which animals are used as objects or instruments to control others.

A bizarre instance of animal killing is tucked with apparent nonchalance into a letter to Anne from Davy in *Anne of the Island*: "Mr Harrison wanted to get rid of his dog. So he hunged him once but he come to life and scooted for the barn while Mr Harrison was digging the grave, so he hunged him again and he stayed dead that time."[37] According to Pierce

Beirnes, the practice of hanging dogs and other animals survived from the Middle Ages, when judiciary hearings of animals (particularly dogs, cattle, and pigs) were held and they were sometimes "executed" for their crimes in this manner.[38] In the case of Mr Harrison, the killing of an adult dog without any apparent cause and the fact that it is reported by a child who does not interrogate the deed suggests that this kind of practice continues unquestioned in Avonlea. Anne is great friends with Mr Harrison and most incidents involving him (including Davy's offhand report) are treated with humour (Anne is not overtly horrified by the incident), but this episode needs to be reread in a different light as a more disturbing confirmation of this man as a hot-tempered "crank"[39] who wishes to assert his right to make unilateral decisions that affect others' lives.

Many of Montgomery's characters seem to take for granted that surplus kittens and puppies should be drowned (in the days before it became more commonplace for pets to be neutered), but her protagonists never make peace with this practice, a sign of changing discourses. A notable instance of a clash in views occurs in *Emily of New Moon*, when Aunt Elizabeth orders Mike II to be drowned and the kitten escapes from the burlap bag, leading Emily to use the "Murray look" to rescue him, as also discussed by Kate Sutherland in her chapter in this volume.[40] Perhaps the most poignant of all cat drownings in Montgomery's fiction is the drowning, in *Rilla of Ingleside*, of the cat Stripey by young Bruce Meredith as a sacrifice to bring Jem Blythe back from the war safely: "I just told God I would give Him Stripey if He would send Jem back." Perhaps more than any other, the horror of this act – which Rilla assesses as "so splendid – and sad – and beautiful" – brings home to readers the distortion of human feelings, even for those not directly involved in war, under the inhumane stresses imposed by the situation.[41] In view of Montgomery's comment in her journal that she did not believe in a God who "is 'a changeable Being whom our prayers can alter' – who will give or withhold according as we do or do not ask,"[42] Bruce's attempt at negotiation would seem futile from the outset. Moreover, despite the approval of this act implied by surrounding characters in the novel, Bruce's willingness to sacrifice his cat nevertheless creates a fissure in the text, what Paul Tiessen in his essay "Opposing Pacifism" calls a "deconstructive wedge … a tiny but disruptive crack in the narrative";[43] since it is Bruce's choice and not Stripey's to make this sacrifice, the incident raises serious questions about the ideal of sacrifice that is celebrated throughout this novel. As Marian Scholtmeijer points out about animal sacrifice, the "actual animal, the animal who suffers terror and dies, appears to be negligible in these practices. He or she is merely a means to spiritual ends."[44] This passage, the reading of which is complicated both by Scholtmeijer's reminder and by a comment Montgomery makes in her journal, thus creates a counterdiscourse that undercuts the surface idealism of Rilla's assessment, which is in line with Montgomery's self-professed view of the war.[45]

Montgomery also uses a child and an animal's death in *A Tangled Web* to open a further fissure relating to religious platitudes in a sickening instance of cruelty to both an animal and a child. In a world in which God can only become manifest in the love that people experience from others, neglected orphan Brian Dark has only one being to love and to love him back – a kitten he calls Cricket, who comes to sleep with him in his miserable loft bed at night. When he returns home after a night away, praying "desperately" that Cricket is unharmed, his Uncle Duncan tells him that Cricket "won't come again. I wrung its neck." In visceral detail, the narrator embodies both the affection between the boy and the kitten, and the physical brokenness of Cricket's "glazed eyes" when Brian picks up the discarded kitten, whom he buries "lying cold and stiff," incarnating the soul-threatening disillusionment and sorrow of the loss: "Never again would he hear the pad-pad of little feet on the porch roof – never again would a soft paw touch his face in the darkness – never again would a purring thing snuggle against him lovingly. There was no God. Not even a young careless God could have let a thing like this happen."[46]

In contrast to the lighter treatment of human–animal relations in most of Montgomery's earlier works, the motif of animal cruelty increases from *Emily of New Moon* onwards, coinciding with Montgomery's concerns about the war and anxiety about her husband and her eldest son. It may have been a motif she found in her reading of material on psychology, given that animal cruelty has been held to be a marker of sociopathy for some time. The strategy culminates in explicit links between animal abuse and the moral character of humans in stories in *The Blythes Are Quoted*, showing that Montgomery's use of animals in her fiction persisted to her final contribution to literature. In "Some Fools and a Saint," Alice Harper terrorizes her cousin Lucia, escalating from nasty pranks to strangling a dog and hanging Lucia's pet kitten, leaving the minister who solves the mystery to comment on Alice's "warped nature." In "The Road to Yesterday," Susette King believes she has run into a distant relative, Dick, whom she hated as a child because he was a bully and particularly because of "what he did to the kitten." The narrator does not explain, leaving readers to imagine the very worst, especially given Susette's horror at the "intolerable" memory. The omission of detail of the actual death or animal torture is perhaps a strategy adopted in deference to the potential target audiences of Montgomery's texts. Nevertheless, the specific inclusion of these deaths raises questions about human hierarchies and the abuse of both the animals themselves, and the abuse of human victims by people who are prepared to objectify and use animals as instruments to gain control over other human beings.

In *Emily of New Moon*, readers encounter the neurotic and jealous love of Aileen Kent, typified by her killing her son Teddy's pets and her attempts to isolate her son by monopolizing and manipulating his affections – a kitten is drowned, two cats are probably poisoned, and Teddy only manages to dissuade his mother from poisoning his dog by threatening (acting on Emily's advice) that he will stop loving his mother if she does.[47] The extreme nature of these acts makes readers aware of an implicit threat to Emily, if Emily should come between Mrs Kent and her son, heightening the Gothic ominousness of the text. Montgomery allows readers to feel some sympathy for Mrs Kent but only by emphasizing how "*haunted*" she is by the mysterious events of her past.[48] In *Emily's Quest*, she admits to Emily that she resorted to this tactic before, killing a dog her husband "loved … so much that I hated it … I don't know what possessed me," adding that this action had a devastating backlash as it led to the quarrel preceding her husband's death.[49] Aileen Kent's (s)mothering attempts to monopolize her son's love may be understandable, but Mrs Kent's shaky mental balance is underscored by the fact, noted by Carol J. Adams, that killing an animal is wilful and purposeful, a "conscious, deliberate, planned strategy,"[50] a dual betrayal of both the person deprived of a beloved pet and the animal itself, since a pet trusts and relies on the humans with whom it lives.

Animal killing as an indicator of moral bankruptcy returns in particularly sinister form in *Jane of Lantern Hill*, in which we are given the apparently minor but illuminating detail that Robin Stuart once had a dog but that it died under mysterious circumstances – indeed, the cook who reveals this information believes Mrs Kennedy poisoned the dog because she was "bitterly jealous of her daughter's love" for it.[51] Mrs Kennedy's action parallels Mrs Kent's pathologically jealous love for her son, but Mrs Kennedy's calculated, manipulative behaviour prevents sympathy for a character who, as Jean Little puts it, is "all the wicked witches and selfish stepmothers rolled into one."[52] Not only does this incident show how far this woman will go to hold on to her daughter, but it casts a long shadow over the novel as a whole: the death of this animal hangs over Mrs Kennedy's veiled threats to Jane. Again, the animal abuse is a manifestation of the distorted relationships explored in the novel.

Threatening or harming pets (and children) is a technique frequently used by men in achieving dominance and in enforcing power on physically or psychologically battered women, as Carol Adams shows in her essay "Woman-Battering and Harm to Animals." (This mode of abusive male domination is demonstrated in "A Commonplace Woman," as discussed below.[53]) Ironically, Montgomery shows similar examples of abuse of animals by *women* to show such dominance – Mrs Kennedy is not physically abusive toward her daughter or her granddaughter but employs all the techniques that Adams records of severe psychological abuse, threat, and loss usually practised by men in abusive relationships in order to control her daughter. Mrs Kennedy effectively imprisons Robin as the object of her affections to replace the late Mr Kennedy, whom she would "never … let … out of her sight for a moment."[54] Adams discusses a number of coercive tactics that I can trace in the treatment of Robin. First, Mrs Kennedy isolates her daughter, limiting her time alone with Jane, cutting her off from competing relationships (including that with Robin's dog), and increasing her reliance on her mother. Then, she introduces debility by inducing the grief resulting from these losses and then repeatedly denying Robin the right to grieve any of them. She offsets this cruelty with apparent indulgences such as the luxuries with which she showers Robin. The demonstration of Mrs Kennedy's omnipotence over life and death through her treatment of animals in her household, in killing the dog and banishing a kitten that Jane picks up to the bitter cold outside, holds an implicit threat to Robin of the loss of Jane, whom Robin is not permitted to love openly. As a result, Jane, like the children of a battered wife, has to endure not only Robin's enforced show of indifference and her inability to escape or protect Jane[55] but also has to contend with the guilt of being unable to protect her mother, leaving both of them without agency. When Jane exposes her grandmother's destruction of Andrew Stuart's letter to his wife seeking a reconciliation, Mrs Kennedy's response is categorical: "*Leave her alone.* She is *my* daughter … no outsider shall ever come between us again."[56] Mrs Kennedy does not use physical violence on Robin or Jane, but the infliction of such harm on animals as third parties instils a layer of menace to her verbal vindictiveness that includes readers in the abusive cycle, leaving them feeling as imprisoned as Jane herself in the scenes set in the Toronto house, and destabilizing notions of female nurture.[57]

Montgomery uses the objectification and exploitation of an animal by a male as a means to dominate in a male–female relationship in the late short story "A Commonplace Woman." Geoffrey Boyd hangs up his own fox terrier and deliberately whips it to death and later goes over to whipping his son "mercilessly." Boyd's strategy, which turns both the animal and the child into objects, without agency or voice, is followed explicitly to inflict anguish on his wife, Isabel, "who crouched on the floor and moaned in her helpless anguish."[58] In Montgomery's portrayal of the incident, Boyd speaks (delivering a threat and an insult), but Isabel remains inarticulate in the face of torture; the dog and the child as instruments are mute; everything is witnessed by equally silent (and silenced) Ursula Anderson. The story's linking of the voicelessness of the helpless and nameless animal to that of the child and two women ironically equates the decentering of the marginalized humans and that of the animal. The scene, including the unspeakable death of the dog, opens up another fissure in the text – by inviting sympathy and empathy for the dog and humans, Montgomery can challenge a lack of connection, as suggested by Wendy Woodward, in *The Animal Gaze*.[59] The scene also invites full understanding of Ursula Anderson's subsequent action, as it motivates her finally to speak and thus claim agency to end the spiral of violent abuse by killing the drunk Boyd to protect her daughter and grandson.

Conclusion

Writing in a time in which human–animal relations – and indeed the relation of humans to nature in general – were becoming an increasingly contested arena, Montgomery keeps her focus firmly on humans, and does not yet challenge anthropocentrism, but does present animals who have some subjectivity,[60] inasmuch as they are depicted as suffering, sentient beings, whose suffering has "ontological implications for the human subject."[61] She has perfected a nuanced and realistic depiction of people's relationships to animals to show the nature of the beast within her human characters and perhaps her readers – their capacity for love is measured by their ability to respond to the unconditional and natural responses of the animals they encounter. In particular, her depiction of animal suffering opens fissures in the texts that urge the reader to engage in a dialogue with that suffering, drawing on the inherent interconnectedness between people and animals to elicit moral outrage at that which breaks down the connective interstices of mutuality and reciprocity to which Bode and Mitchell point in their Introduction. Montgomery's world is no longer one in which Emerson's idealistic comment that "every animal function from the sponge up to Hercules, shall hint or thunder to man the laws of right and wrong"[62] can elicit an unambiguous response, but it does set up what Epperly calls a "dialogic treatment of opposing tensions" in her chapter in this volume. Thus Montgomery anticipates the stance adopted by Jacques Derrida, who argues that animals become moral agents who bring humans to an awareness of human good and evil,[63] and the insights of more recent animal studies – she invites us to work towards the belonging and community that Epperly discusses, in our humane relations with both animals and humans. Let us close, then, with Montgomery's musing on her own affection for some of the cats she has loved (and perhaps their influence on her), when she wonders if they "will meet [her] with purrs of gladness at the pearly gates", adding: "Ah, I am afraid they sleep forever, those little ghosts of gray and white and black that pad softly through the years. But I hope there will be cats in whatever galaxy my future incarnations may lie."[64]

Notes

Abbreviations

LMM L.M. Montgomery

Fiction

AA *Anne of Avonlea*
AGG *Anne of Green Gables*
AGG*(Br)* *Anne of Green Gables, Broadview Edition*
AHD *Anne's House of Dreams*
AIn *Anne of Ingleside*
AIs *Anne of the Island*
BC *The Blue Castle*
BQ *The Blythes Are Quoted*
DS *The Doctor's Sweetheart and Other Stories*
EC *Emily Climbs*
ENM *Emily of New Moon*
EQ *Emily's Quest*
GR *The Golden Road*
JLH *Jane of Lantern Hill*
KO *Kilmeny of the Orchard*
MM *Magic for Marigold*
MP *Mistress Pat*
PSB *Pat of Silver Bush*
RI *Rilla of Ingleside*
RV *Rainbow Valley*
TW *A Tangled Web*

Life-Writing

AP *Alpine Path*
UJ Unpublished journals (University of Guelph archives)
CJ *1989–1900* *Complete Journals: The PEI Years 1989–1900*
CJ *1901–11* *Complete Journals: The PEI Years 1901–1911*
CJ *1911–17* *Complete Journals: The Ontario Years 1911–1917*
CJ *1918–21* *Complete Journals: The Ontario Years 1918–1921*
CJ *1926–29* *Complete Journal: The Ontario Years 1926–1929*
SJ *Selected Journals*

For entries that the *Complete Journals* do not cover, the *Selected Journals* are used.

Published Letters

AfGG *After Green Gables: L.M. Montgomery's Letters to Ephraim Weber, 1916–1941*

GGL *The Green Gables Letters from L.M. Montgomery to Ephraim Weber, 1905–1909*

MDMM *My Dear Mr M.: Letters from L.M. Montgomery to G.B. MacMillan*

Introduction

1 LMM, *CJ 1901–1911*: 208.

2 Epperly, *Fragrance of Sweet-Grass* (2014), 10.

3 Bennett, *Vibrant Matter*, 8, 19.

4 Iovino and Oppermann, "Theorizing Material Ecocriticism," 448.

5 Abram, *The Spell of the Sensuous: Perception and Language in a More-Than-Human World.*

6 In exploring the "interiority of outdoor experience," literary environmentalist Scott Slovic associates notebook writing, in its foregrounding of immediate experience, with several literary genres. He writes: "Many literary naturalists imitate the notebooks of scientific naturalists, the logbooks of explorers, or even the journals of non-scientific travelers in order to entrench themselves in the specific moment of experience" (352). Such a connection is suggestive for Montgomery's methods and achievements and the materiality of her writing practices that links her fictional and nonfictional worlds.

7 Atwood, quoted in Rubio, "Subverting the Trite," 9.

8 Williams, *Keywords*, 219.

9 Clark, *The Cambridge Introduction to Literature and the Environment*, 7, 6, 7.

10 Haraway, *The Companion Species Manifesto*, 3, passim.

11 Buell, "Ecocriticism: Some Emerging Trends," 87.

12 Glotfelty, "Introduction," *The Ecocriticism Reader*, xviii.

13 Soper and Bradley, *Greening the Maple*, xv.

14 Kern, "Ecocriticism: What Is It Good For?", 18.

15 Wordsworth, " Preface' to the *Lyrical Ballads*," 204.

16 Bentley, "On the Confederation Poets' Companionship with Nature: Lampman."
17 Bentley, "On the Confederation Poets' Companionship with Nature: Carman."
18 This section is indebted to Bentley's conclusions about and positioning of the Confederation poets in the three "On the Confederation Poets" articles in *Canadian Poetry*.
19 Under the section of the "new nation" in Carl Klinck's and Reginald Watters's first edition of *Canadian Anthology*, which appeared in 1955, the Confederation poets receive ample representation, and by 1982–83, coeditors Russell Brown and Donna Bennett of the *Anthology of Canadian Literature in English*, while not embracing the merits of all the Confederation poets, continued the representation of their work as well as their critical reappraisal. In Charles G.D. Roberts's "best poems," for instance, they appreciate the "manifestations of nature in New Brunswick from season to season" and discover "a surprisingly modern vision" (I. 156).
20 Bentley, "On the Confederation Poets' Companionship with Nature: Contexts."
21 LMM, *CJ, 1901–1911*: 207; Bentley, "On the Confederation Poets' Companionship with Nature: Contexts"; Rubio, *Lucy Maud Montgomery*, 331.
22 Ruskin, "Of the Pathetic Fallacy," 156.
23 Day, *Romanticism*, 40.
24 Rubio, *Lucy Maud Montgomery*, 300–1.
25 Frye, "Conclusion," 227; Atwood, *Survival*, 45.
26 Soper and Bradley, *Greening the Maple*, xxvii, xxix.
27 Relke, *Greenworld(l)ds*, passim. See especially "Introduction: A Literary History of Nature," 11–37; Boyd, *Garden Plots.*
28 Buss, "Women and the Garrison Mentality," 126, 128.
29 Peterman and Ballstadt, "Introduction" to *Forest and Other Gleanings*, 12; Steffler and Steffler, "If We Would Read It," 124.
30 Urquhart, *L.M. Montgomery*, 53.
31 Fetterley and Pryse, *Writing out of Place*; Kilcup, *Fallen Forests*, 3.
32 Iovino and Oppermann, "Material Ecocriticism: Materiality," 80. See also their edited collection of essays, *Material Ecocriticism*.

33 Bennett, *Vibrant Matter*, 120.
34 Barad, *Meeting the Universe Halfway*, 137.
35 Iovino and Oppermann, "Material Ecocriticism: Materiality," 79.
36 Gammel, and Epperly, eds. *L.M. Montgomery and Canadian Culture*; Gammel, ed. *Making Avonlea*; Gammel, ed. *Intimate Life*; Mitchell, ed. *Storm and Dissonance.*
37 Gammel, ed. *Looking for Anne*; Gammel and Lefebvre, eds. *Anne's World*; Blackford, ed. *100 Years of Anne;* Ledwell and Mitchell, eds. *Anne Around the World.*
38 Fiamengo, "Towards a Theory," 230, 228, 236.
39 Doody, *The Annotated Anne of Green Gables*, 25; Holmes, "How Green," 386.
40 Gammel, "Safe Pleasures for Girls," 126n2, 118.
41 Gammel, "Embodied Landscape Aesthetics," 243.
42 Posey, "Ethereal Etchings," 102.
43 Grafton, "Girls and Green Space," 118.
44 Salah, "Girls in Bonds," 99.
45 At the 2016 LMM Institute Conference, University of Prince Edward Island, Carolyn Strom Collins's opening plenary paper, " Pure as Pearls of Dew': Searching for the Ideal Woman in the Poetry of L.M. Montgomery," and its reception signalled the growing interest in Montgomery's verse. Also in 2016, the annual Lucy Maud Montgomery Day of the LMM society of Ontario, honouring Montgomery's contribution to Canadian literature, had as its theme "A Celebration of Poetry."
46 Rodman, "Empowering Place," 643.
47 Heise, *Sense of Place*, 114.
48 Kilcup, *Fallen Forests*, 11.
49 Soper, *What Is Nature?* 155.
50 Alaimo, *Bodily Natures*, 2, 4.
51 Whitman, "Song of Myself," l. 99–101, l. 663, l. 1340–1.

Chapter One

1 A much revised and expanded version of the section "Queer Ecologies: Islands, Fires, and *After the Fire*" appears in Sandilands,

"Queer Life?" My thanks to the reviewers of this chapter, anonymous and otherwise, for their helpful comments.

2 LMM, *MP*, 270, 271; ellipses in original.

3 LMM, *PSB*, 278; ellipses in original.

4 Mitchell, "Introduction," *Storm*, 6.

5 In the field of social anthropology, "patrilocality" refers to the tradition whereby a married couple resides near or with the husband's parents, rather than the wife's.

6 LMM, *MP*, 179; ellipses in original.

7 Montgomery emphasizes that Pat has a particular attachment to the trees of Silver Bush (and even the trees on other people's land that she can see from Silver Bush, as her sense of place is not entirely confined to her family's property). She mourns the loss of every one and especially refuses to allow anyone to touch the birch grove.

8 LMM, *MP*, 273; ellipses added. He had also been sent a deathbed note by Judy Plum telling him of the end of Pat's engagement to neighbour David Kirk, but that fact alone was not enough to bring him back to Prince Edward Island. Of course, it is clear that Hilary loves Pat and that his visit is also motivated by compassion, but he clearly arrives with a sense of entitlement: the words to possess her are the very first he utters.

9 Doody, "L.M. Montgomery," 46.

10 MacDonald, "Reflections of the Great Depression," 155.

11 Sheckels, *Island Motif*, 138.

12 Garrard, "Problems Concerning Islands," 12.

13 See ibid., 17.

14 See ibid., 20–1.

15 Botkin, *Discordant Harmonies*, 69.

16 For a fascinating study of the role of fire in social/ecological relationships, see Stephen J. Pyne's *Fire: A Brief History*. Pyne might argue that one of the reasons the birch grove burns so readily is the fact that Pat insists that no trees in it get cut down: "And no tree was ever cut in the grove of white birches behind the house. *That* would have been sacrilege" (*MP*, 9). Not clearing trees and undergrowth, and simultaneously preventing broadcast burning,

is a recipe for out-of-control wildfire. Pyne's work is indispensable to understanding the large boreal wildfires that have made so much news in recent Canadian history; see also Sandilands, "Combustion."

17 Rule, *After the Fire*, 1.

18 Ibid., 164.

19 See Rule, "Stumps."

20 Rubio, *Lucy Maud Montgomery*, 423. Although I agree with Doody that the Pat novels (especially *Mistress Pat*) include Montgomery's rather melancholic exploration of the nature of nostalgia, I would argue that they also involve her increasing regret over the heteronormative conventions (marriage and motherhood) in which her own life was so clearly mired at the time.

21 LMM, *PSB*, 135.

22 Sheckels, *Island Motif*, 139.

23 Doody, "L.M. Montgomery," 42.

24 LMM, *PSB*, 30.

25 Ibid., 221. I emphasize, here, that Joe's departure enables Sid – who is also attached to Silver Bush but whose attachment is never pathologized – to be the inheritor of the farm without contest. His relationship to place is naturalized by patrilocal institution; Pat's is not.

26 LMM, *MP*, 210. One of the clearest examples of this reflectiveness comes after Bets's death, in which Pat notes the ways in which memory becomes part of the landscape: "And the Secret Field was changed somehow … more beautiful than ever but still … not just the same" (*PSB*, 231; ellipses in original).

27 There is much to say about Judy Plum and surprisingly little has been written about her. Although Silver Bush is every bit as much Judy's spiritual and physical home as Pat's (she also dreads the possibility of a move), she cannot even *imagine* inheriting it because she is a servant, legally related to the land only because she is employed by the family that owns it. Yet, as Aoife Emily Hart notes in a very smart article that challenges a reading of Judy as only and always a fool-like stock caricature of Irishness, Judy's magical agency

(combined, I would add, with her exceptional domestic competence) also allow her to act "as an alternative feminist figure of performative womanhood for Pat's own negotiations with patriarchal authority" ("There's Minny a One," 210): this feminism is very much grounded in place. It is fitting, then, that Judy never has to leave: she dies at Silver Bush before the fire.

28 MacDonald, "Reflections of the Great Depression," 154.

29 LMM, *PSB*, 5; ellipses in original. It is noteworthy that, even at age seven, Pat never considers that she might not really need Sid at all.

30 Sheckels, *Island Motif*, 141.

31 LMM, *PSB*, 128.

32 LMM, *MP*, 121.

33 It is important to remember, here, that fire can be an agent of renewal as well as destruction: Indigenous communities in many parts of North America and elsewhere use broadcast burning as a form of environmental management, both to prevent wildfire and to create habitats suitable for certain kinds of plants and animals. Along with settler colonialism came the imposition of a regime of private property that was decidedly pyrophobic: fire was to be prohibited at all costs in order to protect white settler interests and spatial arrangements (see Pyne, *Fire*; Sandilands, "Combustion"). Of course, settler colonial private property relations are inextricably linked to heteronormativity: it is not, then, much of a stretch to argue that white settler heteronormativity (of which May Binnie is a poster child) creates a fire hazard.

34 Holmes, "How Green Is *Green Gables*?" 377.

35 LMM, *PSB*, 188; *MP*, 1. I would argue that the Pat novels play with a variety of familial, social, and community metaphors for nature; there are certainly large trees that are felled in the heights of their masculine adulthood but the overall impression is of a familial and domestic ecology, full of flowers and secrets and old-woman rows of trees and "'Kiss-me-quicks' … but you couldn't call [them] that to a boy" (*PSB*, 146).

36 In her biographical account, Rubio suggests that Montgomery reacted with absolute disgust at the thought of Isabel Anderson's

homoerotic fantasy of lying "spoon fashion" with her "all through a long long night," (Rubio, *Lucy Maud Montgomery*, 397; see also LMM, 1 March 1930, *SJ*, 4: 35).

37 LMM, *PSB*, 72.

38 LMM, *MP*, 273; ellipses in original.

39 Ibid.; ellipsis in original.

40 On this note, it is worth pointing out that there is a connection between the fantasy of stasis portrayed in the Pat novels and the real landscape of Prince Edward Island in which the novels are set. Ernest and Myrtle Webb, to whom *Mistress Pat* is dedicated, in the 1920s operated "a tearoom and tourist home in 'Green Gables'" (Rubio, *Lucy Maud Montgomery*, 485), the former home of Montgomery's cousins David and Margaret Macneill; Montgomery would often stay with them when she went back to Cavendish for visits, and it is reasonable to say that the "Green Gables" site is not only the basis for Avonlea but also partly the inspiration for Silver Bush (in spite of the fact that the Campbell home in Park Corner, PEI, is now dubbed "Silver Bush"). That tearoom was included in the land purchased by the federal government in 1936 to be Cavendish (and later Prince Edward Island) National Park. If there is any modern nature institution that resembles a pastoral fantasy for an unchanging nature, it would be the national park, a form of nature "preserve" that is truly caught in the middle of conflicting desires for stasis (recreational value) and change (ecological succession). Indeed, one of the most plaguing problems for national park management concerns fires: in order for park-natures to remain "in pristine condition," many Canadian parks have for decades suppressed the forest fires that, under other circumstances, would have periodically cleared the trees and bush and allowed them to grow again. Although park managers are now actively involved in controlled burning, many national parks are nonetheless, tinderboxes now, so choked with dead undergrowth that any fire would be virtually uncontrollable; in addition, many species that rely on the periodic destruction and regeneration of forests find parks to be entirely unsuitable habitats. In the case of Green Gables and PEI National Park, then, the pastoral fantasy that is so clearly unsus-

tainable in Silver Bush has, rather unfortunately, trapped nature itself quite directly and partly in Montgomery's name. For discussions of Montgomery's ambivalence about the park, see Holmes, "How Green Is *Green Gables*?" 387; Gerson, "Seven Milestones," 23.

Chapter Two

I am indebted to Professor Mary Rubio, who made Charles Macneill's diary and Montgomery's comments on it available to me during my research visit to the University of Guelph archives in 1994, and to Benjamin Lefebvre for encouraging me to write this paper and sharing his copy of "Come Back with Me to Prince Edward Island."

1 LMM, *JLH*, 117.

2 Trillin, "Anne of Red Hair," 217.

3 Review of *Anne of Green Gables* (*Spectator*), 426.

4 LMM, 15 October 1908, *CJ 1901–1911*: 199.

5 Fiamengo, "Towards a Theory," 232, 227, 228.

6 Ibid., 228, 233, 237.

7 LMM, 27 January 1911, *CJ 1901–1911*: 347–57. For more on the links between Cavendish and Avonlea, see Brouse, "Maud Squad"; Lefebvre, "'Small World After All'"; MacLeod, "On the Road."

8 Gartmore is located some twenty-five miles from Stirling in Scotland; there is a country house (Gartmore House) and estate in the village. Charles Macneill's Perthshire ancestors likely came from near this settlement.

9 LMM, 1 March 1925, UJ, 6: 325.

10 LMM, *AGG*, 2; 1 March 1925, UJ, 6: 345. These comments by LMM form part of the extensive reminiscences that follow the diary's transcription. Both are included under the journal entry heading of 1 March 1925.

11 LMM, 1 March 1925, UJ, 6: 327.

12 LMM, 1 March 1925, *SJ*, 3: 220.

13 "'Old-Timers' Stories," 5.

14 LMM, 1 March 1925, *SJ*, 3: 222.

15 Rubio, *Lucy Maud Montgomery*, 333.

16 See LMM and Lefurgey, " … where has my yellow garter gone?'" The diary is transcribed in the second volume of LMM's typescript journal within entries dated 1903 (see Litster, "'Secret' Diary," 105n3).

17 LMM, 1 March 1925, UJ, 6: 327.

18 Ibid.; quoted in LMM, "Notes," 1 March 1925, *SJ*, 3: 421.

19 LMM, 1 March 1925, UJ, 6: 325. Like Marilla Cuthbert, who goes to town to see a travelling oculist, Charles Macneill had to trek to New Glasgow or Charlottetown in search of medical care for his eye.

20 LMM, 1 March 1925 (Charles Macneill, 12 October 1892; 16 February 1893; 5 May 1896) UJ, 6: 249, 260, 269. The Clarks and McKenzies were longstanding Cavendish families; nearby Rustico is, as the names suggest, a notable Acadian settlement – presumably Messrs Doucet(te) and Gallant kept a store there.

21 LMM, 1 March 1925 (Charles Macneill, 2 January 1898, 26 February 1898, and 16 July 1898) UJ, 6: 287–8, 298, 324. Mr Robertson was the Presbyterian minister in Cavendish until 1899, Mr Jackson the Baptist. The Robertsons and Stewarts were Cavendish families; Albert, Russell, Leila, and Alexander were four of Charles Macneill's children. Lorenzo Toombs was the husband of another daughter, Minnie, and Letty (Albert's daughter) was Charles Macneill's young grandchild. Montana was the name local farmers gave to a piece of land. The Cosgroves would have been Irish Catholics thus, in part, Macneill's disapproval.

22 Quoted in LMM, 1 March 1925 (Charles Macneill, 8 March 1898), UJ, 6: 300–1. A diary entry of 3 February 1898 alludes to "great consternation" in Cavendish when James Laird's will cannot be found (UJ, 6: 295).

23 LMM, 1 March 1925, UJ, 354–5; *EQ*, 22; *PSB*, 31; *MP*, 216.

24 See Macneill's diary entries of 24 February 1896, 13 February 1897, and 14 March 1897, quoted in LMM, 1 March 1925, UJ, 6: 264, 273, 275. LMM wrote that Charles Macneill "was always very satirical about his boys'" little outings. He had an odd habit of writing that they had "gone on a mission" to the Scotch or "'to the American

Jews' when they took some of their lady friends driving," LMM, 1 March 1925, UJ, 6: 349.

25 LMM, 1 March 1925, UJ, 6: 344–5. In fact, Macneill's diary contains a number of references to reading the *Guardian*, the *Patriot*, and the *Montreal Witness*.

26 Ibid., 350.

27 Ibid.

28 Ibid., (Charles Macneill, 2 February 1896), 262. The problems the weather posed for ministers and congregations was also captured in LMM's and Nora Lefurgey's comic diary, where Lefurgey writes, "we went to church on Sunday night but Mr Mac [Rev Major MacIntosh] did not come" (3 March 1903) and "It is pouring rain and we have no preaching anywhere within come-at-able distance" (22 March 1903), Montgomery and Lefurgey, "'where has my yellow garter gone?'" 53, 56.

29 LMM, 1 March 1925, UJ, 6: 328, 330–1, 332.

30 Ibid., 333, 331.

31 LMM, *AGG*, 126, 76.

32 Ibid., 206. As the editors of *The Annotated Anne of Green Gables* point out, "No prime minister would choose to visit Charlottetown in the dead of winter, because of the danger of having the Strait freeze over and not being able to get out" (Barry et al, *The Annotated Anne*, 199n1).

33 LMM, *AGG*, 200.

34 LMM, *AA*, 209.

35 LMM, 2 January 1905, *CJ 1901–1911*: 119.

36 LMM, 1 March 1925, UJ, 6: 343.

37 Ibid., 339.

38 LMM, *AGG*, 2.

39 Maud Montgomery attained top marks in agriculture when she studied at Prince of Wales College (see LMM, *CJ 1889–1900*: 216n1). Anne Shirley also studies agriculture, where she finds out "at last what makes the [Island] roads red" (LMM, *AGG*, 139).

40 LMM, *AIS*, 81.

41 LMM, *RI*, 275.

42 LMM, *AIS*, 128.
43 LMM, 1 March 1925, UJ, 6: 353.
44 In these years LMM was pursuing her education and her teaching career: college in Charlottetown (1893), teaching in Bideford (1894–5), university in Halifax (1895–6), and teaching again in Belmont (1896–7) and in Lower Bedeque (1897–8).
45 LMM, 1 March 1925, UJ, 6: 362; ellipsis in original.
46 Rubio, *Lucy Maud Montgomery*, 481. This commission is referred to by LMM as coming in some months previously in a journal entry of 9 April 1936.
47 LMM, 9 April 1936, *SJ*, 5: 60.
48 Changing nature in Prince Edward Island was also in LMM's mind in 1936 as plans were beginning to take shape for the creation by the Canadian government of a national park on the North Shore, a location chosen partly for the shoreline's natural beauty and partly to honour Montgomery's books. In *Jane*, Montgomery sought to capture Island nature before another change altered it forever.
49 LMM, "Come Back with Me," 37.
50 Waterston, Untitled lecture.
51 LMM, *JLH*, 65; ellipses in original.
52 Waterston, *Magic Island*, 201.
53 LMM, *JLH*, 60.
54 Ibid., 136, 211.
55 Waterston, *Magic Island*, 202.
56 LMM, *JLH*, 107, 90, 106.

Chapter Three

1 LMM, *BQ*, 115.
2 Copeland, "The Wild and Wild Animal Characters in the Ecofeminist Novels of Beatrix Potter and Gene Stratton-Porter," 79.
3 Stratton-Porter, *Freckles*, 23, 55.
4 Brooks, *Speaking for Nature*, 178, 180.
5 Long, *Gene Stratton-Porter*, 148–9.
6 MacEachern, "Changing Ecologies," 361.
7 See "National Parks of Canada," and "Canada National Parks Act."

8 Altmeyer, "Three Ideas of Nature," 96–7.
9 LMM, *BC*, 217; Stratton-Porter, *Girl of the Limberlost*, 195; LMM, *RI*, 13.
10 Altmeyer, "Three Ideas of Nature," 103.
11 See LMM, 30 July 1922, *SJ*, 3: 61–2.
12 Brooks, *Speaking for Nature*, 11.
13 Rubio, *Lucy Maud Montgomery*, 331.
14 Long, *Gene Stratton-Porter*, 174.
15 Qtd. in ibid., 164.
16 Richards, *Gene Stratton-Porter*, 39.
17 Meehan, *Lady of the Limberlost*, 127.
18 The description of this experience in the Long biography is nearly identical to the situation in *Freckles* where the Bird Woman photographs his chickens (Long, *Gene Stratton-Porter*, 155–8; Stratton-Porter, *Freckles*, 84–5).
19 Ford, "How to Cocoon," 150.
20 See Epperly, *Through Lover's Lane*, 146, 158, 160–2; Rubio, *Lucy Maud Montgomery*, 650.
21 LMM, "Spring in the Woods," 59; *BC*, 25.
22 Booth, *Rhetoric of Fiction*, 73.
23 Rubio, *Lucy Maud Montgomery*, 330.
24 Moslund, "The Presencing of Place in Literature," 31.
25 Ibid.
26 Merleau-Ponty as qtd in Moslund, "The Presencing of Place in Literature," 31.
27 Clark, "Phenomenology," 279.
28 Stratton-Porter, *Freckles*, 61.
29 Gifford, *Pastoral*, 2.
30 Frank, *Idea of Spatial Form*, 33, 63.
31 Mickelsen, "Types of Spatial Structure," 65, 76, 63.
32 Friedman, "Spatial Poetics," 192.
33 Moslund, "The Presencing of Place," 30.
34 Mazel, "American Literary Environmentalism," 139, 141.
35 Lotman, "Origin of Plot," 161, 167.
36 Gifford, *Pastoral*, 148.
37 Wadland, "Wilderness and Culture," 13.
38 Jackson, *Becoming Native*, 15.

39 Marx, *Machine in the Garden*, 364.
40 Gifford, *Pastoral*, 81.
41 Long, *Gene Stratton-Porter*, 174.
42 LMM, "Spring in the Woods," 61; *BC*, 18.

Chapter Four

1 Thoreau, *Walden*, 90–1.
2 Karr, *Authors and Audiences*, 129; *GGL*, 24.
3 LMM, *AIS*, 160.
4 Merchant, *Reinventing Eden*, 226.
5 LMM, *AGG*(Br), 77, 318.
6 Conlogue, *Working the Garden*, 20.
7 Pollan, *Second Nature*, 193.
8 Pollan, *Botany of Desire*, xvi, subtitle, xv.
9 Mezei and Briganti, "Reading the House," 840, 839.
10 LMM, *AGG*(Br), 73.
11 LMM, 23 May 1911, *CJ 1901–1911*: 404.
12 Steffler, "Barriers and Portals," passim.
13 Alaimo, *Undomesticated Ground*, 39.
14 LMM, *AGG*(Br), 137, 138.
15 Sullivan, "The Tall Office Building," 408.
16 LMM, *AGG*(Br), 138.
17 Ibid., 212.
18 LMM, *AHD*, 223–4.
19 LMM. *JLH*, 1, 22, 1, 2, 22, 23.
20 Ibid., 57, 56, 72, 73, 74.
21 Ibid., 71, 76, 75, 74, 77, 75, 82; ellipses in original.
22 For a fuller discussion of the significance of Jane's housekeeping, see Bode, "Mediating Landscapes."
23 LMM, *JLH*, 163, 164, 165, 164.
24 LMM, *ENM*, 53, 65, 122, 1.
25 Mumford, "Form Follows Nature," 26, 35–6; Madden, "Transcendental Influences," 286, passim.
26 For a brief summary of Wright's architectural principles, see the Frank Lloyd Wright Foundation website.

27 The coverage of Wright's work was limited but nonetheless present in the Canadian press. See, for example, "The City Glorious," and "Modern Architecture is Slowly Creeping In" in the *Toronto Daily Star*.

28 Wright, "In the Cause," 339.

29 LMM, *JLH*, 164, 165.

30 Epperly, *Through Lover's Lane*, 8.

31 LMM, *JLH*, 217.

Chapter Five

I thank Dr Anne-Louise Brookes for countless hours of stimulating conversation that have made the writing of this paper possible and especially for sharing her interest in Christopher Alexander's *The Timeless Way of Building*.

1 See the Introduction for the more recent Canadian interpretations of "nature."

2 Soper, *What Is Nature? Culture, Politics and the Non-Human*, 155–6, qtd. in Bate, 33–4.

3 Bate, *The Song of the Earth*, 34.

4 Wordsworth, "Lines Written a Few Miles Above Tintern Abbey," *The Major Works*, lines 93–4; 100–3.

5 Bate, *The Song of the Earth*, 145.

6 "To be interested in Emerson," Montgomery noted in her journals shortly after her seventeenth birthday, "you must get right into the groove of his thought and keep steadily in it. Then you can enjoy him. There can be no skipping or culling if you want to get at his meaning. I admire and appreciate Emerson, although I do not always understand him – I suppose I am too young." Interestingly, she goes on to compare him with Irving: "What a difference there is between Emerson and Irving. Yet each is a fine writer in his own way. Emerson had the great *intellect*, Irving the greater *heart* – 'which is the better the gods alone know'" (LMM, 10 January 1892, *CJ*, *1889–1900*: 111).

7 For more on the Emersonian distinctions between sublime Nature and common nature, see Oliver, Introduction, xiii.

8 Emerson, *Essential Writings*, 8.
9 Epperly, *Through Lover's Lane*, 17–20.
10 Emerson, *Essential Writings*, 14.
11 Lakoff and Johnson, *Metaphors We Live By*, 193, 4.
12 Feldman, *From Molecule to Metaphor*, 106.
13 Greg Garrard credits Donna Haraway with this term and explains it in his *Ecocriticism*, 2nd ed., 17, 208.
14 Lakoff and Johnson, *Metaphors We Live By*, 5, 265, 256, 274.
15 See the chapter "Nature and Nurture" in Feldman, *From Molecule to Metaphor*, 71–82.
16 I developed my idea about architecture, bridges, and bridging by drawing on the common conceptual metaphors described by Lakoff, Johnson, and Turner and usefully outlined by Kövecses: "creation is building," (Kövecses, 140) where "creation" can also be understood as the creative acts of writing and seeing; "abstract complex systems are buildings" (158); "life is a building" (137); and "relationships are buildings" (136–7). What these conceptual metaphors all have in common is the effortless way we draw from what we know about building and buildings to think automatically about constructing, composing, foundations, strength of materials, patterns, shapes, and so on.
17 "The fore part of him slowly rose from the water; for an instant his whole marbleized body formed a high arch, like Virginia's Natural Bridge, and warningly waving his bannered flukes in the air, the grand god revealed himself, sounded, and went out of sight" (Melville, *Moby Dick*, 784).
18 Emerson, *Essential Writings*, 16, 17.
19 Ibid., 22.
20 Fontanella, "Washington Irving's *Tales*," 113.
21 See Epperly, *Through Lover's Lane*, 83.
22 For a detailed discussion, see ibid., 145–64; see also Karr, "Addicted to Reading," 24.
23 Alexander, *Timeless Way of Building*, 93, 548.
24 Woodman, "Arch," 298, 293.
25 Jung, *Archetypes*, 78, 79, 384.
26 See Arrien, *Signs of Life*, 31–70.

27 Bradbury, "Washington Irving's Europe," 79. For more on Irving's Romanticisms, see Brodwin, *Old and New World*.

28 Washington reputedly etched his initials on Natural Bridge when he surveyed it, and so the arches of Natural Bridge, the Alhambra, and Irving's creations, are all, at least metonymically, connected.

29 Johnson, *Washington Irving's Sunnyside*, 6.

30 Ibid., 13.

31 Gammel, *Looking*, 47–8. Gammel reproduces the painting (n.p.), though without reference to Washington Irving in this context.

32 LMM, 15 April 1914, *CJ 1911–1917*:153.

33 See, in particular, Epperly, *Through Lover's Lane*, 66–71.

34 Emerson, *Essential Writings*, 35, 32.

35 LMM, *AGG*, 19.

36 Ibid., 62, 63; emphasis added.

37 Epperly, *Fragrance of Sweet-Grass*, 75.

38 LMM, *AHD*, 52–3; see also Epperly, *Fragrance of Sweet-Grass*, 80.

39 LMM, *AHD*, 219. Ibid.

40 See also Lorna Drew, "The Emily Connection: Ann Radcliffe, L.M. Montgomery and the 'Female Gothic.'"

41 See Epperly, *Fragrance of Sweet-Grass*, 161–3.

42 LMM, *EQ*, 88, 89.

43 It may take years to understand what one has somehow intuited because, as Daniel Kahneman suggests, an "experiencing self" may be tyrannized by a narratively monopolizing "remembering self," who actually tells stories of experiences. See Daniel Kahneman, "The Riddle of Experience vs Memory." I thank Elizabeth Waterston for bringing Kahneman's work to my attention.

44 Epperly, "L.M. Montgomery and the Colour of Home." For more on synaesthesia, see Cytowic, *Man who Tasted Shapes*; Cytowic and Eagleman, *Wednesday Is Indigo Blue*.

45 Cacciari, "Crossing the Senses," 437, 436.

46 Gammel, "Reading," 86, 95, 87.

47 See Epperly, *Fragrance of Sweet-Grass*, 20.

48 Gammel, "Reading," 87, quoting Kay Redfield Jamison's *Exuberance: The Passion for Life*, 7.

49 How interesting it will be to consider further, as Mitchell suggests

in this volume, Montgomery's creativity in light of her knowledge-of-the-time about herself as neurasthenic.

50 Feldman, *From Molecule to Metaphor*, 110.

51 Be they pastoral, georgic, paradisal, or artistic visionary.

Chapter Six

1 LMM, 7 February 1910, *CJ 1901–1911*, 282.

2 LMM, *MDMM*, 200.

3 LMM, 7 February 2010, *CJ 1901–1911*, 281.

4 Beard, *American Nervousness*, xi.

5 Ibid., vi, ix

6 LMM, 27 January 1905, *CJ 1901–1911*, 122.

7 Irene Gammel in *Looking for Anne* explores Montgomery's cosmopolitism.

8 Lutz, "Varieties of Medical Experience," 59. For a discussion of neurasthenia as a disorder that preceded the development and acceptance of Freud's psychoanalysis, see Gosling, *Before Freud*, 143–63.

9 Scheper-Hughes and Lock, "Mindful Body," 31.

10 Jordanova, "A Slap in the Face," 122.

11 See Schuster's *Neurasthenic Nation* and Jasen's *Wild Things*.

12 Fiamengo, "'… refuge of my sick spirit …'" 171, 175, 176.

13 Lawson, "Victorian Sickroom," 236.

14 Prycer, "The Hectic Flush," 271.

15 Bode, "The Anguish of Mother Loss," 55.

16 Hingston, "Montgomery's 'Imp,'" 201–3.

17 Meyer, "The Fresh-Air Controversy," 209–20.

18 Pike, "Propriety and Proprietary," 187–200.

19 Rubio and Waterston, "Introduction," *SJ* 5: xiii.

20 Caplan, *Mind Games*, 45. Lutz argues that in some ways neurasthenia bridged the divide between *soma* and psyche ("Varieties of Experience," 70). He provides an interesting discussion of this complex relationship embedded in the formulations of neurasthenia.

21 Gosling argues that "the somatic style in medicine" rose to promi-

nence from 1870 and began to decline after 1910 as new formulations of mind and body emerged (*Before Freud*, 17).

22 Medicalization broadly refers to the process of transferring social distress into a biological phenomenon that can be treated by medical expertise. Scheper-Hughes and Lock contend that medicalization "entails a missed identification between the individual and the social bodies, and a tendency to transform the social into the biological" ("Mindful Bodies," 10).

23 Gosling, *Before Freud*, 169. Lutz, "Varieties of Medical Experience," 51–70.

24 Oppenheim, "*Shattered Nerves*," 5.

25 Thomson, "Neurasthenia in Britain," 77.

26 Beard, *American Nervousness*, 96; Oppenheim, "*Shattered Nerves*," 92–3. Oppenheim points out that although neurasthenia was widely associated with Dr George Beard, the medical superintendent of the Michigan Asylum for the Insane, Dr E.H. Van Deusen, independently identified a disorder resembling neurasthenia in 1869, the year Beard published his first article on the subject. It is interesting to note that Beard, a New Yorker, attributed neurasthenia to a disorder associated with urban life while Van Deusen, working in a rural area, identified rural isolation as the cause. This, as Oppenheim, argues, "illustrated neurasthenia's immense capacity to be all things to all medical men" (ibid., 93).

27 Lutz, *American Nervousness*, 31.

28 Showalter, "Hysteria, Feminism and Gender," 306.

29 Davis, "George Beard and Lydia Pinkham," 96.

30 Schuster, *Neurasthenic Nation*, 5, 6.

31 Oppenheim, "*Shattered Nerves*," 83–6.

32 Beard, *Sexual Neurasthenia*, 36; Porter, in "Nervousness," also discusses the importance of metaphors used to describe neurasthenia and other nervous disorders (38).

33 Schuster, *Neurasthenic Nation*, 3.

34 Douglas, *Purity and Danger*, 122.

35 Gallagher and Laquer, "Introduction," vii.

36 Campbell, "The Making of 'American,'" 159–61.

37 Porter, "Nervousness," 32; see also Campbell, "The Making of 'American,'" 162.
38 Beard, *American Nervousness*, 26.
39 Mary Douglas, *Natural Symbols*, 4.
40 Scheper-Hughes and Lock, "The Mindful Body," 7.
41 Rubio, *Lucy Maud Montgomery*, 212.
42 Frawley, *Invalidism and Identity*, 5.
43 Jordanova, "A Slap in the Face," 120.
44 Crozier, "What Was Tropical," 525; Porter, "Nervousness," 39.
45 Sicherman, "Uses of a Diagnosis," 38.
46 Theriot, "Women's Voices in Nineteenth-Century Medical Discourse," 24, 2.
47 Ibid.; Schuster, *Neurasthenic Nation*, 4. See also Pike's "Propriety and Proprietary," where she discusses Muskoka as a place of natural revitalization.
48 Campbell, "The Making of 'American,'" 165–6.
49 LMM, 7 February 1910, *CJ 1901–1911*: 282.
50 Lutz, "Varieties of Medical Experience," 59; See also Jasen who notes that in 1889 Daniel Clark, the medical superintendent of Toronto's Asylum for the Insane, addressed the Ontario Medical Association telling them that the number of neurasthenic patients was "growing larger day by day in this nerve-exhausted age" (*Wild Things*, 108).
51 Mitchinson, *The Nature of Their Bodies*, 277.
52 Foucault writes: "Doctor and patient are caught up in an ever-greater proximity, bound together, the doctor by an ever-more attentive, more insistent, more penetrating gaze, the patient by all the silent, irreplaceable qualities that, in him [or her], betray – that is, reveal and conceal – the clearly ordered forms of the disease" (*The Birth of the Clinic*, 16).
53 Davis, "George Beard and Lydia Pinkham," 93.
54 Pike, "Propriety and Proprietary," 187–202.
55 Lawson, "Victorian Sickroom," 240.
56 Lurhmann, *Of Two Minds*, 19. Theriot also delineates the important distinction between illness and sickness, 3.
57 Rubio, *Lucy Maud Montgomery*, 509–11; Howard H. Chiang discusses

the early research regarding the efficacy of bromide in the treatment of nervous and sleep disorders as well as addictions. He also outlines the drug's adverse effects on patients in a number of studies from the turn of the century ("Early Hope of Psychopharmacology,"1).

58 Oppenheim, "*Shattered Nerves*," 115.

59 LMM, 27 November 1924, *SJ*, 3: 209.

60 Ibid., 3 May 1938, *SJ*, 5: 251; 250.

61 Caplan, *Mind Games*, 55. Physicians, as discussed, faced mounting competition not only from emerging specialists within medicine but also from a range of populist healers and remedies.

62 Porter, "Nervousness," 40.

63 Schuster, "Personalizing Illness and Modernity," 29.

64 Mitchell cited in Schuster, "Personalizing Illness and Modernity," 709.

65 Gilman, "Yellow Wallpaper," 3–20.

66 Showalter, "Hysteria, Feminism, and Gender," 286; see also Wood, *Passion and Pathology*, 176.

67 LMM, 10 November 1908, *CJ 1901–1911*: 203.

68 Oppenheim. "*Shattered Nerves*," 124.

69 Buss, *Mapping Our Selves*, 168.

70 Lawson "'Disappointed' House," 87.

71 A rest cure was available in Toronto from 1894 when Dr Donald Meyer established a private hospital and sanatorium for the treatment of nervous diseases including neurasthenia and the application of Mitchell's rest cure. See Wherret, "History of Neurology in Toronto," 325.

72 Mitchinson. *The Nature of the Bodies*, 282.

73 LMM, 18 October 1934, *SJ*, 4: 310. On this date, for instance, Montgomery wrote, "And I am so tired. As soon as the strain relaxes at all I realize how tired I am. I know what I would like to do. Go to bed for a month … I feel cold and tired all the time."

74 Rubio, *Lucy Maud Montgomery*, 572, 640n102.

75 LMM, 5 February 1937, *SJ*, 5: 144; 14 May 1937, *SJ*, 5: 164; 27 August 1937, *SJ*, 5: 199; 22 July 1937, *SJ* 5: 191.

76 Crellin, *Social History of Medicines*, 270n123; see also Gosling, *Before Freud*, 116.

77 Schuster, *Neurasthenic Nation*, 134.
78 Thoreau cited in Buell, *The Environmental Imagination*, 209.
79 Schuster, *Neurasthenic Nation*, 5.
80 Rubio, *Lucy Maud Montgomery*, 331.
81 Schuster, *Neurasthenic Nation*, 137.
82 Jasen, *Wild Things*, 109, 111.
83 Ibid., 126. See also Pike, "Propriety and Proprietary."
84 LMM, 27 March1924, *SJ:* 3: 177.
85 Pike, "Propriety and Proprietary," 200.
86 Buss, *Mapping Our Selves*, 167.
87 LMM, 22 November 1934, *SJ*, 4: 323, emphasis in original; 27 November 1934, *SJ*, 4: 325; 30 November 1934, *SJ*, 4: 327; 3 December 1934 *SJ*, 4: 327.
88 LMM, 12 September 1938, *SJ*, 5: 278, emphasis in original.
89 Rubio, *Lucy Maud Montgomery*, 575. See also Rubio, "Uncertainties Surrounding the Death," 60–1.
90 Scheper-Hughes and Lock, "Mindful Body," 31.
91 Alaimo, *Bodily Natures*, 17.

Chapter Seven

1 Morrison, "Stories for Good Children," 113; Hamilton, "Over the Rainbow," 75; Manderson, "From Hunger to Love," 95.
2 Roberts, "Once Upon the Bench," 509, 515.
3 Hamilton, "Over the Rainbow," 76; Manderson, "From Hunger to Love," 126.
4 See for example Lurie, *Don't Tell the Grown-ups*, 4; Mickenberg and Nel, *Tales for Little Rebels*, 1–3; and, Reynolds, *Radical Children's Literature*, 2, 16.
5 Klein, "Imperfect Order." Ian Ward makes a similar point, albeit as a brief aside rather than as a central feature in his analysis, of Huck's decision not to return Jim to his "owner" in Mark Twain's *The Adventures of Huckleberry Finn*: "There is no doubt that Twain presents a conception of natural justice bounded by an ethics which lies above the positive law" (Ward, *Law and Literature*, 110).
6 Klein, "Imperfect Order," 303, 315, 316.

7 For helpful histories of natural law theory, see Bix, "Natural Law Theory"; Harris, *Legal Philosophies*, 6–23; Wacks, *Understanding Jurisprudence*, 12–29; and Wolfe, *Natural Law Liberalism*, 152–84.
8 Harris, *Legal Philosophies*, 7. Raymond Wacks echoes these three tenets and notes that they can be gleaned from Cicero's classic definition of natural law (Wacks, *Understanding Jurisprudence*, 16).
9 Bix, "On the Dividing Line," 1615.
10 Harris, *Legal Philosophies*, 8.
11 Bix, "Natural Law Theory," 214–15; see also Wacks, *Understanding Jurisprudence*, 19.
12 Harris, *Legal Philosophies*, 10; see also Wacks, *Understanding Jurisprudence*, 24.
13 Coleman and Leiter, "Legal Positivism," 228.
14 McLeod, *Legal Theory*, 22; see also Leslie Green, "Legal Positivism," in *Stanford Encyclopedia of Philosophy*, http://plato.stanford.edu/entries/legal-positivism/.
15 For a discussion of a modest revival of natural law theory in the twentieth century, see McLeod, *Legal Theory*, 27.
16 Klein, "Imperfect Order," 305, 317.
17 Davison, "A Natural Law Based Environmental Ethic," 2. See also French, "Natural Law and Ecological Responsibility," 30–3.
18 I have drawn the details of the legal battles described below from Montgomery's own account of them in her journals and also in her letters to G.B. MacMillan and Ephraim Weber. See, for instance, Montgomery to Weber, 26 May 1919, in *AfGG*, 74–5; Montgomery to MacMillan, 10 February 1929, in *MDMM*, 140–7.
19 LMM, 8 April 1920, *CJ 1918–1921*: 251; emphasis in original. Entry is dated 9 April in *SJ* 2: 375. 9 April was a Friday in 1920.
20 LMM, 7 May 1917, *CJ 1911–1917*: 294.
21 LMM, [9] 8 April 1920, *CJ 191–1921*: 251.
22 LMM, 5 January 1924, *SJ*, 3: 155.
23 LMM, 20 May 1920, *CJ 1918–1921*: 255; 24 June 1920, *CJ 1918–1921*: 266; 20 May 1920, *CJ 1918–1921*: 255; 22 June 1920, *CJ 1918–1921*: 265; 24 June 1920, *CJ 1918–1921*: 266.
24 Based on Montgomery's own account of the accident, it is possible to conclude that Macdonald was partially responsible for it owing

to a failure to keep a proper lookout for other cars on the road. However, the damages awarded against him included substantial sums to cover Marshall Pickering's prostate condition and his wife's diabetes, both of which it should have been apparent, even given the limits of medical knowledge of the time, were preexisting conditions that could not have been caused by the accident. For a full account and analysis of this litigation, see Sutherland, "'Even a Successful Lawsuit.'"

25 Melissaris, *Ubiquitous Law*, 27–30, 34; see also Griffiths, "What Is Legal Pluralism?"

26 Melissaris, *Ubiquitous Law*, 34; Macdonald, *Lessons of Everyday Law*, 6; see also Merry, "Legal Pluralism"; Kleinhans and Macdonald, "What Is a *Critical* Legal Pluralism?"

27 Macdonald, *Lessons of Everyday Law*, 8.

28 Morrison, "Stories for Good Children," 123.

29 Manderson, "From Hunger to Love," 95.

30 In her chapter in this volume, Rita Bode highlights this dwelling as the one "that pushes Montgomery's architectural vision of a partnership between built structures and their environs … towards a paradigm circumventing the threat of human domination of and imposition on the earth."

31 LMM, *ENM*, 1.

32 Ibid., 41.

33 Ibid., 51, 54, 55, 58, 59.

34 Ibid., 62, 95 (emphasis in the original), 100.

35 Ibid., 117.

36 Ibid., 112.

37 In her chapter in this volume, Idette Noomé points out that, beyond simply being an animal lover, Montgomery evidences in her novels and stories an awareness of the animal rights discourse that gained in prominence in Canada and elsewhere in the world during her lifetime, and of active animal rights organizations including Canada's first Society for the Prevention of Cruelty to Animals.

38 LMM, *ENM*, 147.

39 Ibid., 166.

40 Ibid., 167.
41 Ibid., 171.
42 Ibid., 309, 310.
43 Ibid., 313, 315.
44 For an illuminating analysis of the significance of the Murray look in the Emily trilogy, and of the relationship between Elizabeth Murray and her father, see McMaster, "'Murray Look.'"
45 There are interesting connections between the transformation of Emily that I describe here and that detailed by Lesley D. Clement in her chapter in this volume of Emily's progression from an intimate to an empathetic relationship with nature. Clement, quoting from *Emily Climbs*, emphasizes the "wild, lawless strain hidden deep in Emily's nature" that marks a more profound relationship with the natural world that has the power to unleash Emily's art. Alas, this wild strain is at odds with "society's control of when and how she will write," a constraint by which Emily remains strongly bound. I describe a similar conflict in her moral life, where she is caught not between lawlessness and law, but natural law and positive law. But perhaps that "wild, lawless strain hidden deep in Emily's nature" does not equate so easily with the deep commitment to natural justice that I posit. Perhaps for Emily positive law is simultaneously in conflict with natural law and a pagan lawlessness akin to a Hobbesian state of nature. This line of speculation raises interesting questions about the relationship between Emily's individual sense of morality and her art.
46 My analysis here parallels Margaret Atwood's insightful consideration of the relationship between Anne and Marilla, in which she notes that the novel "is not about Anne becoming a good little girl: it is about Marilla Cuthbert becoming a good – and more complete – woman." She adds further: "It may be the ludicrous escapades of Anne that render the book so attractive to children, but it is the struggles of Marilla that give it resonance for adults" (Atwood, "Reflection Piece," 225, 226).

Chapter Eight

1 LMM, *AGG*, 20–1, 21.

2 LMM, *AGG*, 21.

3 For more information on Seton, Wright, and Porter, see Armitage, *Nature Study Movement*, 71–91; Philippon, *Conserving Words*, 72–105; Copeland, "The Wild and Wild Animal Characters."

4 LMM, *AA*, 53.

5 Kohlstedt, *Teaching Children Science*, 20–2, 27–8.

6 LMM, *AGG*, 191.

7 LMM, 7 January 1910, *CJ 1901–1911*: 272.

8 Crawford, *Guide to Nature Study*, 6.

9 Kohlstedt, *Teaching Children Science*, 11–12.

10 Armitage, *Nature Study Movement*, 1.

11 L.H. Bailey, *Nature-Study Idea*, 6.

12 Burroughs, "Nature Study," 326.

13 LMM, *AIn*, 141.

14 Comstock, *Handbook of Nature Study*, 1, 2, 24, 6.

15 LMM, *RV*, 16, 17.

16 Ibid., 17, 56.

17 Comstock, *Handbook of Nature Study*, 2.

18 LMM, *RI*, 162, 291, 329.

19 Scott, *Nature Study*, 123.

20 LMM, *AA*, 85.

21 Comstock, *Handbook of Nature Study*, 2.

22 Kohlstedt, *Teaching Children Science*, 45–6.

23 LMM, *AIn*, 71, 72, 73.

24 Ibid., 80.

25 Fiamengo, "Towards a Theory," 231, 232; Holmes, "How Green Is *Green Gables*?" 377.

26 L.H. Bailey, *Nature-Study Idea*, 10; Comstock, *Handbook of Nature Study*, 5; *AIn*, 127.

27 Crawford, *Guide to Nature Study*, 26.

28 Kohlstedt, *Teaching Children Science*, 231.

29 Armitage, *Nature Study Movement*, 201. For a discussion of the shift in attitudes following the First World War and how these changes

affected the reception of Montgomery's novels, see Waterston, "Marigold and the Magic."

30 LMM, *AIn*, 100, 62.

31 Epperly, *Fragrance of Sweet Grass*, 141.

32 L.H. Bailey, *Nature-Study Idea*, 20; Crawford, *Guide to Nature Study*, 1; L.H. Bailey, *Nature-Study Idea*, 36.

33 LMM, *AIn*, 151.

34 L.H. Bailey, *Nature-Study Idea*, 44.

35 Wilson, *Biophilia*, 1; Louv, *Last Child in the Woods*, 351.

36 Carson, "Help Your Child," 26, 46.

37 LMM, *AIn*, 17; emphasis in original.

Chapter Nine

1 Reimer, "Daughter of the House," 330.

2 Lippa, *Gender, Nature, and Nurture*, xv.

3 Kaplan and Rogers, *Gene Worship*, 4, 9.

4 LMM, *AGG*, 249, 276.

5 Ibid., 1; Epperly, *Fragrance of Sweet-Grass*, 18–20.

6 Crockett, "Outlaws, Outcasts, and Orphans," 58–9.

7 R. Bailey, "Little Orphan Mary," 12.

8 LMM, *AGG*, 7.

9 Reimer, "Daughter of the House," 331.

10 LMM, *AA*, 8, 2; second ellipsis in original.

11 Robinson, "'Born Canadian,'" 23.

12 Ibid.

13 Lefebvre, "Fitness of Things," 178.

14 Bhabha, *Location of Culture*, 89.

15 LMM, *AGG*, 8. The phrase resonated powerfully enough that Montgomery returned to it in *Anne of Avonlea*. "Mrs Rachel Lynde was sitting at her kitchen window, knitting a quilt, just as she had been sitting one evening several years previously when Matthew Cuthbert had driven down over the hill with what Mrs Rachel called 'his imported orphan'" (LMM, *AA*, 56).

16 LMM, *AGG*, 6.

17 Needham, *Street Arabs*, 21, iii.
18 Ibid., 22–3.
19 LMM, *AGG*, 7.
20 Ibid., 249, 15, 29, 298.
21 Ibid., 38.
22 Jones, "Exceptional Orphan Anne," 427.
23 LMM, *AGG*, 98.
24 Ibid., 307, 67–8.
25 Ibid., 265, 277, 24.
26 Reimer, "Daughter of the House," 330.
27 Stanley, *London Street Arabs*, 5–6.
28 Ibid., 8.

Chapter Ten

1 LMM, *AHD*, 39.
2 The term "the race that knows Joseph" also recurs in Montgomery's journals; see, for example, LMM, 16 December 1912, *CJ 1911–17*: 92). For detailed discussions of the latter two terms, see Dull, "Kinship and Nation"; Robinson, " Born Canadian."'
3 Alaimo and Hekman, Introduction: Emerging Models, 6; Tuana, "Viscous Porosity" 193–4; Alaimo, "Trans-Corporeal Feminisms," 238.
4 Doody, "L.M. Montgomery," 40, 41; Robinson, "'Born Canadian,'" 25; Chlebek, "Canadian Family," 152.
5 Ceraldi, "Utopia Awry," 255; Said, *The World, the Text*, 17.
6 Lefebvre, "Pigsties and Sunsets," 127.
7 Franklin and McKinnon, Introduction, 15.
8 Carsten, *After Kinship*, 30, 7.
9 Butler, *Undoing Gender*, 126, 127.
10 LMM, *AGG*, 33.
11 LMM, 11 April 1915, *CJ 1911–17*: 183.
12 LMM, *BC*, 145.
13 LMM, *AA*, 237; ellipsis in original.
14 LMM, *AIS*, 14.
15 LMM, *AHD*, 4.

16 LMM, 3 November 1936, *SJ*, 5: 115.
17 LMM, *AHD*, 72, 76.
18 Ibid., 174.
19 LMM, *BC*, 13.
20 Åhmansson, "Textual/Sexual Space," 152; Waterston, *Magic Island*, 133.
21 LMM, *BC*, 11, 15.
22 Ibid., 6, 12; see also ibid., 23, 51, 92, 123.
23 Ibid., 143.
24 LMM, *AHD*, 176.
25 Epperly, *Fragrance of Sweet-Grass*, 75.
26 Hingston, "Montgomery's 'Imp,'" 203.
27 Pike, "Propriety and the Proprietary," 189.
28 LMM, *AHD*, 167.
29 LMM, *BC*, 215.
30 Butler, *Antigone's Claim*, 10; *BC*, 101.
31 Åhmansson, "Textual/Sexual Space," 151.
32 LMM, *BC*, 50.
33 Ibid., 72, 149, 216.
34 LMM, *AHD*, 189, original italics.
35 Ibid., 63, 65, 99, 187, 188.
36 Ibid., 213.
37 Waterston, *Magic Island*, 83. In Åhmansson's view, "Leslie Moore's transformation from tragic heroine to a happily married woman detracts substance from her previous suffering in the manner of sentimental novelettes, where the final kiss obliterates years of misfortune in an instant" (*Life and Its Mirrors*, 155).
38 Åhmansson, *Life and Its Mirrors*, 155.
39 Epperly, *Fragrance of Sweet-Grass*, 239.
40 LMM, *BC*, 218.

Chapter Eleven

1 de Waal, *Age of Empathy*, 43, 2, 9, 208–9, 222, 7.
2 LMM, *AHD*, 25.
3 LMM, *GR*, 191, 188. Montgomery repeated, several times verbatim,

the sentiments articulated in this passage before and after they appeared in *The Golden Road*; for examples, see her 1911 nature essay "Spring in the Woods," her 1917 memoir *The Alpine Path* (AP, 11), and extracts from John Foster's books in *The Blue Castle* (BC, 17–18). These self-borrowings lead Nancy Holmes, in chapter 3 of this collection, to conclude that Foster is an alias for Montgomery, who is barely disguised through the name-shifting that occurs in *The Blue Castle*.

4 Smith, *Theory of Moral Sentiments*, 11–12.

5 Rifkin, *Empathic Civilization*, 13. Rifkin bases his definitions and observations primarily on those provided by Martin L. Hoffman, who posits that "the key requirement of an empathic response ... is the involvement of psychological processes that make a person have feelings that are more congruent with another's situation than with his own situation" (Hoffman, *Empathy and Moral Development*, 30; emphasis in original).

6 de Waal, *Age of Empathy*, 9, 124.

7 Hoffman, *Empathy and Moral Development*, 197.

8 de Waal, *Age of Empathy*, 203.

9 For fuller development of these concepts, see Clement, "Apprenticeship of Anne Shirley."

10 LMM, *AGG*, 12.

11 Ibid., 35, 62; LMM, *AWP*, 12–13, 127; *AGG*, 76, 106; *AA*, 74; *AIS*, 46.

12 LMM, *AGG*, 31.

13 LMM, *AA*, 157; *AIS*, 211, 240.

14 As Montgomery writes in her essay "The Woods in Summer," "Trees have as much individuality as human beings to those who love and learn them." Some "love to grow sociably together," but others "like to stand apart in solitary majesty and hold commune only with the winds of heaven. Yet these trees are often the best worth knowing, and have all the charm that attaches to the strong and lonely and reserved" (LMM, "The Woods in Summer," 401).

15 LMM, *AHD*, 40–1.

16 LMM, *AIS*, 8, 9; *AHD*, 41.

17 LMM, *AHD*, 11, 10, 23.

18 Ibid., 54.

19 Ibid., 63, 64.
20 Ibid., 54, 64.
21 Ibid., 97, 117.
22 Ibid., 85.
23 LMM, *AA*, 53.
24 LMM, *AHD*, 15. In Montgomery's *The Blythes Are Quoted*, we learn for the first time that Anne gave up writing "occasional stories" after her children were born, turning her creative impulses into the writing of "occasional poems" instead (*BQ*, 68). Anne is prone to use her verse for confessional and therapeutic purposes, particularly after Walter's death. As Gilbert reflects, "It does seem as if in some queer way Walter's gift had descended to her instead of the reverse. Well, I daresay it is some outlet for the pain we feel when we think of him" (*BQ*, 375).
25 LMM, *AIn*, 265; de Waal, *Age of Empathy*, 11. For a discussion of Anne as domestic artist, see Miller, "Weaving a Tapestry," which presents further ways in which "the import of Anne's social artistry rests in her ability to see people and the world as she imagines them and then to make other people view things in this way too" (31).
26 LMM, *ENM*, 1.
27 Ibid., 60, 80.
28 Ibid., 8, 108, 129.
29 "Writing Herself Out," the title of chapter 1 of *Emily Climbs*, is a phrase that is played with throughout the early parts of this novel as Emily, an emerging artist, channels her feelings and perceptions through her writing, "the working out of her creative impulse" (LMM, *EC*, 14).
30 Ibid., 151.
31 Ibid., 175, 176, 177.
32 Roberts, "The Animal Story," 29. On 7 November 1928, Montgomery had the opportunity to meet Roberts and expressed the desire to "thank him for writing *The Heart of the Ancient Wood* [1900]" (LMM, *SJ* 3: 381).
33 LMM, *EC*, 246–7. To build up this scene in *Emily Climbs*, Montgomery borrowed extensively from earlier sources: see Montgomery,

18 November 1907, in LMM, *CJ 1901–1911*: 177; LMM, "The Woods in Autumn," 577.

34 LMM, *EC*, 252.

35 Roberts, "The Poetry of Nature," 276–7. This essay was originally published in *Forum* (New York), December 1897.

36 Fiamengo, "Looking at Animals, Encountering Mystery," 47.

37 While this is a theme to which a number of Montgomery scholars have returned, the most extensive discussion of mentorship and gender in the development of Emily's conception of herself as writer–heroine is found in Epperly's three chapters on the *Emily* trilogy in Part II of *The Fragrance of Sweet-Grass*: "The Struggle for Voice," "Testing the Voice," and "Love and Career."

38 LMM, *EC*, 257. Keats is, however, a poet whom both Emily and Montgomery deem "too full of beauty" (ibid., 257; see also Montgomery, 11 July 1909, in LMM, *CJ 1901–1911*: 235–6). In this same passage, Emily criticizes Tennyson for never letting his sense of himself as artist be "swept away by some splendid mountain torrent of feeling," again a sentiment with which Montgomery would concur (LMM, *EC*, 257; LMM, *CJ 1901–1911*: 237).

39 LMM, *EC*, 324–5.

40 LMM, *EQ*, 2.

41 Ibid., 5; see also ibid., 156–8.

42 Ibid., 221.

43 Epperly, "L.M. Montgomery's," 40.

44 LMM, *RV*, 17; see also ibid., 224; LMM, *RI*, 45, 162, 215, 245.

45 LMM, *RI*, 199.

46 LMM, *AIn*, 86.

47 LMM, *RI*, 215, 347.

48 Ibid., 244.

49 Ibid., 215; Epperly, Foreword to LMM, *BQ*, xi. Benjamin Lefebvre makes further observations about Montgomery's writing and the inclusion of these two particular poems in *Rilla of Ingleside* and *The Blythes Are Quoted* (Lefebvre, "'That Abominable War!'" 120–3).

50 LMM, *BQ*, 509–10 (ellipses in original).

51 LMM, 30 December 1928, *SJ* 3: 388; cf. 25 February 1932, in LMM, *SJ* 4: 172.

52 LMM, *RI*, 215; *BQ*, 509–10.
53 LMM, *RI*, 348; see also ibid., 244–6.
54 de Waal, *Age of Empathy*, 25, 220, 45.
55 Rifkin, *Empathic Civilization*, 5–6.
56 LMM, *BQ*, 510.
57 LMM, *RI*, 54, 81–3, 123–4, 62, 106–7, 153–4.
58 Ibid., 27–8, 44, 210–11, 313, 44, 265–6, 298, 310.
59 Ibid., 246; LMM, *BQ*, 510. While Gilbert, Rev. Meredith, and Jem all give their own interpretation of "the Idea," Walter articulates it most fully in the letter he writes to Rilla on the evening before he dies, an Idea for which not "only the *living* … are fighting – the *dead* are fighting too" (LMM, *RI*, 212–13, 348, 246; emphasis in original).
60 LMM, 23 November 1901, *CJ 1901–1911*: 34.
61 de Waal, *Age of Empathy*, 90.

Chapter Twelve

1 LMM, 10 June 1932, *SJ*, 4: 184.
2 Waterston, *Magic Island*, 168.
3 LMM, *BC*, 8, 18.
4 LMM, *BC*, 156; *JLH*, 26.
5 An exception is the side road where Little Aunt Em lives in *Jane of Lantern Hill*, a "timid little red road, laced with firs and spruces" where rabbits play and a squirrel is "impudent" to Jane (121), but the wildlife is neither threatening nor explicitly wild.
6 Fiamengo, *Other Selves*, see essays by Gwendolyn Guth, "(B)othering the Theory," 29–49; Albert Braz, "St Archie of the Wild," 206–26; and Brian Johnson, "National Species," 333–52.
7 Armstrong, *What Animals Mean*, 6, 7. See also Thomas, *Man and the Natural World*, 17–39, 36–41.
8 Ibid., 1; see also Berger, *About Looking*, 3–28.
9 Armstrong, *What Animals Mean*, 39. People kept pets much earlier (e.g. Chaucer's Prioress in *The Canterbury Tales*, who keeps pet dogs) but views on pets changed.
10 Woodward, *The Animal Gaze*, 5, in line with Bekoff, *The Emotional Lives*, 109.

11 Thomas, *Man and the Natural World*, 119.
12 Armstrong, *What Animals Mean*, 39.
13 Darwin, *Expression of the Emotions*, 12.
14 Alcott, *Journals*, 55; emphasis added.
15 LMM, (7 January 1910) *CJ, 1901–1911*, 263.
16 LMM, *BQ*, 215.
17 LMM, *AHD*, 58–9.
18 LMM, *DS*, 129.
19 As Elizabeth Rollins Epperly notes, cats are also a central motif in the scrapbooks – clippings of cat photographs, articles, jokes, and cat fur make up about a tenth of the Red and Blue Island scrapbooks (Epperly, *Imagining Anne*, 140). Mary Henley Rubio calls Montgomery's "loving portrait" of her departed cat Lucky, in a journal entry of forty handwritten pages, "a tour de force in the annals of pet obituaries" (Rubio, *Lucy Maud Montgomery*, 498). See also LMM, 9 January 1938, in *SJ*, 5: 120–38, compared to a shorter eulogy for her cat Paddy, LMM, 27 July 1935, in *SJ*, 5: 25–9. *Jane of Lantern Hill* is dedicated to Lucky's memory. There are no poems in *The Poetry of Lucy Maud Montgomery* or *The Blythes Are Quoted* on pets, but "In Memory of Maggie" appears in *The Watchman and Other Poems* (145).
20 Montgomery's books rarely extend this treatment to farm animals, just as she does not include wildlife. See Litster's comment in this volume, as noted above. The namelessness and facelessness of these animals is particularly striking in view of the fact that Montgomery's heroines tend to name almost everything, from a favourite geranium to cooking utensils, e.g in LMM, *AGG*(Br), 86; LMM, *JLH*, 104. In *Anne of Avonlea*, Anne mistakenly sells Mr Harrison's cow instead of Dolly, whom Matthew gave her as a calf (LMM, *AA*, 5, 14–17); this cow has a name, but Anne cannot tell the two cows apart, showing how little cows as farm animals interest Anne (and possibly her creator).
21 LMM, *SJ*, 5:163; (13 October 1919; 28 October 1919) *CJ 1918–1921*, 197; 203. See also Gwendolyn Davies, "Marshall Saunders and the Urbanization of the Animal," 170.
22 Mason, *Civilized Creatures*, 13, 14.

23 Kreilkamp, "Petted Things," 92.

24 These assumptions about the emotions and intuitive wisdom of dogs are the closest that she moves to anthropomorphizing animals in her texts – she does not speak for animals or adopt a first person animal persona.

25 LMM, *AIn*, 138; ellipsis in original.

26 Epperly, *Imagining Anne*, 140; LMM, *AIS*, 214. Earlier in the novel, Anne's attitude to cats had softened when she and Philippa fail in an attempt to chloroform a stray, based on a successful real-life instance of cat euthanasia (ibid., 120–3; LMM, 26 September 1912, *CJ 1911–17*, 81–2).

27 LMM, 3 December 1932, *SJ*, 4: 211; LMM, *PSB*, 154.

28 LMM, *PSB*, 27; LMM, *MP*, 270; LMM, *PSB*, 5, 86.

29 There is a precedent for this strategy in one of Montgomery's favourite novels, Olive Schreiner's *The Story of an African Farm*, as described by Wendy Woodward, in her assessment of Schreiner's novel (*The Animal Gaze*, 96–7).

30 LMM, *MP*, 22.

31 The cook and chauffeur believe it is a bribe to reconcile Jane to having to come back from Prince Edward Island, but as always with Mrs Kennedy, there are multiple agendas. The animal is objectified. The "gift" is used to coerce Jane to show gratitude for Mrs Kennedy's magnanimity (or alternatively to demonstrate how ungrateful Jane is not to like the "superior" cat provided to her).

32 LMM, *ENM*, 264.

33 See Dunayer, "Sexist Words, Speciest Roots."

34 LMM, *AIS*, 201, 38; emphasis in original.

35 LMM, *JLH*, 56, 64; *TW*, 11, 13, 148, 143.

36 LMM, *ENM*, 45; *BC*, 64; *PSB*, 182.

37 LMM, *AIS*, 129.

38 See Beirnes, "Law Is an Ass."

39 LMM, *AA*, 2. His erratic behaviour includes leaving his wife, who follows him to Avonlea.

40 LMM, *ENM*, 146–7; see McMaster, "'Murray Look.'" Sutherland, in her chapter, argues that Emily's intense and instinctive reaction to seeing the "suffering or tortured animal" makes her "obey a

higher law than that of Aunt Elizabeth," choosing natural law over positive law.

41 LMM, *RI*, 331.

42 LMM, 1 December 1912, *CJ 1911–1917*, 89. The unacknowledged quotation is from Schreiner, *Story of an African Farm*, 150.

43 Tiessen, "Opposing Pacifism," 136.

44 Scholtmeijer, "Animals and Spirituality," 376.

45 Montgomery's views and treatment of the First World War have been discussed in detail: see Edwards, "L.M. Montgomery's *Rilla*"; Edwards and Litster, "End of Canadian Innocence"; Epperly, *Fragrance of Sweet-Grass*, 95–130; Lefebvre, "'That Abominable War!'"; Lefebvre and McKenzie, Introduction; McKenzie, "Women at War"; Tector, "Righteous War?"; Tiessen, "Opposing Pacifism"; and most recently, MacKenzie and Ledwell, eds., *L.M. Montgomery and War.*

46 LMM, *TW*, 240–1. Only Margaret Penhallow's budding love for the grieving child saves him.

47 LMM, *ENM*, 125, 183, 280–1.

48 LMM, *EC*, 78.

49 LMM, *EQ*, 197.

50 Adams, "Woman-Battering and Harm," 74.

51 LMM, *JLH*, 31.

52 Little, "But What About Jane?" 78.

53 LMM, *BQ*, 470.

54 LMM, *JLH*, 3.

55 Many readers see Robin Stuart as frivolous or at best weak, incapable, "ineffectual" (Rothwell, "Knitting Up the World," 141), and insufficiently motherly, as "she embodies many qualities of the maternal ideal, but fails … to fulfil them" (Bode, "L.M. Montgomery," 61).

56 LMM, *JLH*, 207; ellipsis in original. Tellingly, Jane is constructed as an "outsider."

57 This instability is compounded in *JLH* by the depiction of Aunt Irene's jealous, interfering love, but finds a counterpoint in warmly, wholesomely loving mother figures like Aunt Em, Mrs Snowbeam, Mrs Meade, and Mrs Jimmy John (all animal lovers).

58 LMM, *BQ*, 470. This incident is the most deliberate torture of an animal Montgomery mentions.

59 Woodward, *The Animal Gaze*, 1. Woodward advocates challenging the "human–self and animal–other divide" (1), to destabilize notions of human superiority and perhaps, by extension, the superiority of men over women, of adults over children.

60 Woodward, *The Animal Gaze*, 5; Woodward suggests resisting anthropocentrism by insisting on animal subjectivity, which she defines as representing an animal as an "individual, sentient being who experiences emotions, who, possibly, enacts morality, who has agency, intentionality, a sense of the teleology of her or his life, as well as an ability to recognise and fear death and its advent" (7).

61 Ibid., 16.

62 Emerson, "Nature," ch. 5, section 2, 51.

63 Jacques Derrida, "The Animal That Therefore I Am (More to Follow)," 378–80; see also Woodward, *The Animal Gaze*, 2.

64 LMM, 6 April 1934 *SJ*, 4: 257.

Bibliography

Abram, David. *The Spell of the Sensuous: Perception and Language in a More-Than-Human World*. New York: Vintage, 1997.

Adams, Carol J. "Woman-Battering and Harm to Animals." In *Animals and Women*, edited by Carol J. Adams and Josephine Donovan, 55–84. Durham: Duke University Press, 1995.

Adams, Carol J. and Josephine Donovan, eds. *Animals and Women: Feminist Theoretical Explorations*. Durham: Duke University Press, 1995.

Åhmansson, Gabriella. *A Life and Its Mirrors: A Feminist Reading of L.M. Montgomery's Fiction*, Volume 1: *An Introduction to L.M. Montgomery, Anne Shirley*. Uppsala: University of Uppsala 1991.

– "Textual/Sexual Space in *The Blue Castle*: Valancy Stirling's 'Room of Her Own.'" In *Harvesting Thistles*, edited by Mary Henley Rubio, 146–54. Guelph: Canadian Children's Press, 1994.

Alaimo, Stacy. *Bodily Natures: Science, Environment, and the Material Self*. Bloomington: Indiana University Press 2010.

– "Trans-Corporeal Feminisms and the Ethical Space of Nature." In *Material Feminisms*, edited by Stacy Alaimo and Susan Hekman, 237–64. Bloomington: Indiana University Press, 2008.

– *Undomesticated Ground: Recasting Nature as Feminist Space*. Ithaca: Cornell University Press, 2000.

Alaimo, Stacy, and Susan Hekman. "Introduction: Emerging Models of Materiality in Feminist Theory." In *Material Feminisms*, edited by Stacy Alaimo and Susan Hekman, 1–19. Bloomington: Indiana University Press, 2008.

– eds. *Material Feminisms*. Bloomington: Indiana University Press, 2008.

Alcott, Louisa May. *The Journals of Louisa May Alcott*. Edited by Joel Myerson and Daniel Shealy. Athens: University of Georgia Press, 1989.

Alexander, Christopher. *The Timeless Way of Building*. New York: Oxford University Press, 1979.

Alexander, Joy. "Anne with two 'G's: Green Gables and Geographical Identity." In *100 Years of Anne with an "e": The Centennial Study of Anne of Green Gables*, edited by Holly Blackford, 41–60. Calgary: University of Calgary Press, 2009.

Altmeyer, George. "Three Ideas of Nature in Canada: 1893–1914." In *Consuming Canada: Readings in Environmental History*, edited by Chad Gaffield and Pam Gaffield, 96–118. Toronto: Copp Clark, 1995.

Armitage, Kevin C. *The Nature Study Movement: The Forgotten Popularizer of America's Conservation Ethic*. Lawrence: University Press of Kansas, 2009.

Armstrong, Philip. *What Animals Mean in the Fiction of Modernity*. London: Routledge, 2008.

Arrien, Angeles. *Signs of Life: The Five Universal Shapes and How to Use Them*. New York: Tarcher/Putnam, 1992.

Atwood, Margaret. "Reflection Piece – Revisiting Anne." In *L.M. Montgomery and Canadian Culture*, edited by Irene Gammel and Elizabeth Epperly, 222–6. Toronto: University of Toronto Press, 1999.

– *Survival: A Thematic Guide to Canadian Literature*. Toronto: Anansi, 1972.

Bailey, Liberty Hyde. *The Nature-Study Idea: An Interpretation of the New School-Movement to Put the Young in Relation and Sympathy with Nature*. 4th ed. New York: The Macmillan Company, 1909.

Bailey, Rosamund. "Little Orphan Mary: Anne's Hoydenish Double." *Canadian Children's Literature/Littérature canadienne pour la jeunesse* 55 (1989): 10–19.

Barad, Karen. *Meeting the Universe Halfway: Quantum Physics and the Entanglement of Matter and Meaning*. Durham and London: Duke University Press, 2007.

– "Posthumanist Performativity: Toward an Understanding of How Matter Comes to Matter." In *Material Feminisms*, edited by Stacy

Alaimo and Susan Hekman, 120–54. Bloomington: Indiana University Press, 2008.

Barry, Wendy E., Margaret Anne Doody, and Mary E. Doody Jones, eds. *The Annotated Anne of Green Gables.* New York: Oxford University Press, 1997.

Bate, Jonathan. *The Song of the Earth.* Cambridge, Massachusetts: Harvard University Press, 2002.

Beard, George M. *American Nervousness: Its Causes and Consequences, a Supplement to Nervous Exhaustion (Neurasthenia).* New York: G.P. Putman's Sons, 1881.

– *Sexual Neurasthenia (Nervous Exhaustion): Its Hygiene, Causes, Symptoms, and Treatment, with a Chapter on Diet for the Nervous.* New York: T.B. Treat, 1884.

Beirnes, Pierce. "'The Law Is an Ass': Reading E.P. Evans' 'The Medieval Prosecution and Capital Punishment of Animals.'" *Society and Animals* 2.1 (1994): 27–46.

Bekoff, Marc. *The Emotional Lives of Animals.* Novato: New World Library, 2007.

Bennett, Donna and Russell Brown, eds. *An Anthology of Canadian Literature in English.* 2 vols. New York and Toronto: Oxford University Press, 1982–83.

Bennet, Jane. *Vibrant Matter: A Political Ecology of Things.* Durham and London: Duke University Press, 2010.

Bentley, D.M.R. "On the Confederation Poets' Companionship with Nature: Contexts." *Canadian Poetry* 47 (Fall/Winter 2000). http://www.canadianpoetry.ca/cpjrn/vol47/preface.htm

– "On the Confederation Poets' Companionship with Nature: Lampman." *Canadian Poetry* 48 (Spring/Summer 2001). http://www.canadianpoetry.ca/cpjrn/vol48/preface.htm

– "On the Confederation Poets' Companionship with Nature: Carman." *Canadian Poetry* 49 (Fall/Winter 2001). http://www.canadianpoetry.ca/cpjrn/vol49/preface.htm

Berger, John. *About Looking.* New York: Random House, 1980.

Berman, Marc G., John Jonides, and Stephen Kaplan. "The Cognitive Benefits of Interacting With Nature." *Psychological Science* 19 (2008): 1207–12.

Bhabha, Homi K. *The Location of Culture*. London: Routledge, 1994.

Bix, Brian. "Natural Law Theory." In *A Companion to Philosophy of Law and Legal Theory*, 2nd edition, edited by Dennis Patterson, 211–27. Oxford: Wiley–Blackwell, 2010.

– "On the Dividing Line between Natural Law Theory and Legal Positivism." *Notre Dame Law Review* 75.5 (August 2000): 1613–24.

Blackford, Holly, ed. *100 Years of Anne with an "e": The Centennial Study of Anne of Green Gables.* Calgary: University of Calgary Press 2009.

Bode, Rita. "L.M. Montgomery and the Anguish of Mother Loss." In *Storm and Dissonance: L.M. Montgomery and Conflict*, edited by Jean Mitchell, 50–66. Newcastle-upon-Tyne, United Kingdom: Cambridge Scholars Publishing, 2008.

– "Mediating Landscapes: *Jane of Lantern Hill.*" CREArTA 5 (2005): 167–76.

Bode, Rita and Lesley D. Clement, eds. *L.M. Montgomery's Rainbow Valleys: The Ontario Years, 1911–42*. Montreal and Kingston: McGill-Queen's University Press, 2015.

Booth, Wayne C. *The Rhetoric of Fiction*. 2nd ed. Chicago: University of Chicago Press, 1983.

Botkin, Daniel B. *Discordant Harmonies: A New Ecology for the Twenty-First Century*. New York: Oxford University Press, 1990.

Boyd, Shelley. *Garden Plots: Canadian Women Writers and Their Literary Gardens*. Montreal and Kingston: McGill-Queen's University Press, 2013.

Bradbury, Malcolm. "Washington Irving's Europe." In *The Atlas of Literature*, edited by Malcolm Bradbury, 78–81. London: Prospero, 1996.

Branch, Michael and Scott Slovic, eds. *The ISLE Reader: Ecocriticism, 1993–2003*. Athens: University of Georgia Press, 2003.

Braz, Albert. "St Archie of the Wild: Grey Owl's Account of His 'Natural' Conversion." In *Other Selves: Animals in the Canadian Literary Imagination*, edited by Janice Fiamengo, 206–26. Ottawa: University of Ottawa Press, 2007.

Brinklow, Laurie, Frank Ledwell, and Jane Ledwell, eds. *Message in a Bottle: The Literature of Small Islands*. Charlottetown: Institute of Island Studies, 2000.

Brooks, Paul. *Speaking for Nature: How Literary Naturalists from Henry*

Thoreau to Rachel Carson Have Shaped America. San Francisco: Sierra Club Books, 1980.

Brouse, Cynthia. "The Maud Squad." *Saturday Night* (September 2002).

Buell, Lawrence. "The Ecocritical Insurgency." *New Literary History* 30.3 (1999): 699–712.

– *The Environmental Imagination: Thoreau, Nature Writing, and the Formation of American Culture*. Cambridge, Massachusetts: Harvard University Press, 1995.

– *The Future of Environmental Criticism: Environmental Crisis and Literary Imagination*. Cambridge, Massachusetts: Harvard University Press, 2005.

– "Ecocriticism: Some Emerging Trends" *Qui Parle: Critical Humanities and Social Sciences*. 19.2 (Spring/Summer 2011): 87–115.

Burroughs, John. "Nature Study." *The Outlook* (4 February 1899).

Buss, Helen M. "Women and the Garrison Mentality: Pioneer Women Autobiographers and Their Relation to the Land." In *Re(Dis)covering Our Foremothers:Nineteenth-Century Canadian Women Writers*, edited by Lorraine McMullen,123–36. Ottawa: University of Ottawa Press, 1990.

– *Mapping Ourselves: Canadian Women's Autobiography*. Montreal and Kingston: McGill-Queen's University Press, 1994.

Butler, Judith. *Antigone's Claim: Kinship Between Life and Death*. New York: Columbia University Press, 2000.

– *Undoing Gender*. New York: Routledge, 2004.

Cacciari, Cristina. "Crossing the Senses in Metaphorical Language." In *The Cambridge Handbook of Metaphor and Thought*, edited by Raymond W. Gibbs Jr, 425–43. Cambridge: Cambridge University Press 2008.

Campbell, Brad. "The Making of 'American': Race and Nation in a Neurasthenic Discourse." *History of Psychiatry* 18.2 (June 2007): 157–78.

"Canada National Parks Act." http://laws-lois.justice.gc.ca/eng/acts/n-14.01/, accessed 26 August 2017.

Caplan, Eric. *Mind Games: American Culture and the Birth of Psychotherapy*. Berkeley: University of California Press 1998.

Carson, Rachel. "Help Your Child to Wonder." *Woman's Home Companion* (July 1956).

– *Silent Spring*. 1962; Boston: Houghton Mifflin Harcourt, 2002.

Carsten, Janet. *After Kinship*. Cambridge: Cambridge University Press, 2004.

Ceraldi, Gabrielle. "Utopia Awry: L.M. Montgomery's Emily Series and the Aftermath of the Great War." In *Message in a Bottle: The Literature of Small Islands*, edited by Laurie BrinklowFrank Ledwell, and Jane Ledwell, 247–63. Charlottetown: Institute of Island Studies, 2000.

Chiang, Howard H. "An Early Hope of Psychopharmacology: Bromide Treatment in the Turn-of-the-Twentieth-Century Psychiatry." *Historia Medicinae* 1.1 (2009): 1–7.

Chlebek, Diana Arlene. "The Canadian Family and Female Adolescent Development During the 1930s: *Jane of Lantern Hill*." In *L.M. Montgomery and Canadian Culture*, edited by Irene Gammel and Elizabeth Epperly, 145–52. Toronto: University of Toronto Press 1999.

"City Glorious, The." *Toronto Daily Star* (18 April 1935): 6.

Clark, Timothy. *The Cambridge Introduction to Literature and the Environment*. Cambridge: Cambridge University Press, 2011.

– "Phenomenology." In *The Oxford Book of Ecocriticism*, edited by Greg Garrard, 276–90. Oxford: Oxford University Press, 2014.

Clement, Lesley D. "The Apprenticeship of Anne Shirley: Imagining Self/Imagining Others." *Studies in Canadian Literature/Études en littérature canadienne* 36.1 (2011): 51–68.

Coleman, Jules L. and Brian Leiter. "Legal Positivism." In *A Companion to Philosophy of Law and Legal Theory*, 2nd edition, edited by Dennis Patterson, 228–48. Oxford: Wiley–Blackwell, 2010.

Comstock, Anna Botsford. *Handbook of Nature Study*. 1911. Ithaca: Comstock Publishing Company, 1967.

Conlogue, William. *Working the Garden: American Writers and the Industrialization of Agriculture*. Chapel Hill: University of North Carolina Press, 2001.

Copeland, Marion W. "The Wild and Wild Animal Characters in the Ecofeminist Novels of Beatrix Potter and Gene Stratton-Porter." In *Wild Things: Children's Culture and Ecocriticism*, edited by Sidney I. Dobrin and Kenneth B. Kidd, 71–81. Detroit: Wayne State University Press, 2004.

Crawford, Mattie Rose. *Guide to Nature Study for the Use of Teachers*. 1902. Whitefish, Montana: Kessigner Publishing, 2004.

Crellin, John K. *A Social History of Medicines in the Twentieth Century: To Be Taken Three Times a Day*. Binghamton, NY: Pharmaceutical Products Press, 2004.

Crockett, Beverly. "Outlaws, Outcasts, and Orphans: The Historical Imagination and *Anne of Green Gables*." In *Imagining Adoption: Essays on Literature and Culture*, edited by Marianne Novy, 57–81. Ann Arbor: University of Michigan Press, 2001.

Crozier, Anna. "What Was Tropical about Tropical Neurasthenia? The Utility of the Diagnosis in the Management of British East Africa." *Journal of the History of Medicine and Allied Sciences* 64.4 (October 2009): 518–48.

Cytowic, Richard. *The Man Who Tasted Shapes*. 1993. Cambridge, Massachusetts: MIT Press, 2003.

Cytowic, Richard and David Eagleman. *Wednesday Is Indigo Blue: Discovering the Brain of Synesthesia*. Cambridge, Massachusetts: MIT Press, 2009.

Darwin, Charles. *The Expression of the Emotions in Man and Animals*. London: John Murray, 1872.

Davies, Gwendolyn. "Marshall Saunders and the Urbanization of the Animal." In *Other Selves: Animals in the Canadian Literary Imagination*, edited by Janice Fiamengo, 170–83. Ottawa: University of Ottawa Press, 2007.

Davis, Dona. "George Beard and Lydia Pinkham: Gender, Class, and Nerves in Late 19th Century America." *Health Care for Women International* 10.2–3 (1989): 93–114.

Davison, Scott A. "A Natural Law Based Environmental Ethic," *Ethics & the Environment* 14.1 (2009): 1–13.

Day, Aidan. *Romanticism*. 1996. London and New York: Routledge, 2012.

Derrida, Jacques. "The Animal That Therefore I Am (More to Follow)." Translated by David Wills. *Critical Inquiry* 28.2 (2002): 369–418.

de Waal, Frans. *The Age of Empathy: Nature's Lessons for a Kinder Society*. Toronto: McClelland and Stewart, 2009.

Doody, Margaret Anne. "L.M. Montgomery: The Darker Side." In *Storm and Dissonance: L.M. Montgomery and Conflict*, edited by Jean Mitchell, 25–49. Newcastle-upon-Tyne, United Kingdom: Cambridge Scholars Publishing, 2008.

– "Introduction." L.M. Montgomery, *The Annotated Anne*, 9–34.

Doughty, Terri, and Dawn Thompson, eds. *Knowing Their Place? Identity and Space in Children's Literature*. Newcastle-upon-Tyne, United Kingdom: Cambridge Scholars Publishing, 2011.

Douglas, Mary. *Purity and Danger: An Analysis of the Concepts of Pollution and Taboo*. New York: Praeger, 1966.

– *Natural Symbols*. New York: Vintage, 1970.

Drew, Lorna. "The Emily Connection: Ann Radcliffe, L.M. Montgomery and 'the Female Gothic.'" *Canadian Children's Literature* 77 (1995): 19–32.

Duke, David Freeland. *Canadian Environmental History*. Toronto: Canadian Scholars Press 2006.

Dull, Monique. "Kinship and Nation in Amelia (1848) and Anne of Green Gables (1908)." In *The Rhetoric of Canadian Writing*, edited by Conny Steenman-Marcusse, 161–78. Amsterdam: Rodopi, 2002.

Dunayer, Joan. "Sexist Words, Speciest Roots." In *Animals and Women: Feminist Theoretical Explorations*, edited by Carol J. Adams and Josephine Donovan, 11–31. Durham: Duke University Press, 1995.

Edwards, Owen Dudley. "L.M. Montgomery's *Rilla of Ingleside*: Intention, Inclusion, Implosion." In *Harvesting Thistles: The Textual Garden of L.M. Montgomery: Essays on Her Novels and Journals*, edited by Mary Henley Rubio, 126–36. Guelph: Canadian Children's Press, 1994.

Edwards, Owen Dudley, and Jennifer H. Litster. "The End of Canadian Innocence: L.M. Montgomery and the First World War." In *L.M. Montgomery and Canadian Culture*, edited by Irene Gammel and Elizabeth Epperly, 31–48. Toronto: University of Toronto Press, 1999.

Emerson, Ralph Waldo. *Essays: First and Second Series*. London: J.M. Dent, 1906.

– *The Essential Writings of Ralph Waldo Emerson*. Edited by Brooks Atkinson. New York: Modern Library, 2000.

– *Nature*. Boston: James Munroe and Company, 1836. https://archive.org/stream/naturemunroeooemerrich#page/n5/mode/2up

Epperly, Elizabeth Rollins. Foreword to Montgomery, *The Blythes Are Quoted*, ix–xiv.

– *The Fragrance of Sweet-Grass: L.M. Montgomery's Heroines and the Pursuit of Romance.* Toronto: University of Toronto Press, 1992.

– *The Fragrance of Sweet-Grass with New Preface,* Toronto: University of Toronto Press, 2014.

– *Imagining Anne: The Island Scrapbooks of L.M. Montgomery.* Toronto: Penguin Canada, 2008.

– "L.M. Montgomery and the Colour of Home." Paper delivered at "L.M. Montgomery – Writer of the World," Uppsala University, 22 August 2009.

– "L.M. Montgomery's *Anne's House of Dreams*: Reworking Poetry." *Canadian Children's Literature / Littérature canadienne pour la jeunesse* 37 (1985): 40–6.

– *Through Lover's Lane: L.M. Montgomery's Photography and Visual Imagination.* Toronto: University of Toronto Press, 2007.

Feldman, Jerome A. *From Molecule to Metaphor: A Neural Theory of Language.* Cambridge, Massachusetts: MIT Press, 2006.

Fetterley, Judith and Marjorie Pryse. *Writing out of Place: Regionalism, Women, and American Literary Culture.* Urbana-Champaign: University of Illinois Press, 2003.

Fiamengo, Janice. "Looking at Animals, Encountering Mystery: The Wild Animal Stories of Ernest Thompson Seton and Charles G.D. Roberts." *Journal of Canadian Studies/Revue d'études canadiennes* 44.1 (2010): 36–59.

– " … the refuge of my sick spirit …': L.M. Montgomery and the Shadow of Depression." In *The Intimate Life of L.M. Montgomery,* edited by Irene Gammel, 170–86. Toronto: University of Toronto Press, 2005.

– "Towards a Theory of the Popular Landscape in *Anne of Green Gables.*" In *Making Avonlea: L.M. Montgomery and Popular Culture,* edited by Irene Gammel, 225–37. Toronto: University of Toronto Press, 2002.

– ed. *Other Selves: Animals in the Canadian Literary Imagination.* Ottawa: University of Ottawa Press, 2007.

Fontanella, Lee. "Washington Irving's *Tales of the Alhambra* and Early Photography in Spain." In *The Old and New World Romanticism of Washington Irving,* edited by Stanley Brodwin, Stanley113–26. New York: Greenwood Press, 1986.

Ford, Elizabeth. "How to Cocoon a Butterfly: Mother and Daughter in *A Girl of the Limberlost.*" *Children's Literature Association Quarterly* 18.4 (Winter 1993): 148–53.

Foucault, Michel. *The Birth of the Clinic: An Archaeology of Medical Perceptions*. London: Vintage, 1994.

Frank, Joseph. *The Idea of Spatial Form*. New Brunswick, NJ: Rutgers University Press, 1991.

Frank Lloyd Wright Foundation, http://franklloydwright.org/.

Franklin, Sarah, and Susan McKinnon. "Introduction." In *Relative Values: Reconfiguring Kinship Studies*, edited by Sarah Franklin and Susan McKinnon, 1–28. Durham: Duke University Press, 2001.

Frawley, Maria H. *Invalidism and Identity in Nineteenth-Century Britain.* Chicago: University of Chicago Press, 2014.

French, William C. "Natural Law and Ecological Responsibility: Drawing on the Thomistic Tradition," *University of St Thomas Law Journal* 5, no. 1 (2008): 12–36.

Friedman, Susan Stanford. "Spatial Poetics and Arundhati Roy's *The God of Small Things.*" In *A Companion to Narrative Theory*, edited by James Phelan and Peter J. Rabinowitz, 192–205. Malden, Massachusetts: Blackwell, 2005.

Frye, Northrop. "Conclusion to a Literary History of Canada." In *The Bush Garden: Essays on the Canadian Imagination*, edited by Northrop Frye, 215–53. Toronto: Anansi, 1971.

Gaffield, Chad, and Pam Gaffield, eds. *Consuming Canada: Readings in Environmental History*. Toronto: Copp Clark, 1995.

Gallagher, Catherine, and Thomas Laqueur. "Introduction." In *The Making of the Modern Body: Sexuality and Society in the Nineteenth Century*, edited by Catherine Gallagher and Thomas Laqueur. vii–xv. Berkeley: University of California Press, 1987.

Gammel, Irene. "Embodied Landscape Aesthetics in *Anne of Green Gables.*" *The Lion and the Unicorn* 34.2 (April 2010): 228–47.

– *Looking for Anne: How Lucy Maud Montgomery Dreamed Up a Literary Classic.* Toronto: Key Porter Books, 2008.

– "Reading to Heal: *Anne of Green Gables* as Bibliotherapy." In *Anne's World: A New Century of Anne of Green Gables*, edited by Irene Gammel and Benjamin Lefebvre, 82–99. Toronto: University of Toronto Press, 2010.

– “Safe Pleasures for Girls: L.M. Montgomery’s Erotic Landscapes,” In *Making Avonlea: L.M. Montgomery and Popular Culture*, edited by Irene Gammel, 114–27. Toronto: University of Toronto Press, 2002.
– ed. *The Intimate Life of L.M. Montgomery*. Toronto: University of Toronto Press, 2005.
– ed. *Making Avonlea: L.M. Montgomery and Popular Culture*. Toronto: University of Toronto Press, 2002.
Gammel, Irene, and Elizabeth Epperly, eds. *L.M. Montgomery and Canadian Culture*. Toronto: University of Toronto Press, 1999.
Gammel, Irene, and Benjamin Lefebvre, eds. *Anne’s World: A New Century of Anne of Green Gables*. Toronto: University of Toronto Press, 2010.
Garrard, Greg. *Ecocriticism*. 2nd ed. New York: Routledge, 2011.
– “Problems Concerning Islands.” In *“What Is the Earthly Paradise” Ecocritical Responses to the Caribbean*, edited by Chris Campbell and Erin Somerville, 10–22. Newcastle-upon-Tyne, United Kingdom: Cambridge Scholars Publishing, 2007.
– ed. *The Oxford Book of Ecocriticism*. Oxford: Oxford University Press, 2014.
Gerson, Carole. “Seven Milestones: How *Anne of Green Gables* Became a Canadian Icon.” In *Anne’s World: A New Century of Anne of Green Gables*, edited by Irene Gammel and Benjamin Lefebvre, 17–34. Toronto: University of Toronto Press, 2010.
Gibbs, Raymond W., Jr., ed. *The Cambridge Handbook of Metaphor and Thought*. Cambridge: Cambridge University Press, 2008.
Gifford, Terry. *Pastoral*. London: Routledge, 1999.
Gijswijt-Hofstra, Marijke and Roy Porter, eds. *Cultures of Neurasthenia from Beard to the First World War*. Amsterdam: Rodopi, 2001.
Gilman, Charlotte Perkins, “The Yellow Wallpaper.” In *The Charlotte Perkins Gilman Reader*, edited by Ann J. Lane, 3–20. Charlottesville: University of Virginia Press 1999.
Glotfelty, Cheryll. “Introduction.” In *The Ecocriticism Reader: Landmarks in Literary Ecology*, edited by Cheryll Glotfelty and Harold Fromm, xv–xxxvii. Athens: University of Georgia Press, 1996.
Glotfelty, Cheryll and Harold Fromm, eds. *The Ecocriticism Reader: Landmarks in Literary Ecology*. Athens: University of Georgia Press, 1996.
Gosling, F.G. *Before Freud: Neurasthenia and the American Medical Community, 1870–1910*. Urbana: University of Illinois Press, 1987.

Grafton, Jane. "Girls and Green Space: Sickness to Health Narratives in Children's Literature." In *Knowing Their Place? Identity and Space in Children's Literature*, edited by Terri Doughty and Dawn Thompson, 109–26. Newcastle-upon-Tyne, United Kingdom: Cambridge Scholars Publishing, 2011.

Green, Leslie. "Legal Positivism" In *Stanford Encyclopedia of Philosophy*. http://plato.stanford.edu/entries/legal-positivism/

Griffiths, John. "What Is Legal Pluralism?" *Journal of Legal Pluralism and Unofficial Law* 24 (1986): 1–55.

Guth, Gwendolyn. "(B)othering the Theory: Approaching the Unapproachable in *Bear* and Other Realistic Animal Narratives." In *Other Selves: Animals in the Canadian Literary Imagination*, edited by Janice Fiamengo, 29–49. Ottawa: University of Ottawa Press, 2007.

Hamilton, Sarah. "Over the Rainbow and Down the Rabbit Hole: Law and Order in Children's Literature." *North Dakota Law Review* 81.1 (2005): 75–114.

Haraway, Donna. "A Manifesto for Cyborgs: Science, Technology, and Socialist Feminism in the 1980s." In *The Haraway Reader*. New York: Routledge, 2003. 7–45.

– *The Companion Species Manifesto: Dogs, People, and Significant Otherness*. Chicago: Prickly Paradigm Press, 2003.

Harris, J.W. *Legal Philosophies*. London: Butterworths, 1980.

Hart, Aoife Emily. " There's Minny a One in Ould Ireland': Judy Plum's Witchcraft of Irish Stereotypes and Storytelling." *Studies in Canadian Literature* 38 (2), 2013: 205–24.

Heise, Ursula K. *Sense of Place and Sense of Planet: The Environmental Imagination of the Global*. New York: Oxford University Press, 2008.

Hingston, Kylee-Anne. "Montgomery's 'Imp': Conflicting Representations of Illness in L.M. Montgomery's *The Blue Castle*." In *Storm and Dissonance: L.M. Montgomery and Conflict*, edited by Jean Mitchell, 192–208. Newcastle-upon-Tyne, United Kingdom: Cambridge Scholars Publishing, 2008.

Hoffman, Martin L. *Empathy and Moral Development: Implications for Caring and Justice*. Cambridge: Cambridge University Press, 2000.

Holmes, Nancy. "How Green Is *Green Gables*? An Ecofeminist Perspective on L.M. Montgomery." In *Storm and Dissonance: L.M. Mont-*

gomery and Conflict, edited by Jean Mitchell, 373–90. Newcastle-upon-Tyne, United Kingdom: Cambridge Scholars Publishing, 2008.

Iovino, Serenella, and Serpil Oppermann, eds. *Material Ecocriticism.* Bloomington: Indiana University Press, 2014.

– "Material Ecocriticism: Materiality, Agency, and Models of Narrativity." *Ecozon@ European Journal of Literature, Culture and Environment* 3.1 (2012): 75–91. http://ecozona.eu/article/view/452

– "Theorizing Material Ecocriticism: A Diptych." ISLE 19.3 (Summer 2012): 448–75.

Irving, Washington. *The Alhambra.* 1832. New York: Caldwell, n.d.

– *The Sketch Book.* 1819. New York: Signet Classic, 1961.

– *Tales of the Alhambra.* 1832. Granada: Ediciones Miguel Sanchez, 1994.

Jackson, Wes. *Becoming Native to This Place.* New York: Counterpoint, 1994.

Jasen, Patricia. *Wild Things: Nature, Culture, and Tourism in Ontario, 1790–1914.* Toronto: University of Toronto Press, 1995.

Johnson, Brian. "National Species: Ecology, Allegory, and Indigeneity in the Wolf Stories of Roberts, Seton, and Mowat." In *Other Selves: Animals in the Canadian Literary Imagination*, edited by Janice Fiamengo, 333–52. Ottawa: University of Ottawa Press, 2007.

Johnson, Kathleen Eagen. *Washington Irving's Sunnyside.* Tarrytown, NY: Historic Hudson Valley Press, 1995.

Johnston, Rosemary Ross. ed. *L.M. Montgomery's Interior and Exterior Landscapes.* Special Issue. CREArTA 5 (2005).

Jones, Mary E. Doody. "The Exceptional Orphan Anne: Child Care, Orphan Asylums, Farming Out, Indenturing, and Adoption." In *The Annotated Anne of Green Gables.* Edited by Wendy E. Barry, Margaret Anne Doody, and Mary E. Doody Jones, 422–9. New York and London: Oxford University Press, 1997.

Jordanova, Ludmilla. "'A slap in the face for old Mother Nature': Disease, Debility, and Decay in Huysmans's *A Rebours.*" *Literature and Medicine* 15.1 (Spring 1996): 112–28.

Jung, Carl G. *The Archetypes and the Collective Unconscious.* Translated by R.F.C. Hull. 2nd ed. Bollingen Series 20. Princeton: Princeton University Press, 1959.

Kahneman, Daniel. "The Riddle of Experience vs. Memory." TED video,

20:06. February 2010. https://www.ted.com/talks/daniel_kahneman_the_riddle_of_experience_vs_memory/transcript?language=en

Kaplan, Gisela, and Lesley J. Rogers. *Gene Worship: Moving beyond the Nature/Nurture Debate over Genes, Brain, and Gender*. New York: Other Press, 2003.

Karr, Clarence. "Addicted to Reading: L.M. Montgomery and the Value of Reading." *Canadian Children's Literature/Littérature canadienne pour la jeunesse* 113–14 (Spring–Summer 2004): 17–33.

– *Authors and Audiences: Popular Canadian Fiction in the Early Twentieth Century.* Montreal and Kingston: McGill-Queen's University Press, 2000.

Kern, Robert. "Ecocriticism: What Is It Good For?" *ISLE* 7.1 (2000): 9–32

Kilcup, Karen L. *Fallen Forests: Emotion, Embodiment, and Ethics in American Women's Environmental Writing, 1781–1924*. Athens and London: University of Georgia Press, 2013.

Klein, Thomas C. "Imperfect Order: Reflections of the Law in Two Classic Children's Novels." *Texas Wesleyan Law Review* 12.1 (Fall 2005): 303–18.

Kleinhans, Martha-Marie, and Roderick A. Macdonald. "What Is a *Critical* Legal Pluralism?" *Canadian Journal of Law and Society* 12.2 (Fall 1997): 25–46.

Klinck, Carl and Reginald Watters, eds. *Canadian Anthology*. Toronto: Gage, 1955.

Kohlstedt, Sally Gregory. *Teaching Children Science: Hands-on Nature Study in North America, 1890–1930*. Chicago: University of Chicago Press, 2010.

Kövecses, Zoltán. *Metaphor: A Practical Introduction.* New York: Oxford University Press, 2002.

Kreilkamp, Ivan. "Petted Things: *Wuthering Heights* and the Animal." *The Yale Journal of Criticism* 18.1 (Spring 2005): 87–110.

Kristeva, Julia. *Strangers to Ourselves*. Translated by Leon S. Roudiez. New York: Columbia University Press, 1991.

Lakoff, George, and Mark Johnson. *Metaphors We Live By*. 1980. Chicago: University of Chicago Press, 2003.

Lakoff, George, and Mark Turner. *More than Cool Reason: A Field Guide to Poetic Metaphor.* Chicago: University of Chicago Press, 1989.

Lawson, Kate. "The Victorian Sickroom in L.M. Montgomery's *The Blue*

Castle and *Emily's Quest*: Sentimental Fiction and the Selling of Dreams." *The Lion and the Unicorn* 31.3 (2007): 232–49.

– "The 'Disappointed' House: Trance, Loss, and the Uncanny in L.M. Montgomery's *Emily* Trilogy." *Children's Literature* 29 (2001): 71–90.

Ledwell, Jane, and Jean Mitchell, eds. *Anne Around the World: L.M. Montgomery and her Classic*. Montreal and Kingston: McGill-Queen's University Press, 2013.

Lefebvre, Benjamin, "The Fitness of Things: *Anne of Green Gables*, Social Change, and Montgomery's 'Discerning Extraordinary Observer.'" In *Diversity and Change in Early Canadian Women's Writing*, edited by Jennifer Chambers, 170–93. Newcastle-upon-Tyne, United Kingdom: Cambridge Scholars Publishing, 2008.

– "Pigsties and Sunsets: L.M. Montgomery, *A Tangled Web*, and a Modernism of Her Own." *English Studies in Canada* 31.4 (December 2005): 123–46.

– "'A Small World After All': L.M. Montgomery's Imagined Avonlea as Virtual Landscape." In *The International Handbook of Virtual Learning Environments*, edited by Joel Weiss, et al, 1121–40. Dordrecht: Springer, 2006.

– "'That Abominable War!': *The Blythes Are Quoted* and Thoughts on L.M. Montgomery's Late Style." In *Storm and Dissonance: L.M. Montgomery and Conflict*, edited by Jean Mitchell, 109–30. Newcastle-upon-Tyne, United Kingdom: Cambridge Scholars Publishing, 2008.

Lefebvre, Benjamin, ed. *The L.M. Montgomery Reader*. 3 Vols. Toronto: University of Toronto Press, 2013–15.

Lefebvre, Benjamin, and Andrea McKenzie. "Introduction." In *Rilla of Ingleside*, by L.M. Montgomery, edited by Bejamin Lefebvre and Andrea McKenzie, ix–xix. Toronto: Viking Canada, 2010.

Lippa, Richard A. *Gender, Nature, and Nurture*. Mahwah, NJ: Lawrence Erlbaum Associates, 2002.

Litster, Jennifer H. "The 'Secret' Diary of Maud Montgomery, Aged 28¼." In *The Intimate Life of L.M. Montgomery*, edited by Irene Gammel, 88–105. Toronto: University of Toronto Press, 2005.

Little, Jean. "But What about Jane?" *Canadian Children's Literature* 1.3 (Autumn 1975): 71–81.

Long, Judith Reick. *Gene Stratton-Porter: Novelist and Naturalist*. Indianapolis: Indiana Historical Society, 1990.

Lotman, Jurij M. "The Origin of Plot in the Light of Typology." Translated by Julian Graffy. *Poetics Today* 1.1–2 (Autumn 1979): 161–84.

Louv, Richard. *Last Child in the Woods: Saving Our Children from Nature-Deficit Disorder*. Rev. ed. Chapel Hill: Algonquin Books, 2008.

Luhrmann, T.M. *Of Two Minds: An Anthropologist Looks at American Psychiatry*. New York: Vintage Books, 2001.

Lurie, Alison, *Don't Tell the Grown-ups: Subversive Children's Literature*. Boston: Little, Brown and Company, 1990.

Lutz, Tom. *American Nervousness, 1903: An Anecdotal History*. Ithaca: Cornell University Press, 1991.

– "Varieties of Medical Experience: Doctors and Patients, Psyche and Soma in America." In *Cultures of Neurasthenia from Beard to the First World War*, edited by Marijke Gijswijt-Hofstra and Roy Porter, 51–76. Amsterdam: Rodopi, 2001.

MacDonald, Heidi. "Reflections of the Great Depression in L.M. Montgomery's Life and Her Pat Books." In *Storm and Dissonance: L.M. Montgomery and Conflict*, edited by Jean Mitchell, 142–58. Newcastle-upon-Tyne, United Kingdom: Cambridge Scholars Publishing, 2008.

Macdonald, Roderick A. *Lessons of Everyday Law*. Montreal and Kingston: McGill-Queen's University Press, 2002.

MacEachern, Alan. "Changing Ecologies: Preservation in Four National Parks, 1935–1965." In *Canadian Environmental History*, editec by David Freeland Duke, 361–86. Toronto: Canadian Scholars Press, 2006.

MacLeod, Alexander. "On the Road from Bright River: Shifting Social Space in *Anne of Green Gables*." In *Anne's World: A New Century of Anne of Green Gables*, edited by Irene Gammel and Benjamin Lefebvre, 134–49. Toronto: University of Toronto Press, 2010.

Madden, Edward H. "Transcendental Influences on Louis H. Sullivan and Frank Lloyd Wright." *Transactions of the Charles S. Peirce Society* 31.2 (Spring 1995): 286–321.

Manderson, Desmond. "From Hunger to Love: Myths of the Source, Interpretation, and Constitution of Law in Children's Literature." *Law and Literature* 15.1 (2003): 87–141.

Marshall, Ian. *Story Line: Exploring the Literature of the Appalachian Trail*. Charlottesville: University Press of Virginia, 1998.

Marx, Leo. *The Machine in the Garden: Technology and the Pastoral Ideal in America*. 1964. Oxford: Oxford University Press, 2000.

Mason, Jennifer. *Civilized Creatures: Urban Animals, Sentimental Culture and American Literature, 1850–1900*. Baltimore: Johns Hopkins University Press, 2005.

Mazel, David. "An American Literary Environmentalism as Domestic Orientation." In *The Ecocriticism Reader: Landmarks in Literary Ecology*, edited by Cheryll Glotfelty and Harold Fromm, 137–46. Athens: University of Georgia Press, 1996.

McKenzie, Andrea. "Women at War: L.M. Montgomery, the Great War, and Canadian Cultural Memory." In *Storm and Dissonance: L.M. Montgomery and Conflict*, edited by Jean Mitchell, 83–108. Newcastle-upon-Tyne, United Kingdom: Cambridge Scholars Publishing, 2008.

McKenzie, Andrea and Jane Ledwell, eds. *L.M. Montgomery and War*. Montreal and Kingston: McGill-Queen's University Press, 2016.

McLeod, Ian. *Legal Theory*. 5th ed. London: Palgrave Macmillan, 2010.

McMaster, Lindsey. "The 'Murray Look': Trauma as Family Legacy in L.M. Montgomery's *Emily of New Moon* Trilogy." *Canadian Children's Literature/Littérature canadienne pour la jeunesse* 34.2 (Fall 2008): 50–74.

McMullen, Lorraine, ed. *Re(Dis)covering Our Foremothers: Nineteenth-Century Canadian Women Writers*. Ottawa: University of Ottawa Press, 1990.

Meehan, Jeannette Porter. *The Lady of the Limberlost: The Life and Letters of Gene Stratton-Porter*. Garden City: Doubleday, Doran and Company, 1928.

Melissaris, Emmanuel. *Ubiquitous Law: Legal Theory and the Place for Legal Pluralism*. Burlington, VT: Ashgate, 2009.

Melville, Herman. *Moby Dick: or The Whale*. 1851. New York: Modern Library, 2000.

Merchant, Carolyn. *Reinventing Eden: The Fate of Nature in Western Culture*. New York: Routledge, 2003.

Merry, Sally Engle. "Legal Pluralism." *Law and Society Review* 22.5 (1988): 869–96.

Meyer, Susan, "The Fresh-Air Controversy, Health and Art in Montgomery's *Emily* Novels." In *Storm and Dissonance: L.M. Montgomery and Conflict*, edited by Jean Mitchell, 194–208. Newcastle-upon-Tyne, United Kingdom: Cambridge Scholars Publishing, 2008.

Mezei, Kathy and Chiara Briganti. "Reading the House: A Literary Perspective." *Signs: Journal of Women in Culture and Society*, 27.3 (2002): 837–46.

Mickelsen, David. "Types of Spatial Structure in Narrative." In *Spatial Form in Narrative*, edited by Jeffrey R. Smitten and Ann Daghigstany, 63–78. Ithaca: Cornell University Press, 1981.

Mickenberg, Julia L., and Philip Nel. *Tales for Little Rebels*. New York: New York University Press, 2008.

Miller, Kathleen A. "Weaving a Tapestry of Beauty: Anne Shirley as Domestic Artist." *Canadian Children's Literature/Littérature canadienne pour la jeunesse* 34.2 (Fall 2008): 30–49.

Mitchell, Jean. "Introduction: Storm and Dissonance: L.M. Montgomery and Conflict." In *Storm and Dissonance: L.M. Montgomery and Conflict*, edited by Jean Mitchell, 1–21. Newcastle-upon-Tyne, United Kingdom: Cambridge Scholars Publishing, 2008.

Mitchell, Jean, ed. *Storm and Dissonance: L.M. Montgomery and Conflict*. Newcastle-upon- Tyne, United Kingdom: Cambridge Scholars Publishing 2008.

Mitchinson, Wendy. *The Nature of Their Bodies: Women and Their Doctors in Victorian Canada*. Toronto: University of Toronto Press, 1991.

"Modern Architecture is Slowly Creeping In." *Toronto Daily Star*, 12 July 1930. 4.

Montgomery, L.M. "Abel and His Great Adventure." In *The Doctor's Sweetheart and Other Stories*, selected by Catherine McLay, 124–39. 1979. Seal Books, 1993.

– *After Green Gables: L.M. Montgomery's Letters to Ephraim Weber, 1916–1941*. Edited by Hildi Froese Tiessen and Paul Gerard Tiessen. Toronto: University of Toronto Press, 2006.

– *The Alpine Path: The Story of My Career*. 1917. Don Mills: Fitzhenry and Whiteside, n.d.

– *Anne of Avonlea*. 1909. Toronto: Seal Books (Collector's Edition), 1996.

– *Anne of Green Gables*. 1908. Toronto: Seal Books (Collector's Edition), 1996.

– *Anne of Green Gables*. 1908. Edited by Cecily Devereux. Peterborough, ON: Broadview, 2004.

– *Anne of Ingleside.* 1939. Toronto: Seal Books (Collector's Edition), 1996.
– *Anne of the Island.* 1915. Toronto: Seal Books (Collector's Edition), 1996.
– *Anne's House of Dreams.* 1917. Toronto: Seal Books (Collector's Edition), 1996.
– *Anne of Windy Poplars.* 1936. Toronto: Seal Books (Collector's Edition), 1996.
– *The Annotated Anne of Green Gables.* Edited by Wendy E. Barry, Margaret Anne Doody, and Mary E. Doody Jones. New York and London: Oxford University Press, 1997.
– *The Blue Castle.* 1926. Toronto: Bantam/Seal Books, 1989.
– *The Blythes Are Quoted.* Edited by Benjamin Lefebvre. Toronto: Viking Canada, 2009.
– "Come Back with Me to Prince Edward Island." *The Maritime Advocate and Busy East* (Sackville, NB), May–June 1936, 3–8, 37.
– *The Complete Journals of L.M. Montgomery: The PEI Years, 1889–1900.* Edited by Mary Henley Rubio and Elizabeth Hillman Waterston. Toronto: Oxford University Press, 2012.
– *The Complete Journals of L.M. Montgomery: The PEI Years, 1901–1911.* Edited by Mary Henley Rubio and Elizabeth Hillman Waterston. Toronto: Oxford University Press, 2013.
– *The Doctor's Sweetheart and Other Stories.* Selected by Catherine McLay. 1979. Toronto: Seal Books, 1993.
– *Emily Climbs.* 1925. Toronto: Bantam/Seal Books, 1983.
– *Emily of New Moon.* 1923. Toronto: Bantam/Seal Books, 1983.
– *Emily's Quest.* 1927. Toronto: Bantam/Seal Books, 1983.
– *Further Chronicles of Avonlea.* 1920. Toronto: Seal Books, 1987.
– *The Golden Road.* 1910. Toronto: Seal Books, 1987.
– *The Green Gables Letters from L.M. Montgomery to Ephraim Weber, 1905–1909.* Edited by Wilfrid Eggleston. 1960. Ottawa: Borealis Press, 1981.
– *Jane of Lantern Hill.* 1937. Toronto: Seal Books, 1993.
– *Kilmeny of the Orchard.* 1910. Toronto: Seal Books, 1987.
– *L.M. Montgomery's Complete Journals: The Ontario Years, 1911–1917.* Edited by Jen Rubio. Oakville, Ontario: Rock's Mills Press, 2016.
– *L.M. Montgomery's Complete Journals: The Ontario Years, 1918–21.* Edited by Jen Rubio. Oakville, Ontario: Rock's Mills Press, 2017.

– *Magic for Marigold*. 1925. Toronto: Seal Books, 1988.
– *Mistress Pat*. 1935. Toronto: Bantam/Seal Books, 1988.
– *My Dear Mr M: Letters to G.B. MacMillan from L.M. Montgomery*. Edited by Francis W.P. Bolger and Elizabeth R. Epperly. 1980. Toronto: Oxford University Press, 1992.
– *Pat of Silver Bush*. 1933. Toronto: Bantam/Seal Books, 1989.
– *The Poetry of Lucy Maud Montgomery*. Selected by John Ferns and Kevin McCabe. Toronto: Fitzhenry and Whiteside, 1987.
– *Rainbow Valley*. 1919. Toronto: Seal Books (Collector's Edition), 1996.
– *Rilla of Ingleside*. 1921. Edited by Benjamin Lefebvre and Andrea McKenzie. Toronto: Viking Canada, 2010.
– *The Selected Journals of L.M. Montgomery*. Volumes 2–5. Edited by Mary Rubio and Elizabeth Waterston. Toronto: Oxford University Press, 1985–2004.
– "Spring in the Woods." *The Canadian Magazine* (May 1911): 59–62.
– *The Story Girl*. 1911. Toronto: Seal Books, 1987.
– *A Tangled Web*. 1931. Toronto: Seal Books, 1989.
– *The Watchman and Other Poems*. Toronto: McClelland, Goodchild, and Stewart, 1916.
– "The Woods in Autumn." *The Canadian Magazine* (October 1911): 574–7.
– "The Woods in Summer." *The Canadian Magazine* (September 1911): 399–402.
Montgomery, L.M. and Nora Lefurgey. " … where has my yellow garter gone?' The Diary of L.M. Montgomery and Nora Lefurgey." In *The Intimate Life of L.M. Montgomery*, edited by Irene Gammel, 19–87. Toronto: University of Toronto Press, 2005.
Morrison, John. "Stories for Good Children." In *Tall Stories? Reading Law and Literature*, edited by John Morrison and Christine Bell, 113–43. Brookfield, VT: Dartmouth, 1996.
Moslund, Sten Pultz. "The Presencing of Place in Literature: Toward an Embodied Topopoetic Mode of Reading." In *Geocritical Explorations: Space, Place, and Mapping in Literary and Cultural Studies*, edited by Robert T. Tally Jr, 29–43. New York: Palgrave Macmillan 2011.
Mullally, Sasha. "'Daisy,' 'Dodgie,' and 'Lady Jane Grey Dort': L.M. Montgomery and theAutomobile." In *L.M. Montgomery and Canadian Cul-*

ture, edited by Irene Gammel and Elizabeth Epperly, 120–30. Toronto: University of Toronto Press, 1999.

Mumford, Mark. "Form Follows Nature: The Origins of American Organic Architecture." *Journal of Architectural Education* 42.3 (Spring, 1989): 26–37.

"National Parks of Canada," *Canadian Encyclopedia*, http://www.thecanadianencyclopedia.ca/en/article/national-parks-of-canada/, accessed 26 August 1917.

Needham, George. *Street Arabs and Gutter Snipes: The Pathetic and Humorous Side of Young Vagabond Life in the Great Cities, with Records of Work for Their Reclamation*. Boston: D.L. Guernsey, 1884.

" Old-Timers' Stories Source for Author." *The Globe and Mail* (11 November 1937): 5.

Oliver, Mary. Introduction to Emerson, *The Essential Writings*, xi-xvii.

Oppenheim, Janet. "*Shattered Nerves*:" *Doctors, Patients, and Depression in Victorian England*. New York: Oxford University Press, 1991.

Patterson, Dennis, ed. *A Companion to Philosophy of Law and Legal Theory*. 2nd ed. Oxford: Wiley–Blackwell, 2010.

Peterman, Michael, and Carl Ballstadt. "Introduction." In *Forest and Other Gleanings: The Fugitive Writings of Catharine Parr Traill*, edited by Michael Peterman and Carl Ballstadt, 1–16. Ottawa: University of Ottawa Press, 1994.

Philippon, Daniel J. *Conserving Words: How American Nature Writers Shaped the Environmental Movement*. Athens: University of Georgia Press, 2004.

Pike, E. Holly. "(Re)Producing Canadian Literature: L.M. Montgomery's Emily Novels." In *L.M. Montgomery and Canadian Culture*, edited by Irene Gammel and Elizabeth Epperly, 64–76. Toronto: University of Toronto Press, 1999.

– "Propriety and the Proprietary: The Commodification of Health and Nature in *The Blue Castle*." In *L.M. Montgomery's Rainbow Valleys: The Ontario Years, 1911–42*, edited by Rita Bode and Lesley D. Clement, 187–202. Montreal and Kingston: McGill-Queen's University Press, 2015.

Pollan, Michael. *The Botany of Desire: A Plant's-Eye View of the World*. 2001. New York: Random House, 2002.

– *Second Nature: A Gardener's Education*. New York: Grove Press, 1991.

Porter, Roy. "Nervousness, Eighteenth and Nineteenth Century Style: From Luxury to Labour." In *Cultures of Neurasthenia from Beard to the First World War*, edited by Marijke Gijswijt-Hofstra and Roy Porter, 31–49. Amsterdam: Rodopi, 2001.

Posey, Catherine. "Ethereal Etchings: Connecting with the Natural World in Lucy Maud Montgomery's *Anne of Green Gables* (2008), *Emily of New Moon* (1923), and *Magic for Marigold* (1929)." In *Knowing Their Place? Identity and Space in Children's Literature*, edited by Terri Doughty and Dawn Thompson, 95–108. Newcastle-upon-Tyne, United Kingdom: Cambridge Scholars Publishing, 2011.

Prycer, Melissa. "The Hectic Flush: The Fiction and Reality of Consumption in L.M. Montgomery's Life." In *The Intimate Life of L.M. Montgomery*, edited by Irene Gammel, 258–72. Toronto: University of Toronto Press, 2005.

Pyne, Stephen J. *Fire: A Brief History*. Seattle: University of Washington Press, 2001.

Reimer, Mavis. "A Daughter of the House: Discourses of Adoption in L.M. Montgomery's *Anne of Green Gables*." In *The Oxford Handbook of Children's Literature*, edited by Julia L. Mickenberg and Lynne Vallone, 329–50. Oxford: Oxford University Press 2011.

Review of *Anne of Green Gables*, by L.M. Montgomery. *The Spectator* (London) (13 March 1909): 426–7.

Relke, Diana M.A. *Greenwor(l)ds: Ecocritical Readings of Canadian Women's Poetry*. University of Calgary Press, 1999.

Reynolds, Kimberley. *Radical Children's Literature: Future Visions and Aesthetic Transformation in Juvenile Fiction*. New York: Palgrave Macmillan, 2007.

Richards, Bertrand F. *Gene Stratton-Porter*. Boston: Twayne, 1980.

Rifkin, Jeremy. *The Empathic Civilization: The Race to Global Consciousness in a World in Crisis*. New York: Jeremy P. Tarcher/Penguin, 2009.

Roberts, Charles G.D. "The Animal Story." *The Kindred of the Wild: A Book of Animal Life*. Boston: L. C. Page and Company, 1935. http://www.uwo.ca/english/canadianpoetry/confederation/roberts/kindred_of_the_wild/index.htm

– "The Poetry of Nature." In *Selected Poetry and Critical Prose, Charles*

G. D. Roberts, edited by W. J. Keith, 276–81. Toronto: University of Toronto Press, 1974.

Roberts, Katherine J. "Once upon the Bench: Rule under the Fairy Tale." *Yale Journal of Law and the Humanities* 13.2 (Summer 2001): 497–529.

Robinson, Laura M. " A Born Canadian': The Bonds of Communal Identity in *Anne of Green Gables* and *A Tangled Web*." In *L.M. Montgomery and Canadian Culture*, edited by Irene Gammel and Elizabeth Epperly, 19–30. Toronto: University of Toronto Press, 1999.

– " Sex matters': L.M. Montgomery, Friendship, and Sexuality." *Children's Literature* 40 (2012): 167–90.

Rodman, Margaret C. "Empowering Place: Multilocality and Multivocality." *American Anthropologist* 94.3 (1992): 650–6.

Ross, Ellen. "Dorothy Tennant (Lady Stanley)." In *Slum Travelers: Ladies and London Poverty, 1860–1920*, edited by Ellen Ross, 239–43. Berkeley: University of California Press, 2007.

Rothwell, Erika. "Knitting Up the World: L.M. Montgomery and Maternal Feminism in Canada." In *L.M. Montgomery and Canadian Culture*, edited by Irene Gammel and Elizabeth Epperly, 133–44. Toronto: University of Toronto Press, 1999.

Rubio, Mary Henley, ed. *Harvesting Thistles: The Textual Garden of L.M. Montgomery: Essays on Her Novels and Journals*. Guelph: Canadian Children's Press 1994.

– *Lucy Maud Montgomery: The Gift of Wings*. Toronto: Doubleday Canada (Random), 2008.

– "Montgomery, Lucy Maud." In *Encyclopedia of Literature in Canada*, edited by William H. New, 748–51. Toronto: University of Toronto Press, 2002.

– "Subverting the Trite: L.M. Montgomery's Room of Her Own." *Canadian Children's Literature* 65 (1992): 6–39.

– "Uncertainties Surrounding the Death of L.M. Montgomery." In *Anne Around the World: L.M. Montgomery and her Classic*, edited by Jane Ledwell and Jean Mitchell, 45–62. Montreal and Kingston: McGill-Queen's University Press, 2013.

Rubio, Mary Henley, and Elizabeth Hillman Waterston, eds. *The Complete Journals of L.M. Montgomery: The PEI Years, 1889–1900*. Toronto: Oxford University Press, 2012.

– *The Complete Journals of L.M. Montgomery: The PEI Years, 1901–1911.* Toronto: Oxford University Press, 2013.

– *The Selected Journals of L.M. Montgomery*, Volumes 2–5. Toronto: Oxford University Press, 1987–2004.

Rule, Jane. *After the Fire*. Toronto: MacMillan, 1989.

– "Stumps." In *Outlander*, by Jane Rule. Tallahassee, FL: Naiad Press, 1981.

Ruskin, John. "Of the Pathetic Fallacy." *Modern Painters*. Vol 3. 1856. New York: John Wiley 1863. 156–72. https://archive.org/details/modernpainters21ruskgoog

Said, Edward. *Orientalism*. New York: Vintage, 1978.

– *The World, the Text, and the Critic*. Cambridge, Massachusetts: Harvard University Press, 1983.

Salah, Christiana. "Girls in Bonds: Prehensile Place and the Domestic Gothic in L.M. Montgomery's Short Fiction." *Tulsa Studies in Women's Literature* 32, no. 1 (Spring 2013): 99–117.

Sandilands, Catriona. "Queer Life? Ecocriticism After the Fire." In *The Oxford Handbook of Ecocriticism*, edited by Greg Garrard, 305–19. New York: Oxford University Press, 2014.

– "Combustion." *The Goose: A Journal of Arts, Environment and Culture in Canada* 15, 2016. www.http://scholars.wlu.ca/thegoose/.

Scheper-Hughes, N. and Margaret M. Lock. "The Mindful Body: A Prolegomenon to Future Work in Medical Anthropology." *Medical Anthropology Quarterly* 1 (March 1987): 6–41.

Scholtmeijer, Marian. "Animals and Spirituality: A Skeptical Animal Rights Advocate Examines Literary Approaches to the Subject." *Literature, Interpretation, Theory* 10.4 (1999): 371–94.

Schreiner, Olive. *The Story of an African Farm*. 1883. London: Penguin Books, 1995.

Schuster, David G. *Neurasthenic Nation: America's Search for Health, Happiness, and Comfort, 1869–1920*. New Brunswick: Rutgers University Press, 2011.

– "Personalizing Illness and Modernity: S. Weir Mitchell, Literary Women, and Neurasthenia, 1870–1914." *Bulletin of the History of Medicine* 79.4 (Winter 2005): 695–722.

Scott, Charles B. *Nature Study and the Child.* Boston: D.C. Heath and Company, 1900.

Sheckels, Theodore F. *The Island Motif in the Fiction of L.M. Montgomery, Margaret Laurence, Margaret Atwood, and Other Canadian Women Novelists.* New York: Peter Lang, 2003.

Showalter, Elaine. "Hysteria, Feminism, and Gender." In *Hysteria Beyond Freud*, edited by Sander L. Gilman, Helen King, Roy Porter, G.S. Rousseau, and Elaine Showalter, 286–344. Berkeley: University of California Press, 1993.

Sicherman, Barbara. "The Uses of a Diagnosis: Doctors, Patients, and Neurasthenia." *Journal of the History of Medicine and Allied Sciences* 32.1 (January 1977): 33–54.

Slovic, Scott. "Nature Writing and Environmental Psychology: The Interiority of Outdoor Experience." In *The Ecocriticism Reader: Landmarks in Literary Ecology*, edited by Cheryll Glotfelty and Harold Fromm, 351–70. Athens: University of Georgia Press, 1996.

Smith, Adam. *The Theory of Moral Sentiments.* 1759. Edited by Knud Haakonssen. Cambridge: Cambridge University Press, 2002.

Soper, Kate. *What Is Nature?: Culture, Politics, and the Non-Human.* Oxford: Wiley-Blackwell, 1995.

Soper, Ella, and Nicholas Bradley, eds. *Greening the Maple: Canadian Ecocriticism in Context.* Calgary: University of Calgary Press, 2012.

Stanley, H.M. *London Street Arabs.* London: Cassell and Company, 1890.

Steenman-Marcusse, Conny, ed. *The Rhetoric of Canadian Writing.* Amsterdam: Rodopi, 2002.

Steffler, Margaret. "Brian O'Connal and Emily Byrd Starr: The Inheritors of Wordsworth's 'Gentle Breeze.'" In *Windows and Words: A Look at Canadian Children's Literature in English*, edited by Aïda Hudson and Susan-Ann Cooper, 87–96. Ottawa: University of Ottawa Press, 2003.

– "Barriers and Portals: Writing through the walls, windows and doors of the Leaskdale manse." *CREArTA* 5 (2005): 63–75

Steffler, Margaret and Neil Steffler. " If We Would Read It Aright': Traill's 'Ladder to Heaven.'" *Journal of Canadian Studies/Revue d'études canadiennes* 38.3 (Fall 2004): 123–52.

Stratton-Porter, Gene. *Freckles*. 1904. New York: Golden Press, 1965.

– *A Girl of the Limberlost*. New York: Grosset and Dunlap, 1909.

– *The Song of the Cardinal: A Love Story*. Indianapolis: The Bobbs-Merrill Company 1903.

Sullivan, Louis. "The Tall Office Building Artistically Considered." *Lippincott's Magazine*. March 1896. 403–9. https://archive.org/stream/tall officebuildioosull#page/n9/mode/2up

Sutherland, Kate. " Even a Successful Lawsuit Will Be a Worry:' Law and Community Relations in L.M. Montgomery's Life and Work." In *Storm and Dissonance: L.M. Montgomery and Conflict*, edited by Jean Mitchell, 295–307. Newcastle-upon-Tyne, United Kingdom: Cambridge Scholars Publishing, 2008.

Tector, Amy. "A Righteous War? L.M. Montgomery's Depiction of the First World War in *Rilla of Ingleside*." *Canadian Literature* 179 (Winter 2003): 72–86.

Theriot, Nancy M. "Women's Voices in Nineteenth-Century Medical Discourse: A Step toward Deconstructing Science." *Signs: Journal of Women in Culture and Society* 19.1 (Autumn 1993): 1–31.

Thomas, Keith. *Man and the Natural World: Changing Attitudes in England 1500–1800*. Harmondsworth: Penguin, 1984.

Thomson, Matthew. "Neurasthenia in Britain: An Overview." In *Cultures of Neurasthenia from Beard to the First World War*, edited by Marijke Gijswijt-Hofstra and Roy Porter, 77–95. Amsterdam: Rodopi, 2001.

Thoreau, Henry David. *Walden*. Edited by J. Lyndon Shanley. Princeton, NJ: Princeton University Press, 1971.

Tiessen, Paul. "Opposing Pacifism: L.M. Montgomery and the Trouble with Ephraim Weber." In *Storm and Dissonance: L.M. Montgomery and Conflict*, edited by Jean Mitchell, 131–40. Newcastle-upon-Tyne, United Kingdom: Cambridge Scholars Publishing, 2008.

Trillin, Calvin. "Anne of Red Hair: What Do the Japanese See in *Anne of Green Gables*?" In *L.M. Montgomery and Canadian Culture*, edited by Irene Gammel and Elizabeth Epperly, 213–21. Toronto: University of Toronto Press, 1999.

Tuana, Nancy. "Viscous Porosity: Witnessing Katrina." In *Material Feminisms*, edited by Stacy Alaimo and Susan Hekman, 188–213. Bloomington: Indiana University Press, 2008.

Urquhart, Jane. *L.M. Montgomery*. 2009. Toronto: Penguin Canada, 2012.

Wacks, Raymond. *Understanding Jurisprudence: An Introduction to Legal Theory*. Oxford: Oxford University Press, 2009.

Wadland, John. "Wilderness and Culture." In *Consuming Canada: Readings in Environmental History*, edited by Chad Gaffield and Pam Gaffield, 12–15. Toronto: Copp Clark, 1995.

Ward, Ian. *Law and Literature: Possibilities and Perspectives*. Cambridge: Cambridge University Press, 1995.

Waterston, Elizabeth. *Magic Island: The Fictions of L.M. Montgomery*. Don Mills, Ontario: Oxford University Press, 2008.

– "Marigold and the Magic of Memory." In *Harvesting Thistles: The Textual Garden of L.M. Montgomery: Essays on Her Novels and Journals*, edited by Mary Henley Rubio, 155–66. Guelph: Canadian Children's Press, 1994.

– Untitled lecture, University of Prince Edward Island, June 2006.

Watson, Albert Durrant, and Lorne Pierce, eds. *Our Canadian Literature: Representative Prose and Verse*. Toronto: Ryerson, 1922.

Weiss, Joel, et al, eds. *The International Handbook of Virtual Learning Environments*. Dordrecht: Springer, 2006

Wherrett, J.R. "History of Neurology in Toronto 1892–1960 Part Two." *Canadian Journal of Neurological Sciences* 22.4 (November 1995): 322–32.

Whitman, Walt. "Song of Myself." *Leaves of Grass and Other Writings*. Edited by Michael Moon. New York: Norton 2002. 26–78.

Williams, Raymond. *Keywords: A Vocabulary of Culture and Society*. 1976. Oxford: Oxford University Press, 1985.

Wilson, Edward O. *Biophilia*. Cambridge, Massachusetts: Harvard University Press, 1984.

Wolfe, Christopher. *Natural Law Liberalism*. Cambridge: Cambridge University Press, 2006.

Wood, Jane. *Passion and Pathology in Victorian Fiction*. Oxford: Oxford University Press, 2001.

Woodman, Francis. "Arch." In *The Dictionary of Art* vol. 2, edited by Jane Turner, 292–98. New York: Grove, 1996.

Woodward, Wendy. *The Animal Gaze: Animal Subjectivities in Southern African Narratives*. Johannesburg: Wits University Press, 2008.

Wordsworth, William. In *The Major Works*, edited by Stephen Gill. Oxford: Oxford University Press, 1984.

– "Preface to the *Lyrical Ballads*." 1802. In *The Broadview Anthology of British Literature: The Age of Romanticism* vol. 4, edited by Joseph Black, Leonard Conolly, et al., 202–9. Peterborough, Ontario: Broadview Press, 2006.

Wright, Frank Lloyd. "In the Cause of Architecture." In *On and by Frank Lloyd Wright: A Primer of Architectural Principles*, edited by Robert McCarter, 338–44. New York: Phaidon 2005.

Contributors

RITA BODE is professor of English literature at Trent University. She is coeditor, with Lesley D. Clement, of *L.M. Montgomery's Rainbow Valleys: The Ontario Years, 1911–1941* (MQUP, 2015). Her work on Montgomery has appeared in CREArTA and in *Storm and Dissonance: L.M. Montgomery and Conflict* (2008). Other recent work includes chapters on George Eliot and Harriet Beecher Stowe in *Transatlantic Women* (UNEP 2012) and *Transatlantic Conversations* (University Press of New England 2017), and George Eliot and Edith Wharton in *Edith Wharton and Cosmopolitanism* (University of Florida Press 2016).

LESLEY D. CLEMENT has held teaching and administrative positions in various Canadian universities and is currently at Lakehead University Orillia. She is the author of *Learning to Look: A Visual Response to Mavis Gallant's Fiction* and has published on (among others) Judith Thompson in the *Encyclopedia of Literature in Canada*, death in children's picture books in *Bookbird*, and L.M. Montgomery in *Studies in Canadian Literature*. She coedited *Global Perspectives on Death in Children's Literature* (Routledge, 2015) with Leyli Jamali and authored a chapter on picture books on Emily Dickinson for that volume. She is coeditor, with Rita Bode, of *L.M. Montgomery's Rainbow Valleys: The Ontario Years, 1911–1942* (MQUP, 2015) and contributed a chapter on "Toronto's Cultural Scene: Tonic or Toxin for a Sagged Soul?" Her current research explores visual literacy, the visual imagination, empathy, and death in children's and YA literature.

ELIZABETH ROLLINS EPPERLY is professor emerita of English at the University of Prince Edward Island and founder of the L.M. Montgomery Institute. Her numerous contributions to Montgomery Studies include the book-length studies *The Fragrance of Sweet-Grass: L.M. Montgomery's Heroines and the Pursuit of Romance* (1992/2014); *Through Lover's Lane: L.M. Montgomery's Photography and Visual Imagination* (2007), and *Imagining Anne: The Island Scrapbooks of L.M. Montgomery* (2008); edited volumes, *My Dear Mr M: Letters to G.B. MacMillan from L.M. Montgomery*, jointly with Francis W.P. Bolger (1980), and *L.M. Montgomery and Canadian Culture*, jointly with Irene Gammel (1999), and numerous articles and book chapters.

NANCY HOLMES is an associate professor in the Department of Creative Studies at the University of British Columbia (Okanagan), where she teaches creative writing. She is the author of five collections of poems: *Valancy and the New World* (1988), *Down to the Golden Chersonese: Victorian Lady Travellers* (1991), *The Adultery Poems* (2002), *Mandorla* (2005), and *The Flicker Tree: Okanagan Poems* (2012). She is the editor of *Open Wide a Wilderness: Canadian Nature Poems* (2009). Her poetry and fiction have been published in *Arc*, *Room of One's Own*, *Lichen*, *The Malahat Review*, *Matrix*, *Prairie Fire*, *Grain*, *The Harpweaver*, and *The Antigonish Review*. Beside writing and teaching, she organizes eco art projects in the Okanagan valley, especially with her collaborator Denise Kenney through The Eco Art Incubator.

PAUL KEEN is a professor of English at Carleton University. He is the author of *The Age of Authors: An Anthology of Eighteenth Century Print Culture* (2013); *Literature, Commerce, and the Spectacle of Modernity, 1750–1800* (2012), and *The Crisis of Literature in the 1790s: Print Culture and the Public Sphere* (1999). His edited books include *The Radical Popular Press in Britain, 1817–1821* (2003), *Revolutions in Romantic Literature: An Anthology of Print Culture, 1780–1832* (2004), *Bookish Histories: Books, Literature, and Commercial Modernity, 1700–1900* (with Ina Ferris, 2009). His current SSHRC-funded research project explores the development of ideas about the humanities in a utilitarian age.

JENNIFER H. LITSTER completed her PhD on "The Scottish Context of L.M. Montgomery" at the University of Edinburgh in 2001. Her articles on Montgomery have been published in the journal *Canadian Children's Literature/Littérature canadienne pour la jeunesse* and in *L.M. Montgomery and Canadian Culture* (1999) and *The Intimate Life of L.M. Montgomery* (2005). From 2005 to 2016 she worked for NRDC (Institute of Education, University of London), a centre dedicated to conducting research and development projects to improve adult literacy, numeracy, language, and related skills and knowledge.

JEAN MITCHELL is an associate professor of Anthropology at the University of Prince Edward Island. She edited *Storm and Dissonance: L.M. Montgomery and Conflict* and coedited *Anne Around the World: L.M. Montgomery and her Classic.* She conducts research in the South Pacific and her most recent article (2016) is entitled "The War on the *Anopheles* Mosquito: Malaria, Labour and Race in New Hebrides." She is currently undertaking a project on the ecologies of gardens in Vanuatu.

IDETTE NOOMÉ has lectured in English language, literature, and editing in the Department of English at the University of Pretoria (South Africa) since 1985, specialising in medieval and seventeenth-century literature. Her DLitt explored the translation of legal anthropology texts on indigenous law. She has also published on girls' school stories and the possibilities of the *Bildungsroman* for girls in English, German, and Afrikaans, which included a discussion of Montgomery's Anne books.

TARA K. PARMITER received her PhD from New York University, where she teaches in the Expository Writing Program. Her areas of interest include turn-of-twentieth-century women's literature, literature and the environment, children's literature, and popular culture. She has published articles on the imagined landscapes in *Anne of Avonlea*, summer vacationing in Kate Chopin's *The Awakening*, journey narratives in the Muppet movies, the intimate language of *Pushing Daisies*, and the green gothic of Stephenie Meyer's Twilight saga.

LAURA M. ROBINSON is dean of the School of Arts and Social Science at Grenfell Campus, Memorial University of Newfoundland. She has published articles about Canadian children's literature, Margaret Atwood, Ann-Marie MacDonald, *Pollyanna*, and the television show *The L-Word* in addition to many articles on Montgomery's work, most recently in *L.M. Montgomery and War*, *L.M. Montgomery's Rainbow Valleys*, and *Seriality and Texts for Young People*. Her current project examines Montgomery's depiction of friendship and sexuality, and as part of that she curated an exhibit, "The Canadian Home Front: L.M. Montgomery's Reflections on the First World War" that has travelled to France, England, and various locations in Canada. She and E. Holly Pike are presently working on an edited collection on L.M. Montgomery and gender.

CATRIONA SANDILANDS is professor in the Department of Environmental Studies at York University, where she teaches and writes at the intersections of ecocultural studies, sexuality studies, and environmental politics. Recent publications include the coedited volume (with Bruce Erickon) *Queer Ecologies: Sex, Nature, Politics, Desire* (2010); "Acts of Nature: Literature, Excess, and Environmental Politics" in Critical Collaborations: *Indigeneity, Diaspora, and Ecology in Canadian Literary Studies* (2014); "Violent Affinities: Sex, Gender and Species in *Cereus Blooms at Night*," in *The Cambridge Companion to Ecocriticism*, Cambridge University Press (2014); "Pro/polis: Three Forays into the Political Lives of Bees," in *Material Ecocriticisms* (2014); "Queer Life? Ecocriticism After the Fire," in *The Oxford Handbook of Ecocriticism* (2014). She is currently working on a book on Jane Rule's contributions to queer (and environmental) public culture in Canada.

KATE SUTHERLAND is an associate professor at Osgoode Hall Law School. She teaches and conducts research in the areas of tort law, law and literature, law and sexuality, and feminist legal theory. She contributed chapters to *Storm and Dissonance: L.M. Montgomery* and *Conflict* and *L.M. Montgomery's Rainbow Valleys: The Ontario Years, 1911–*

1942. She is at work on a book about lawsuits involving writers as litigants and literary texts as evidence. She is also the author of two collections of short stories and a book of poems. The latter, titled *How to Draw a Rhinoceros*, was shortlisted for a 2017 Creative Writing Book Award by the Association for the Study of Literature and the Environment.

Index